Praise for *Fl[...]*
by Catherine H[...]

"Who wouldn't want to flourish? Discover how to blossom and grow in a healthy way, living a 'life well lived' and having a positive influence. I know Dr. Catherine can do this for you, because she has done it for me! I am a better person because I know her personally, listen to her wisdom, and live out her God-centered advice. Everyone should read *Flourish* so they can flourish too!"
—**Pam Farrel**, relationship specialist, international speaker, and author of over thirty books, including the bestselling *Men Are Like Waffles—Women Are Like Spaghetti, Red Hot Monogamy, The 10 Best Decisions a Woman Can Make, Woman of Influence, and Woman of Confidence*

"If you long for a healthy, vibrant, productive, and happy life, read this book. *Flourish* is an extraordinary book with so much take-home value. Catherine Hart Weber reveals the secrets of flourishing in our personal, social, and spiritual relationships. Discover how to experience the life you long for, practicing the transformational principles of enjoying God's love, developing a joyful, grateful heart, embracing tranquility, and anticipating a future hope."
—**Carol Kent**, speaker and author of *Between a Rock and a Grace Place*

"Dr. Catherine Hart Weber has mined from her professional and personal life treasures of truth that will help you move from surviving to thriving, from ordinary to extraordinary living, and from life on a mundane plane to a place far above anything we could ever imagine."
—**Linda Mintle**, PhD, PureMedia Group, Inc.

"We were not created to just 'get by' but to 'thrive in the life God has planned for us.' In her latest book, *Flourish: Discover the Daily Joy of Abundant, Vibrant Living*, Dr. Catherine Hart Weber offers a very readable, practical, and well-researched plan for helping you experience God's intended *shalom* for your life. Catherine aptly draws from both positive psychology and Christian spiritual formation in creating this important book."

—**Gary W. Moon**, editor of *Conversations Journal* and author of *Apprenticeship with Jesus*

"Wilt and languish? Or thrive and flourish? Dr. Hart Weber escorts you out of a life of languishing into a refreshed life of faith-based flourishing. She leads you to renewal and intentional living with personal stories, thought-provoking exercises, and practical application. Fascinating! Life-changing!"

—**Katie Brazelton**, PhD, bestselling author and founder of Life Purpose Coaching Centers International®

"Abundant living isn't about just treading water. It's not about mediocrity or settling for second best. It's about learning and thriving and growing. It's about increasing your hope and joy and maximizing your potential to enjoy all that God designed you to be and become. In *Flourish*, Dr. Hart Weber has given readers the gift of a practical, invaluable, and essential resource that will increase your emotional and relational intelligence and make a noticeable difference in how you 'view' life and how you 'do' life. It's a book you'll read more than once and one you'll want to share with your friends."

—**Gary J. Oliver**, ThM, PhD, Executive Director of The Center for Relationship Enrichment and Professor of Psychology and Practical Theology at John Brown University and coauthor of *Mad About Us* and *Raising Sons and Loving It!*

flourish

discover the daily joy of abundant, vibrant living

CATHERINE HART WEBER, PhD

BETHANY HOUSE PUBLISHERS

Minneapolis, Minnesota

Published by Bethany House Publishers
11400 Hampshire Avenue South
Bloomington, Minnesota 55438

Bethany House Publishers is a division of
Baker Publishing Group, Grand Rapids, Michigan.

Printed in the United States of America

Library of Congress Cataloging-in-Publication Data

Weber, Catherine Hart.
    Flourish : discover the daily joy of abundant, vibrant living / Catherine Hart Weber.
      p.   cm.
    Includes bibliographical references.
    Summary: "A leading Christian psychologist offers innovative ways to live an abundant life based on cutting-edge research and biblical wisdom"—Provided by publisher.
    ISBN 978-0-7642-0808-9 (pbk. : alk. paper) 1. Christian life. 2. Christianity— Psychology. I. Title.
    BV4501.3.W393   2010
    248.4—dc22

                                    2010021633

WITH DEEP APPRECIATION TO THOSE WHO HAVE WATERED MY LIFE:

*the Lord Jesus Christ, my parents,
my husband, my daughters, my sisters,
my friends, my teachers, and my mentors.*

❀

Contents

Foreword

Do you feel tired and worn out at times—not just physically, but mentally, emotionally, or spiritually? Perhaps, like so many today, you feel discontent and uneasy, like something deep within is missing. You may feel lax in your relationship with God, longing for more connections, discouraged, stressed, and worried or despairing in your struggles. You may long for more purpose, more love, more joy, peace, and hope.

If so, you are not alone. New research shows that this state of "languishing" is becoming increasingly more prevalent than depression, anxiety, or other mental and emotional challenges.

You aren't meant to merely exist and survive—you are meant to thrive and prosper in the abundant life that God offers—to *flourish*.

That is why the book you are about to read is as important as any I have ever encountered. We have been flooded with all types of "self-help" and "better-health" books in recent times, but this book is different. It directly addresses why we are losing our grip on the flourishing life God intended us to live, and why we struggle daily with languishing. Then you are invited to follow God's design for a life full of love, joy, gratitude, peace, tranquility, and hope.

Dr. Hart Weber has been very passionate about studying and living the topic of human flourishing for many years, and I believe that this book is very timely. Her emphasis is from a Christian perspective, but she is continually reviewing new developments along the theme of flourishing, integrating discoveries from the sciences.

As you will see, the field of psychology, which was languishing for many years, has had a renaissance since the late 1990s. Instead of merely identifying miseries and maladies, psychologists, researchers, and scientists have begun asking some good questions about what makes life well lived. Out of this quest, the field of positive psychology was launched. Not surprisingly, flourishing is one of the keys to living a vibrant life.

In *Flourish*, Dr. Hart Weber deftly weaves these important insights into a biblically based examination of living well in all areas of life. In essence, the message of this book is that flourishing in healthy spiritual emotions is possible when you experience the abundance of the Spirit of God.

I believe that Dr. Catherine Hart Weber (who happens to be my daughter, in case you are wondering) has presented us with a clear pathway and plan of action for a flourishing life. Not only does she cover the hallmarks of flourishing, but she also provides practical tools and exercises that can help us develop the intentional habits and lifestyle patterns essential to the abundant life led by the Holy Spirit.

But most important, Catherine offers the rich fruits of her own experience. She is not writing purely out of an academic interest and expertise on this topic, but out of her own vibrant growth and spiritual formation journey. Without a doubt, she has traveled the flourishing road herself and provides insights that will light your way and guide you through the struggles of languishing. In the depths of her own journey she has found the phenomenal redemption that God can offer in life's challenging moments.

My prayer for you is that this book will infuse the freshness of the power of the Holy Spirit in your life in such a way that you will never be the same again. I challenge you to enter in and discover what God can do when you choose to embrace His abundant life.

Archibald D. Hart, PhD, FPPR
Senior Professor of Psychology and Dean Emeritus
Graduate School of Psychology
Fuller Theological Seminary

PART 1

GOD'S INVITATION TO FLOURISH

You flourish when embracing God's redeeming Shalom

Discovering God's Invitation to Flourish

The godly shall flourish like palm trees, and grow tall as the cedars of Lebanon. For they are transplanted into the Lord's own garden, and are under his personal care. Even in old age they will still produce fruit and be vital and green. This honors the Lord, and exhibits his faithful care.

Psalm 92:12–15 TLB

As I enter the final season of writing this book and we begin our journey together, I am enjoying a few seaside summer days. For hours at a time I have been sitting by the ocean, feeling the refreshing sea mist on my face, watching the waves in a natural rhythm of ebb and flow, internalizing this as a centering image for my life. The sunset gently closes out each day, transforming the sky with the promise of a restful night and the hopes of another new day. As I ride my bike through the natural California terrain along the cliffs of the ocean, the wind blows through my hair and I am reminded of the pure pleasures I experienced as a child in South Africa, laughing and playing with carefree innocence.

Can you remember times like this?

The powerful yet gentle beauty of nature has been reminding me profoundly of something I believe we know deep in our hearts, yet often forget in the press of daily cares: that we are created for Eden; for a life of beauty and harmony with God, ourselves, others, and creation.

It is wonderful and life-giving to savor moments when we delight in feeling fully alive: being out in the beauty of nature or sharing a deep and meaningful conversation and thinking, *At this moment I am being my best self, I am catching a glimpse of what life is all about, I feel what matters most, and I perceive God's deeper intentions for me.* At times like this, my whole being resonates with wanting to show warmth, love, and kindness to those around me. I smile at passersby. I am filled with gratitude that overflows with generosity. I desire to be content with each new day, delighting in simple pleasures. I feel a sense of joy that I desire to spread with others. I yearn for more.

The more I experience peace of mind when I start worrying about problems or the future, the more I hold on to hope and gain strength for the journey to face the mundane times and the challenges of life. I am motivated to become more of my best, most authentic self. We were created for moments like this. We were created for more. We were created to flourish!

If you resonate with these longings, then this book is for you. It's about discovering how to flourish through the Spirit in both character and emotion. It is about discovering how to experience more love, joy, gratitude, peace, and hope—the virtues that bring lasting fulfillment and fruitful impact.

Born to Flourish in Life and Relationships

~ We were not created just to exist and "get by," or languish. God's desire is for all of us to live abundantly. This means becoming who God created us to be, for His delight and glory. This is who I am aiming to be. This is who you can be also.

Right from the beginning of creation it was God's vision to create order, harmony, tranquility, balance, and communion. All the fundamental forces of nature are directed toward our growth and harmony.

⚓ You and I are designed for well-being in all areas of our life systems—our body, brain, mind, emotions, spirit, and relationships—in our marriages, as parents, at school, in our work and community, in our churches, with our money, and in all our daily experiences.

Sadly, however, we live in a fallen, broken world, where life as it was intended to be is violated. I know I won't have uninterrupted bliss every day.

⚓ But I have discovered that if I set aside time and make space for these moments that nourish my soul, that make me feel most fully alive in God, savoring them and seizing them, I will turn my heart and life toward what I was created for: my best, most authentic, flourishing self. Like the restoration of a dilapidated garden, I can cultivate a life that is continually being transformed, redeemed, and restored to thrive with beauty and renewed potential.

We each have to pay attention and continually rediscover what this transformation means for us. It will be a different challenge each day. I want something genuine and realistic, something sensible that I can realize and reach. I get tired of keeping up the pace and battling within and without. Don't you? But I have discovered that there is a way to flourish in all areas of life. It begins now, with the life you have to live, made up of the moments of every day. We don't have to wait to find love, joy, gratitude, peace, and hope when things finally settle down, when it all changes and gets better. We often think that's when we will finally be able to grow, flourish, and be happy.

God created you to be fully alive in Him. You can discover how to find this daily joy in the midst of your current life challenges and a difficult world. It might not be what you think it looks like, but you can access the possibility of flourishing more than you realize.

Longing to flourish is universal—from the wealthy people of Europe to the poor orphans of Africa. I received a letter recently from a little girl in Zambia. Her name is Sharon, and she is one of the children I sponsor. She writes, "At the project, we learn very many important things like reading the Bibles, helping the needy, and even how to keep our bodies clean. I thank you very much for my school fees and everything you are doing for me—so that I live in a good, happy life." This is Sharon's picture of flourishing. It is simple and authentic but summarizes the desires we all feel deep down.

The Science and Theology of Human Flourishing

The topic of human flourishing is becoming a major theme in religious faith and science.[1] Neurologists, psychologists, theologians, and scientists are spending millions of research dollars on topics related to human flourishing, character development, healthy relationships, and emotion virtues.[2] A new generation of scientists is building up this research on positive emotions and character traits.[3] The most popular topic, happiness-boosting practices, has resulted in over five thousand books in just the last few years. Neuroscience is also providing new evidence as to what makes us thrive and what that looks like in the brain. Universities and seminaries are now feverishly examining more closely how we can understand and cultivate character virtues such as forgiveness, gratitude, joy, love, kindness, serenity, generosity, and hope.

The Christian heritage of spiritual formation is also being revived in a new and dynamic way, reminding us that many ancient contemplative practices, liturgical rhythms, and the Spirit-filled power of our faith are relevant to the harsh realities of daily life.[4] There is a growing longing for authentic spiritual formation and a yearning for transformation that a vibrant life with God offers.[5]

In this book I will draw from the best that science, theology, and spiritual formation literature have to offer so that you can discover how to flourish in well-being and harmony, cultivating a life reflecting Christian emotion virtues such as contrition, love, compassion, joy, gratitude, peace, tranquility, and hope. A Christian psychology of spirituality and human emotion considers that a healthy, growing Christian is emotionally mature, showing evidence of spiritual emotions, spiritual emotion virtues, or emotion virtues. I will use these terms interchangeably when referring to the primary New Testament emotions and mental states of the Spirit. Journey with me as I show you how to implement this spiritual, emotional, and relational intelligence in your life.

What It Means to Flourish

In psychological terms, flourishing is influenced by Aristotle's notion of *eudaimonia*, which means "a life well lived."[6]

We flourish when we have a sense of well-being and can function positively in our spiritual, personal, and social lives—when we experience high levels of emotional, psychological, and social well-being. It includes a life of vigor, vitality, goodness, generativity, and continuous growth. Flourishing means we are able to have close relationships and a meaningful and purposeful life. It is a life that has fulfillment, where we contribute in meaningful and productive ways. The journey includes rising to challenges and being resilient through adversity and during struggles, sadness, sickness, and loneliness. We can develop both a spiritual and a psychological immune system, so to speak, to help us effectively deal with life challenges, stress, anxiety, and depression. When we integrate every aspect of our being in a healthy way, we flourish.

This good life of personal fulfillment and joy comes when you discover and become exactly who God created you to be—a flourisher. When you use your life to help others, to do good, and to know and trust God, you will feel good about yourself. This is "the good life."[7]

Faith-Based Flourishing in Shalom

The Christian faith is all about flourishing. I call it "faith-based flourishing," and it can be characterized by the Hebrew word *shalom*. It is the way of living as life ought to be, the way we were designed to be. The Hebrew root word for *shalom* has several variations. *Shalom* is translated as "peace" and is used as a greeting in both comings and goings. It is a blessing that also implies a more profound meaning than just peace or happiness. Shalom also means completeness or welfare of every kind. Shalom infers flourishing.[8]

God gave us the gift of shalom. Everything and every being was created to exist in an integrated and harmonious relationship.[9] "Flourishing in shalom" is a wonderful way to think of embracing well-being in all of your life: emotional security, joy and contentment, sound health, prosperity, meaningful attachments, friendship, and peace of mind and heart. Similar to the psychological and mental health criteria for well-being, shalom implies that we flourish within all our life systems: body, mind, emotions, spirit, relationships, and work. Shalom also embraces well-being outside ourselves, with right relationships with God, human beings, and nature. To live and flourish in shalom is to find delight in living well along with contributing to the well-being of others and our world.

We then become "shalom bringers," spreading a sense of warmth, comfort, hope, and well-being.[10] When we think of shalom bringers in our lives, we feel as if God is reaching out to us through them, restoring His image of us, His vision for us to flourish. The glory of God shines through their faces and touches us through their hands. This is when we truly are the children of God, reflecting the Spirit emotions and virtues of love, joy, gratitude, peace, and hope flowing through us.

Be Fresh and Flourishing

God's loving and prophetic promise to Israel through the wisdom literature of the Old Testament is that we should be *fresh* and *flourish*, and embrace this kind of shalom. Analogies, metaphors, and stories of plant life and gardens are repeatedly used to explain the life and growth of the soul. As a garden lover, I find these botanical metaphors very inspirational. Take a moment to reflect on these with me.

People are like trees and our soul is like a garden. These images call us to be vibrant with life, like a "tree planted by streams of water" (Psalm 1:3), sending roots deep down. We are to "flourish like a palm tree" and "grow like a cedar" (Psalm 92:12), bearing big clusters of fruit in a well-pruned vine (John 15:1–17). We are also to be like wild flowers blooming in luxuriant, vibrant growth (Matthew 6:28–30 THE MESSAGE), even blossoming in sparse, and yes dry, surroundings—like a rose in the desert (Isaiah 35:1) or a "lily among thorns" (Song of Solomon 2:2). Old Testament Scripture is full of these flourishing metaphors, and they are meant to reflect God creating us in His image, with the intention that we keep growing and flourishing through the seasons of life.

In Isaiah 35:1–10, we get a picture of what was once a wasteland becoming a place of abundance. In *The Message*, we read that the "wilderness and desert will sing joyously, the badlands will celebrate and flower—like the crocus in spring, bursting into blossom, a symphony of song and color." Also, in Isaiah 41:18–20, the Lord promises, "I will make the wilderness a pool of water, and the dry land springs of water. I will plant in the wilderness the cedar and the acacia tree, the myrtle and the oil tree; I will set in the desert the cypress tree and the pine and the box tree together, that they may see and know. . . ."

These words are a proclamation of hope for you and me.

Shalom Vandalized

The wasteland and wilderness represent the reality of life. Around 700 BC, when Isaiah wrote about gushing, refreshing streams and blooming in the desert, life had become like a desert for the people of Israel. They were wilting and languishing. They didn't have their freedom. They had suffered disappointment, loss, and devastation. They had become spiritually careless and were not living intentionally in God's way. Life can be like this for us, too. Inevitably, there will be times when the going gets tough and our lives stagnate. We all experience challenging times sooner or later. Our shalom will be vandalized.

The story of the garden of Eden explains how it all began with God's original created design and order for human flourishing. God wired us to feel at home in the garden of Eden, which literally means "pleasure" or "delight."[11]

Then life in Eden took a terrible turn with the fatal fall. Adam and Eve sinned and were sent out of the garden of Eden, away from God's presence and their created intention. Our intended shalom was broken. Although created in the image of God as our most beautiful, flourishing selves, we now have to battle against our conflicted, languishing selves. This fallen nature becomes our default setting—where everything regresses to when we are not obedient. We are all negatively affected by this vandalization of our intended well-being, and from Genesis onward we see the results of living outside of God's original plan. Relationship conflict, deception, lies, blame, and shame become the norm. And the result is that life is hard and painful, filled with loss, illness, disappointment, and struggles. The battle is without and within. The brokenness of a fallen world and our defaulted languishing self hinder our flourishing self.

Languishing

So it is no surprise that we live in challenging times. Sadly, many are wilting because they haven't found their way to the living waters of God. The interior lives of vast numbers of people are empty, parched, and dry. Thoreau observed that most people live lives of "quiet desperation."[12] Many describe their lives as "hollow" or "empty."[13]

> *"No society can surely be flourishing and happy, of which the far greater part of the members are poor and miserable."*
>
> —Adam Smith

Turning to the field of psychology for a moment, we find that this state of languishing is of great concern. Recent studies reveal that only 18 percent of American adults meet the criteria for flourishing. That's only one in five! On the other hand, about 17 percent of adults fall into the category of languishing or being mentally unhealthy.[14] Other studies reveal that women in particular are languishing and becoming more unhappy.[15] They report feeling empty and lost, lacking purpose and fulfillment. They struggle with transitions and changes. Stress, anxiety, and depression loom epidemically. Both people of faith and those who are not are longing for some deep renewal.

One would think that with so many outward conditions favoring us, we should experience greater mental health and more life satisfaction than ever. But even with all the accessories of provision and success—a house, a marriage, kids, an education, and a good job—many still cannot find a way to flourish. Polls and research reveal that many Americans, notwithstanding their social status, still lack a deep sense of well-being. They feel something is missing and want more out of life.[16]

None of us is exempt from dissatisfaction if we become spiritually careless, neglecting to nourish our souls. We can easily get discouraged and give up on our deepest hopes and dreams.

23

Relationships wilt; many don't live freely in joy and delight. Even our teens are failing to flourish. One in four teens is considered to be at risk for a diagnosable mental or emotional disorder, resulting in a failure to transition well into early adult life.[17]

This languishing is not just happening to people out there; this is you and me and our children, our children's friends, our nieces and nephews, and our grandchildren.

The Journey of the Lavender Jacket

Languishing can come upon one suddenly, or it can happen slowly and gradually over time. I barely noticed it at first in my own life. But then I suddenly faced the prospect when I opened the mail one day. There, in an envelope, I was confronted with a photo of myself wearing a lavender jacket. I was shocked. "Who is that woman?" My jacket gaped visibly across my torso. I looked disheveled and worn out.

I had another photo wearing the same lavender jacket from a few years earlier, right there on my desk. I compared the two. In just a few years the impact of ongoing stress and emotional strain—and let's throw in a few years of perimenopausal hormones—was quite obvious. Same jacket, but a different me! The reality hit home. I had been going through a "wilderness season." I was parched and depleted.

How did I allow myself to slowly wilt, letting the languishing deplete my best, most flourishing self? Where was the sparkle in my eyes, the playful, genuine happiness in my smile? I missed having exuberance for life and soul serenity. I wanted more than anything else to get back to the joyful, peaceful persona I had deep within me. I wanted to be that rose in the desert, the beautiful lily among the thorns, or the fresh green tree by streams—not a dried-up, lifeless bush of sticks. No doubt I needed a fresh anointing, some deep soul renewal, and an extreme soul and life makeover. I wanted, above everything else, to once again have more of the freshness

24

of the Spirit flowing through me with love, joy, gratitude, peace, and hope. Do you ever feel like that?

Then the thought struck me: *I should have known better. I have two masters and a PhD, for Pete's sake!* I had experienced renewal and flourishing before, helping many to discover the same. Deep within me was still my best, most flourishing self, longing to be revived, nourished, and cultivated. As I reflected on my awakening, the Holy Spirit began revealing hindrances, pathways, and practices to once again tend the garden of my soul and cultivate my overall well-being. That was the beginning of my pursuit for renewal, intentionally discovering how to flourish and ignite abundant, vibrant living once again. I call it *The Journey of the Lavender Jacket.*

Vibrant, Fruitful, Full of Life

My journey, as well as yours, doesn't end with a season of languishing, or living from our languishing self. The rest of God's story with us is about His redemption and transforming plan to give us abundant life. Most of the Old Testament prophets pointed toward this rescue solution: *Reestablish the shalom, freedom, and well-being that God originally intended.* All the botanical metaphors in the Old Testament are pointing to the promise that when the Messiah comes, our desert places will bloom and flourish. This is what happens when the life of Christ and the Spirit of God come to us. In the New Testament, the new concepts of flourishing are fullness, abundance, and fruitfulness.

In the great prayer of Ephesians, Paul expresses the desire that "you . . . may be filled with the fullness of God" (Ephesians 3:19 NKJV). In the gospel of John, Jesus speaks of himself as the "good shepherd," whose primary purpose was to provide a way for our lives to flourish: "The thief comes only to steal and kill and destroy; I have come that they may have life, and have it to the full" (John 10:10). This new life in Jesus and the Holy Spirit is the freedom we have to become who we are intended to be. Our souls are continually being renewed "like the garden of the Lord" (Genesis 13:10). The flourishing life in Christ not only impacts us, but others, as well. When we flourish in life and relationships, we nourish others.

What does a flourishing life look like?

- **Appearance.** A flourishing plant is attractive. It has lovely fresh foliage. Likewise, the countenance of those who are flourishing is vibrant, radiant, cheerful, tranquil, pleasant, and hopeful. Even during hard times, they draw others to themselves because of their spiritual depth and the pleasant aroma of Christ in them. Their smile reflects a heart of joy that is positively contagious.

  - Are you generally cheerful, calm, grateful, and hopeful?

  - Do you experience love, joy, gratitude, peace, serenity, and hope?

  - Are you facing life challenges with resilience, hope, and optimism?

  - Do you look forward to the future with hope, or are you worried and afraid?

- **Behavior.** Just as evergreen trees are identified by their constant color, people living out faith-based flourishing are identified by their daily habits and practices. They embrace life fully and worship God wholeheartedly. They speak encouraging words, do good, are giving, connect and contribute, show gratitude, and reflect the life and character of Jesus and the Holy Spirit.

  - Are you living as a whole person in all areas of your life?

  - Are you living your life fully alive, or stagnant?

  - Are you excited to learn new things, and develop new skills and talents?

  - Are you growing and improving your life for the better?

- **Fruitfulness.** You will know a good tree by the good fruit it produces. When our lives are planted and growing in Christ, we reflect the fruits of the Spirit—love, joy, peace, longsuffering, kindness, goodness, faithfulness, gentleness, self-control (Galatians 5:22–23 NKJV)—and other spiritual character traits such as courage and compassion.

  - Do you have healthy relationship attachments?

- Are you connected with your family, friends, work, and community?

- Do you have a sense of belonging and contributing in a meaningful way?

- Are you doing good and adding value to those around you?

- Are you motivated to contribute to the lives of others out of gratitude?

- **Purpose.** Each plant purposely adds to God's created order. A group of trees makes a forest. Branches serve as nests for birds. Fruits provide nourishment and replenishing. Trees provide shade for rest and beauty for our delight. We each need to know our special purpose, feel we belong and contribute to a community, and look forward to living well and leaving a legacy.

- Do you have a sense of meaning and purpose in life daily?

- Do you have dreams you still want to fulfill?

- Do you have a plan to flourish, becoming your best possible self in the future?

- What legacy would you like to leave, and are you living it intentionally?[18]

Strength for the Journey

Many of us are inspired by sermons, Bible studies, or helpful books. We also like to attend retreats or go to conferences where we can get spiritually higher than a kite and feel bursts of hope. But when all is said and done, the drudgery of everyday living is what really drains us. The challenges of our journey aren't just the life-strengthening mountain climbs, but the sand in our shoes. It is in the humdrum of daily life where we must truly live out the abundant provisions of God.

In this book, I invite you to discover how to thrive and blossom in all the systems of your life. You will discover how to flourish in your brain, mind, body, emotions, spirit, and relationships. We will explore biblical pathways and practices along with scientifically proven exercises for you to intentionally partner with God in your growth. You can experience renewal and restoration of vibrant life, regardless of where you are struggling.

This doesn't mean having to work harder or having to become more perfect as a person. God did not design His abundant life to be complicated or overwhelming. Obviously, I won't be able to address all the major issues you might be facing in your life, but hopefully this book will help you get back on track so you can keep growing stronger and more beautiful in the Spirit, no matter what you are facing. My prayer is that you will discover a deeper, closer connection with the Spirit of God and that you will impact the world around you for God's glory, becoming a flourisher!

Discover How to Flourish

As we begin our journey into the rest of the book, I'd like to give you a glimpse of the pathway ahead. In the next section, we will address specific principles that are important to consider as a whole person and how to activate genuine transformation in your life. Then we will explore the core emotion virtues of the Spirit—love, joy, gratitude, peace, and hope. There are many more virtues and expressions of the Spirit of God, but these are vital to our spiritual and emotional well-being. When we live and express these emotion virtues, they are a reflection of being transformed into mature Christian character.[19] On this journey, you will discover how to cultivate and shape more of these heartfelt attitudes and emotion virtues in your life.

Each of these emotion virtues forms the core of a system that is integral to our whole being. This is similar to how each aspect of our physical life and our relationships is considered a "system." Emotion virtues of the Spirit aren't isolated feelings or interactions, but a whole systemic interrelated way of living and being transformed.

- **Love and Relationship Attachment System**

  You flourish in the presence of God's love and attachment with others.

- **Joy and Pleasure System**

  You flourish when facing challenging emotions and circumstances with a heart open to joy and gratitude.

- **Peace and Tranquility System**

  You flourish when your mind, soul, and body are at peace and are serene and tranquil.

- **Hope and Resilience System**

  You flourish when trusting and surrendering to God with hope, meaning, and purpose for the future.

Throughout this book, questionnaires will be offered to help you become more attuned to your flourishing journey. Practical exercises and spiritual practices will also help you develop intentional habits and lifestyle rhythms. Stories about amazing people will inspire you.

Keep a journal or notebook so you can interact with what you read. Complete the exercises and respond to the reflective questions. Take notes about what you discover, list your goals, and record your progress. Use the appendix as a coaching guide to help direct you on your journey. Consider going through the book with a friend or small group. You may also want to find a coach or counselor to share your journey with. Go to *www.howtoflourish.com* for additional downloads, resources, and a workbook.

Then, as you flourish, you will become a flourisher—a shalom bringer; a loving, safe place; a joy spreader; a peacemaker; and a hope giver—passing on to others the healing balm of love, the soothing tranquility of peace, the delight of enjoying simple experiences of life, and the seeds of hope. God is getting ready to do something new and wonderful in your life, making you more authentically beautiful. Join me in discovering how to flourish.

Prayer

Lord, fill me with the knowledge of your will, with spiritual wisdom and understanding. Fill me with your Spirit and fullness of life, in love and hope. Show me how to flourish with evidence of good fruit in all areas of my life. Amen.

Adapted from Ephesians 1:17–18; 3:16–19

Reflective Questions and Flourish Practices

1. Make a time line of your life so far. Mark the various seasons you have gone through over the course of your life. What season are you in now?

2. How would you describe and name the road of life you are journeying on?

3. Consider the two tracks of your life. What are your desert places of languishing and what are your places of being fresh and flourishing?

4. What botanical metaphor do you relate to? A tree, a flower, a garden, a desert? What specifics of the plant and of your life made you choose this image?

5. If I met you, besides the usual where you live and what you do for a living, how would you introduce yourself as your best, most beautiful flourishing self? Consider introducing yourself according to your strengths, gifts, or interests to the next person you meet.

6. What is the longing and hope of your heart as you begin to read this book?

7. Write down a vision of how you see being a flourisher in all aspects of your life: God, marriage, parenting, friends, workplace, school, church, community, and everyday life.

PART 2

Transforming Your Life to Flourish

You flourish when you intentionally arrange your life to grow in the Spirit

chapter 2

Exploring
Flourishing Principles

Come to me. Get away with me and you'll recover your life.
I'll show you how to take a real rest. Walk with me and work
with me—watch how I do it. Learn the unforced rhythms of
grace. . . . Keep company with me and you'll learn to live
freely and lightly.

Matthew 11:28–30 THE MESSAGE

Faith-based flourishing is about becoming more of the redeemed
"you" that God wants you to be—your best, most authentic flourishing self—filled with the Spirit of God. This is the abundant,
vibrant life that transforms and matures you in the spiritual emotion virtues of love, joy, gratitude, peace, and hope. In this chapter
we will explore a few principles that are essential for this journey:
be authentic, be fully human and fully alive, be a whole person,
and be self-aware.

Be Authentic

You flourish when you move toward becoming your best, most authentic self.

"The goal of the spiritual journey is the transformation of self." The journey of discovering our true identity requires knowing both our authentic self and God.[1] Thomas Merton considers this the most important thing. "There is only one problem on which all my existence, my peace and my happiness depend: to discover myself in discovering God. If I find Him I will find myself and if I find my true self I will find Him."[2] We are each unique and valuable to God, and as we become more like Christ, we discover the freedom and beauty of our true identity. Becoming fully authentic as our unique most beautiful self, however, can be challenging. We get distracted. We consider other options and doubt ourselves. God desires that we each discover Him (who is God?) and the gift of being our authentic self (who am I?).

I was asked to speak at a large women's event recently, held at the church where I had spent most of my early adult years being mentored and maturing spiritually. As the time drew near, I really started to get nervous, and some of my old insecurities and fears flared up. Voices ran through my mind saying things like, *Everyone will have high expectations of you. You'd better not disappoint them or make a fool of yourself. What if you are a big flop? What if you aren't the dynamic speaker they're expecting?*

Then, as I was reading my Bible in preparation, another thought ran through my mind: *You can't take this old tattered Bible up on stage. It's all taped up and shabby looking. What will people think? You need to take the brand-new one that still has the gold on the edge of the pages. You will look much more put together.* So I pulled out the big-black-status-symbol-gold-edged-image-driven Bible and started making plans to use it instead.

That's what happens when we start comparing, contrasting, and competing. "Look at that beautiful Bible she has (or the wonderful family, or terrific job). I want one like that, too. I would rather have the life she is living than the life I have to live." We try to compensate for what's missing in our lives, and this can lead to corruption of our best, most authentic flourishing self. It is our "false-self"—our languishing self—that wants to put on a mask and build a façade that corrupts our most authentic self. Our deep, painful scars and insecurities make us want to hide or pretend to be someone we aren't. But this never works, and it holds us back from the joy, serenity, and freedom of our authentic, compelling beauty when we are secure in our insecurities.

I realized I was going in the wrong direction when other thoughts started crossing my mind. *What if I lose my place on the page? I don't know my way around this new Bible; it's not familiar to me. It's not where I feel most comfortable. Besides, it doesn't matter what my Bible looks like. It's more important for me to be at home with what I am most familiar with, to be true to who I really am.*

YOUR TRUE IDENTITY

And then it all came together. The Spirit reminded me of a profound truth, and I used it as a powerful illustration in my presentation. It comes from the story of the Velveteen Rabbit, the toy rabbit that desperately wanted to become real. He eventually did become real because he was loved by the boy who played with him. Love makes you real. To be deeply loved, as Christ loves us, transforms us deep within. The Velveteen Rabbit's best friend was the skin horse, who had warned him that "becoming real" doesn't happen all at once, and "generally, by the time you are real, most of your hair has been loved off, and your eyes drop out and you get loose in your joints and very shabby. But these things don't matter at all, because once you are real you can't be ugly, except to people who don't understand."[3]

Like the Velveteen Rabbit, when we are loved—really loved, as only God can love us—we also become real in every sense of the word. Authentic and beautiful. No façades or masks. No trying to impress others with status symbols, or trying to be someone else—secure in our insecurities. So what if we are a little beat up and frayed on the edges, like my Velveteen Bible? As long as we are the "real thing," loving God and living out our passions, personality temperament, gifts, and true identity, we can flourish to become our best, most authentic self.

Dr. Robert Holden, director of the Happiness Project in England, echoes elements of what Thomas Merton found was most important. You feel happiest when you know who you truly are and are able to experience your true self.[4] You can work hard to have it all: a nice home, a good job, even a loving partner. But true meaning and fulfillment in life isn't found by searching outside yourself—it starts inside yourself.

So don't compare yourself with how others are growing or what others are doing. Some of us may have to battle against pressure from others to be someone we aren't, or from ourselves to become someone we think we should be or we want to be. Sometimes we are even afraid of who we think God wants us to be, and we miss out on the spiritual growth and abundant life that moves us toward the best version of ourselves. God invites you on a journey to reach your full potential, your true self, becoming the best person you can be.[5]

Get to know your true self

- What kind of tree or flower do you feel represents you at this time?
- What is the best environment for you to grow?
- What are the factors that will make you thrive and flourish?
- What is the best way you learn—your learning style?
- What are your spiritual gifts?
- What are your character and personality strengths?
- What are your skills and talents—your "sweet spot"?
- What is your personality profile?[6]
- Who does God say is your "true self"? Who are you? Who are you becoming?

Be Fully Human and Fully Alive

You flourish when you live a life full of the fullness of God.

We are created in God's image with a tremendous capacity for thinking, feeling, and relating. To be fully alive you have to be aware of the full range of your human experiences and emotions. Our thoughts, feelings, and experiences are all interrelated and determine our actions. Embracing all our feelings, experiences, weaknesses, and foibles is essential to being a whole person. Being "fully human" is often associated with the darker side of human nature—brokenness, failures, sin—and how we can eliminate it from our lives. "I'm only human" is an excuse for our mistakes. However, Irenaeus reminds us that "a human being fully alive" reflects the glory of God and God's good creation.[7] When we embrace His abundance and beauty, we bring glory to God. We have to integrate, face, and deal with all the good and the not so good of our humanity.

Give yourself permission to just be human and honest about who you are and what you are experiencing. This doesn't mean giving in to every whim of your languishing self or negative emotions, going on a downward spiral. But don't deny or suppress difficult emotions, either. Unresolved anger, sadness, disappointment, and loss can all contribute to anxiety and depression.

Distinguish between emotion and action. Accept the emotion, but then choose how to respond and behave. "Go ahead and be angry—but don't use your anger as fuel for revenge. And don't stay angry" (Ephesians 4:26 THE MESSAGE).

In order to flourish, we need to be aware of and accept the full range of our emotional experience. We need friends who are honest with us, companions, and sometimes counselors to accompany us on our journey. They provide insight, inspire us with courage, and help us discern wisdom. The mantra for Alcoholics Anonymous—"The Serenity Prayer"—is a good example. It uses a very powerful prayer by Reinhold Niebuhr that can help us all in discerning how to be more fully human and alive in God: "God, grant me the serenity to accept the things I cannot change, the courage to change the things I can, and the wisdom to know the difference."

The other part of being fully human and alive is to be fully alive in the fullness of God. As N. T. Wright says, "Being full of God doesn't make you less human. Because humans are made in God's image, the more full of God you are, the more genuine a human being you are."[8] When you have the fullness of God in you, that's when you can become your best, most authentic self. God's love brings out the best of how He created us with our personalities, gifts, and talents. We are naturally supernatural people. Fully human, and fully alive in God at the same time.

Be a Whole Person

You flourish when you are fully alive as a whole person.

You were made to flourish in divine harmony as a whole person. This is particularly important today, since many have embraced a dualist way of thinking about how their spiritual lives connect with the rest of their being. Dualism is when you believe that your spiritual life is totally separate from your physical or emotional life.

You can't truly flourish if you focus on just one part of your being. All your life systems must synchronize into beautiful harmony. Luke gives a physician's perspective of God's desire for us to flourish. Several times he uses the Greek word *sozo* when Jesus heals someone. This word expresses restoration of every part of our life: our relationship with God and one another, our inner brokenness and bondages, our physical health, and our ultimate rescue from death.[9]

In Proverbs 16:24 (NKJV), we read: "Pleasant words are like a honeycomb, sweetness to the soul and health to the bones." And

Proverbs 15:30 (NCV) says, "Good news makes you feel better. Your happiness will show in your eyes." These are body, mind, heart, and soul connections. We are integrated whole beings. Each facet of our life is a complex system that impacts the others, so they must work together if we are to flourish.

Scientific research confirms again and again how all these systems work together. For instance, positive psychology research tells us that thinking and speaking pleasant words produces positive emotions. They don't just go in one ear and out the other; they create changes in our brain, elevate our mood, broaden our capacity to think, help us to have a clearer perspective on life, and allow us to make better decisions. We are more creative and better problem-solvers, and have healthier relationships and well-being when we think positively.[10]

In the next section are some of these complex "life systems" that are essential to our journey to flourish. You can refer to appendix B, "Flourish Practices for Well-Being as a Whole Person," to help you create your personal well-being plan.

FLOURISHING IN THE SPIRIT

You flourish in the presence of God's love and the streaming flow of the Holy Spirit.

All flourishing life is seeded, grows, blossoms, and receives nourishment from God. Likewise, as we receive this life-giving power of the gift of the Spirit, we can daily live in grace, arranging our lives to be guided by and attuned to this ongoing transforming, streaming flow. When you surrender to more of the Spirit of God transforming and growing you, you will be empowered not to live from your languishing self, the hindrances and vandalizing of your shalom. Partnering with God, you stay self-aware and avoid those habits and hindrances that quench the flow of the Spirit such as busyness, worry, anxiety, gluttony, resentment, and despair.

If you are deeply connected to the Spirit of God within, you have a renewable inner wellspring continuously flowing through you, expressed as God-given vitality, being fully alive with emotion virtues like love, joy, gratitude, peace, and hope. The things that aren't of the Spirit, your languishing self, and the natural pull toward your default setting of sin will be less alluring. You won't be so bound by bad habits and escaping behaviors that fill in the voids and longings of your heart. This will impact all areas of your life and relationships for the better.

"It's impossible to be spiritually mature, while remaining emotionally immature."

—Peter Scazzero[11]

FLOURISHING EMOTIONS

You flourish when you are aware of all your emotions and become emotionally healthy.

We were all created with the capacity for a wide range of emotions. Emotional maturity (knowing how to deal with the full range of your emotions) is essential to your journey to flourish. It is in the context of your everyday life and the full range of emotions you experience. The Holy Spirit provides expressions of the inward blossoming of spiritual emotions such as love, joy, gratitude, peace, patience, kindness, generosity, faithfulness, and self-control.

When you experience these deeply nourishing, positive emotions in the context of all the other systems of your being, you will feel more fully alive. The good news is that you can cultivate the continual flow of the Spirit, nurturing these emotion virtues through habits and daily lifestyle practices. When you are faced with negative emotions of fear, anger, or sadness, pay attention to these as signals, and choose constructive ways to respond and take action.

FLOURISHING MIND

You flourish when you think good, great, healthy thoughts.

The biggest battle is fought in the mind. The happiness of your life depends on the quality of the thoughts your mind welcomes. Our thoughts can support us to flourish or sabotage us to languish. Our thoughts can lead us to dwell on the negative in order to deal with our pain. We can be our best encourager or our worst discourager. Thousands of thoughts run through our minds every day, and research shows that many of them tend to be negative. Alice in Wonderland said that sometimes she believed as many as six impossible things before breakfast. Indeed, many of us struggle with believing at least six lies and distortions before breakfast.

We can't believe everything we think or feel that is influenced by our thoughts, since they can undercut our ability to flow in the Spirit and daily live out the emotion virtues. None of us are immune. But you can learn to keep your thoughts from negatively influencing you: Intentionally change your life by changing your mind. You can be "transformed by the renewing of your mind" (Romans 12:2 NKJV). God has given us "the mind of Christ" (1 Corinthians 2:16 NKJV), which is "of love and of a sound mind" (2 Timothy 1:7 NKJV). Healthy habits of the mind and positive self-talk will open up more flourishing possibilities in your life.

FLOURISHING BODY

You flourish when you respect your body as the vessel impacting your spirit and soul.

The body is sacred and requires proper love and care. The Christian practice of honoring the body is founded on the belief that our bodies are the place where His divine presence dwells, so our bodies should be treated as worthy of care and blessing. God has designed us as integrated beings, and there is a strong body/soul/ spirit connection—a connection between our physical well-being,

> *"You should know that your body is a temple for the Holy Spirit who is in you."*
>
> —1 Corinthians 6:19 NCV

emotional well-being, and spiritual well-being.

People often end up in counseling because they have pushed passed the natural limits they were created for. The body and soul will signal that something is wrong and needs to be realigned. The recent field of Positive Health Psychology and medicine have mounds of research showing that exercising regularly and eating well benefit our body, brain, mind, emotions, and overall well-being. Getting enough sleep and rest is essential for managing stress and anxiety and creating a calm soul sanctuary. And if we are doing well, our relationships will go better. So take good care of yourself, and your body, too.

FLOURISHING RELATIONSHIPS

You flourish when you are in the presence of God's love and the company of others.

We flourish, grow, and become our most authentic, best self in the presence of God's love and the company of one another. We do better together. From birth, healthy attachments are crucial for development—our brain, emotions, body, and relationships. We are hardwired for being in meaningful relationships, and when we are not, we don't flourish as God intends. Focus on building healthy relationships. Listen to others. Interact in a way that invites mutual sharing of experiences, thoughts, feelings, hopes, and dreams. Learn healthy ways of relating, even arguing. Discover your and others' styles of attachment, of relating, love languages, and other factors that will help you improve your ability to cultivate meaningful, healthy relationship attachments. Resolve and repair disputes and conflict. Be willing to take responsibility for your failings, let go of grudges, and forgive. Flourishing relationships are so important that I have devoted a full chapter to them later in the book.

FLOURISHING EXPERIENCES

You flourish when you have hope and purpose, contributing to a greater cause beyond yourself.

The purpose of flourishing is to bear fruit in all areas of our life so we can be a blessing to others. Our most authentic self and our flourishing strengths, gifts, and talents are all to be shared and given toward making a difference in helping others flourish. When we live with a sense of hope, purpose, passion, and calling, we experience a sense of meaning and fulfillment. When we focus on doing what we love in meaningful work and creating value rather than money, things, and status, we will flourish and be happy. Research shows that those who volunteer and are generous and altruistic have a higher sense of life satisfaction.[12]

Even during the challenging, dry experiences in life, we can learn to be hopeful, become resilient, and grow stronger as a result. God promises to redeem, restore, and refresh us, to make us flourishers.

Be Self-Aware

You flourish when you are aware and discern hindrances.

My sister Sylvia lives in Virginia, and she tells me that one of the great threats to plants flourishing in the south is a vine called kudzu. It is a climbing, coiling vine that also has the nicknames of "foot-a-night vine" or "mile-a-minute vine" or "the vine that ate the South," because of its out-of-control growth. Although this vine flourishes in its own way, it is destructive. It grows all over the tree, choking it from the carbon dioxide it needs, blocking out the light and strangling the potential life out of it. Likewise, there are factors in our lives and our environment that can hinder and prevent us from flourishing in the fullness of life that God has for us.

Becoming self-aware in a healthy way is an important beginning to the renewal journey, as I rediscovered on my Journey of the

Lavender Jacket. We can grow accustomed to the hectic pace, the pain and discomfort, the neglect of our souls, or having our own way. We rationalize, justify, and deny. We get used to life the way it is, thinking, *That's just who I am.* Then it gets a hold of us, blocking out the flow of the life of the Spirit. We were created for more. God wants us to live lightly, free from the cords that entangle us and overrun us with bad habits, issues, weaknesses, and our vandalized fallen human nature.

> *"One reason sin flourishes is that it is treated like a cream puff instead of a rattlesnake."*
>
> —Billy Sunday

SPIRITUAL CARELESSNESS

In pursuit of purity of heart, the early mothers and fathers of the Christian faith identified what they called "eight negative thoughts" that are present in all human hearts. This is where we get the concept of the seven deadly sins. Most of us half-recognize them, and most of us avoid facing them, but we all experience them. The first three have to do with the body: gluttony, lust, and greed; the next relate to our heart and mind: anger, sadness, and *acedia* (which is spiritual carelessness, apathy, or languishing). The last two thoughts challenge the soul: vanity and pride. These all come from within us, our default human nature, and have the potential to damage our well-being. They throw us off balance and lead us away from happiness and human flourishing.[13]

When we are not filled with the Spirit, we will function on default. In other words, we fall back into our sinful selves. C. S. Lewis puts it this way: "All your life long you are slowly turning . . . either into a heavenly creature or into a hellish creature: either into a creature that is in harmony with God . . . and with itself, or else into one that is in a state of war and hatred with God, and with its fellow creatures, and with itself. To be the one kind of creature is heaven: that is, it is joy and peace and knowledge and power. To be the other means madness, horror, idiocy, rage, impotence, and eternal loneliness. Each of us at each moment is progressing to the one state or the other."[14]

We are all moving toward either a flourishing heavenly life of harmony, or a languishing life. This growth and transformation happens slowly, moment by moment, day by day. Have you ever wondered about this battle within, as the apostle Paul did: "Why do I do the things I don't want to do?" (See Romans 7:15–20.) *Why did I say those hurtful words that I now regret? Why did I stuff myself with those calorie-laden fattening foods when I'm trying to lose weight? Why was I so impulsive to spend all that money that I now have to pay when the Visa bill comes? How did I let myself get to this neglected state? Why am I still dealing with the same old issues years later?* At times, we can all become careless, and our default nature takes over.

Early Christian philosophers like Evagrius Ponticus stated that acedia, considered the state of *languishing*, was the eighth deadly sin. This Greek term denotes indifference, the loss of enthusiasm for the spiritual life, absence of care, similar to apathy. The early Christians identified this spiritual lethargic dozing as sinful. *The Oxford English Dictionary* defines acedia and languishing synonymously.[15]

So *spiritual languishing* is defined as suffering from weariness, and failing to excite interest and be alert about our life. The sin of things done and left undone follows when we allow acedia to replace watchful expectation and attentive listening.[16]

The reality of this spiritual carelessness is a strong concern in our culture today. Rick Warren believes that we currently face five global giants—the first of which is spiritual languishing. In order to flourish and have well-being fully alive in God, we have to overcome this giant.

The remedy for languishing in sin and spiritual carelessness begins with waking up and recognizing where we have become slack in keeping alert and paying attention to the presence of God in our daily lives. Jesus urges us in many parables to be alert and wake up. "Awake, my soul!" is also echoed in Psalm 57:8. Becoming spiritually aware in how we live is the remedy and the way to overcome these deadly sins and embrace the redemption of our shalom.

HONEST, FEARLESS INVENTORIES

When I ask myself and those I coach or counsel, "What is hindering you from flourishing?" or "What could have prevented you from ending up in the depleted or wilting situation you are now in?" I often get a similar response: "I knew something in my life was not going right, but I wasn't aware of what it was or what to do about it." That is how I felt when I saw the photo of me in the lavender jacket. We may be aware of the low-grade nagging symptoms like unhappiness, restlessness, and longing, but we're not sure what to do with them. This is when we need the same kind of reality feedback for our lives that we get from the medical evaluation process, knowing what's really going on in our bodies. The scale never lies. (Well, I think mine does—at least I hope it does.)

Powerful questions serve as a reality check to create awareness. They guide us in the spiritual practice and spiritual emotion of contrition and repentance. Many men and women of God throughout time have created a lifestyle of continual self-awareness and intentional living. We need these in the rhythm of our lives—daily, weekly, quarterly, and annually. The purpose is not to impose guilt and burden but to become more attuned to the Spirit, helping us be self-aware, pay attention, and repent, eventually overcoming this giant of apathy, carelessness, and our human nature of vandalizing our shalom.

Jesus asked many great questions to get into our inner heart, to help us be self-aware and grow. "What do you want?" "Who is it you are looking for?" "Do you love me?" "Do you want to get well?" "What do you want me to do for you?" (John 1:38; 20:15; 21:17; 5:6; Matthew 20:32).

Imagine Jesus being with you now and asking you in a caring and loving way: "How are you living the abundant life I have for you, maturing and growing as a whole person?" What is your immediate response? What are the scenarios playing out in your life right now? What is blocking the flow of the life-giving streams of the Spirit in your life? Are you in a dry, stagnant place, not feeling fully alive? Are you feeling depleted, in need of renewal and new growth? What are you longing for more of in your daily life?

Powerful Questions

- **What depletes you?** What drains you of energy and wilts you?
  - What causes you fear, conflict, strain, stress, anxiety, depression?
  - Where are there dry, stagnant, or wilting places in your life?
  - What are the joy busters, peace quenchers, and spirit blockers?
  - What cords of sin are wilting you, destroying your rest, peace, and connection with God?
- **What energizes you?** What brings you positive energy and emotion?
  - What things and people do you enjoy being around?
  - When do you feel most fully alive in God, and God's delight in you?
  - Where are there vibrant signs of green life and fruitfulness?

I often ponder these questions with friends and spiritual companions:

What am I really longing for? What desire, sin, or darkness in me is hindering me to flourish? How can I be more intentional to flourish in the fullness of abundant life God provides?

As you reflect on the questions in this chapter and the sidebars, listen to the longings of your heart and the questions that the Holy Spirit is prompting you to ask. Take some time to reflect and journal. Write your own powerful probing questions for an honest, fearless inventory. Consider doing this regularly: in the mornings when you have your quiet time and weekly during your Sabbath rest. At the beginning of every new year, take some extra time for reevaluating and considering God's custom remedy for you to awaken spiritually and flourish. Go on a retreat at least once a year to slow down, be quiet, pay attention, and listen to the direction of the Spirit of God. Then begin to envision your plan for how to flourish.

49

What causes your failure to flourish?

Rate each of these as they apply to your life now, using the following scale:

1 = strongly   2 = somewhat   3 = slightly

___ spiritual carelessness/apathy
___ gluttony
___ lust
___ greed
___ anger
___ sadness
___ vanity
___ pride
___ misdirected natural human desires
___ misguided pursuits for happiness
___ insecurities
___ emotional wounds
___ emotional vulnerability
___ low self-esteem and confidence
___ false self
___ negative self-talk
___ relationship difficulties
___ stress overload
___ disappointment
___ worry
___ guilt
___ illness
___ fatigue
___ depletion, burnout
___ feeling stuck in a job, relationship
___ not being authentic—your true self
___ absence of mental health
___ feeling empty or hollow
___ excessive focus on work
___ weakness

___ inappropriate sexuality
___ love of money
___ love of power
___ fear
___ stress
___ busyness with the mundane
___ bitterness, unforgiveness
___ addiction
___ prone to worry, anxiety
___ sadness, depression
___ abusing your pleasure system
___ bad habits
___ chronic negative thoughts and emotions
___ critical spirit
___ discouragement
___ lack of love and connection
___ feeling empty, lonely, alienated
___ no intentional plan to flourish
___ unconscious needs and desires
___ weak personal boundaries
___ unresolved mental and emotional issues
___ neglecting self-care
___ family of origin issues
___ absence of positive emotion
___ accumulating more "stuff" with lack of meaning and purpose in life
___ pride in accomplishments but not in personal growth, relationships, or lasting contributions
___ other

Be Encouraged as You Begin Your Journey

At this point you may be feeling a little overwhelmed by what it takes to flourish. That is not my intent, so please don't get discouraged. As you read further, you will discover that part of flourishing includes different seasons, and that's okay. Life goes a lot more smoothly when you flourish than when you are languishing. So grasp this opportunity to reflect and tend to your life more intentionally, or if you are already on your flourishing journey, keep going.

Honestly, none of us is living up to our full potential, achieving the most authentic, best life God has for us. We don't perfectly reflect positive emotion virtues of the Spirit and good character in every situation. We still have issues we are working through on the journey of our redemption. We will go through winter and fall seasons. But the unexamined, careless life is not on the road to flourishing. We must live carefully and aware, regardless of what road we are on or what season we are going through, always coming to God in prayer with humility and a repentant heart.

When you are honest and genuine about your frustrations and vulnerabilities, you can take them to God in prayer, confessing with a heart of contrition and opening to His forgiveness, healing, and transformation. Then take responsibility, and get your life aligned with the right conditions to naturally flourish and help others around you flourish.

The great hope in the New Testament[17] is that if we choose the way of the Spirit, we have abundant life and vitality to be fresh and flourishing. This will diminish our languishing. Practically, it may look like not filling your life with things that waste time, dealing with bad habits, or reaching out to love someone. Let go and finally feel free from a sin. Think and guard your mouth before you speak. In some cases, it may be helpful to find support from a professional counselor or coaching for your healing journey.

In the next chapter you will discover how you can arrange your life to intentionally be more attuned to your desire for God, live in the Spirit, and learn the art of living well to flourish.

Prayer

Lord God, I pray that you bear lasting fruit in my life through the gift of the Spirit.

You are the fountain of life. Enliven and refresh my listless, thirsting soul and spirit through your love and vibrant life that renews.

You are the tree of life. Make strong the branches of my life that have been weakened by the storms of daily life. Keep me fresh and filled with your life.

Your Spirit is living water. Deepen the roots of my restless and weary life through the river of life in your Word. Refresh me and bring me joy by infusing me with your Holy Spirit and more of your abundant life.

Your Church is the orchard that you feed and prune by your love. Lord, I come to you longing for peace, nourishment, and to find rest in its shade.[18]

Reflective Questions and Flourish Practices

1. Where in your spiritual life have you been careless and are you now languishing? Make a list of the cords of these and other sins that are entangling you. Confess them, ask God for forgiveness, and choose to live differently. Then destroy the list.

2. What distorted or misplaced desires and longings are driving your behaviors and habits, hindering your flourishing? (Refer to *www.howtoflourish.com* for "What Drives Your Life?") What would it look like for you to let go of what drives you in an unhealthy way, and instead realign your

desires to become more authentic and balanced, so you can enjoy the journey—the people, interactions, and learning experiences along the way?

3. What are the natural default settings of your human nature and personality that lead to bad habits?

4. Which of the emotion virtues do you want to cultivate?

5. What is your motivation to flourish and bear good fruit in your life right now? (Be happier? Have better relationships? Be healthier? Live well and live longer?)

6. Refer to appendix B for the flourish practices for well-being inventory. Review the main systems and pillars of your life, and consider where you may begin making changes.

7. As you begin envisioning your journey to flourish, how would you respond to Jesus asking, "What do you want me to do for you?"

chapter 3

Intentional Living
to Flourish

Take your everyday, ordinary life—your sleeping, eating, going
to work, and walking-around life—and place it before God
as an offering. Embracing what God does for you is the best
thing you can do for him.

Romans 12:1 THE MESSAGE

Since 2006, companies in the U.S. and Canada have been infusing
water and edibles with good vibes and positive intentions in an
attempt to provide consumers with a spiritual pick-me-up. How
do they do this? Believe it or not, it's through prayer, meditation,
and music. Water packaged in pretty bottles is infused with wishes
for love, joy, peace, gratitude, and perfect health. During the bot-
tling of this water, restorative music is played; the words, symbols,
and colors on the label are designed to carry good vibrations. The
premise is that our thoughts, emotions, and actions impact those
in the world around us. The label encourages those who drink the

water to also take in and think about these positive emotions and intentions, and let them resonate in and around them throughout the day.

For you chocoholics, there are confections that have been exposed to five days of the electromagnetic brain waves of meditating monks. Does it do any good? Well, some chocolate consumers surveyed actually reported a 67 percent improvement in mood from the infused products, compared to those who ate regular chocolate.[1]

Sound gimmicky? I can imagine you rolling your eyes in dismay with me right now. Do these products really do anything besides make money for those realizing the longing in people for more of these heavenly spiritual emotions? Some psychologists would say that the marketing lure behind these products is the result of the placebo effect. Just the thought of its ability to help you will somehow convince your brain that it is, in fact, helping you.

I'll leave you to decide whether this is legitimate or not. However, new research in the fields of neurology, psychology, and even theology shows evidence supporting the idea that if you directly infuse yourself daily with biblically based spiritual practices such as prayer, meditation, music, and worship, you will benefit immensely.[2] I don't know about you, but I'd rather be infused directly with the real thing myself. Sorry, chocolate lovers!

"Live in me. Make your home in me just as I do in you. In the same way that a branch can't bear grapes by itself but only by being joined to the vine, you can't bear fruit unless you are joined with me. I am the Vine, you are the branches. When you're joined with me and I with you, the relation intimate and organic, the harvest is sure to be abundant. Separated, you can't produce a thing."

—John 15:4–5 THE MESSAGE

Infused With the Spirit of God

The Spirit of God directly flowing through us gives evidence of emotion virtues such as love, joy, peace, gratitude, and hope. You flourish when connected to the life-giving Spirit of God. Jesus says that if we abide—make our home in Him, stay intimately connected and live close to Him—we will keep receiving this unceasing flow of life nourishment and love from God. When we are fused and infused with the Spirit, we will naturally experience these emotion virtues.

When you feel spiritually dry and emotionally depleted, only the direct presence and Spirit of God as your life source will truly satisfy. No physical product, like infused water, prayed-over chocolate, or anything else, will provide the deep, authentic fulfillment we long for in life. The Lord God is known as the fountain of living waters, the streams and rivers in dry places. (See Jeremiah 17:13.) Staying connected to His stream and allowing it to flow through you is the secret and source of your ability to flourish daily. In Psalm 92, Jeremiah 17, and Isaiah 35 there are references to rivers, streams, and springs of water. These beautiful metaphors all bring the hope of gladness and the blossoming of new life.

Ezekiel 47:1–12 and Revelation 22:1–2 reference the sacred rivers of life that come from the throne of God. There are many trees (symbolic of people), and rivers of water (symbolic of the Spirit) flowing into the sea, changing it into fresh water. Everything lives where the river goes. Leaves don't wither, and these trees always bear fruit, because the water is from the sanctuary of God. Living waters flow from Jerusalem. (See Zechariah 14:8.) The fruit of the trees will be for food and the leaves will provide healing. The streams of the river bring life and make people glad. (See Psalm 46:4.)

This is a powerful picture of how we are to flourish. Isn't that what you would like in your life? In your family and community? These prophesies all relate to the flowing waters of blessing we can anticipate when the Holy Spirit lives in us as believers. Water, life, and healing can flow to and through us.

OPEN TO THE SPIRIT'S FLOW

Right now, in the quietness of wherever you are, you can invite the Spirit of God to flow through you, to bring healing, renewed life, and hope. I often pray a simple prayer: "Come, Holy Spirit." That's all it takes for God to work a miracle in your life. In John 7:37–38, Jesus invites you to come to Him and drink of this living water, and out of your heart—your inner being—will flow rivers of living water.

We are assured that the heavenly Father will give the Holy Spirit to those who ask (Luke 11:13). Jesus also said that the Father would send us the Holy Spirit as a friend, a helper, who will be with us, live in us, and give us peace and joy (John 14:15–17).

In contrast to the raging, stressful environments we live in, it's good to know that out of God's sacred sanctuary and Spirit within, we can discover a peaceful, joyful, healing, life-giving river that can refresh us and bless others.

STAYING IN THE FLOW

Our part is to discover moment-by-moment how to stay in the flow, not quenching the Spirit within. He is as close as your breath, continually available. Breathe in the life of the Spirit and let go of the things that get in the way. Then consider how you can be more attuned to the Spirit life in you. Arrange your days and lifestyle around making this a priority. William Paulshell says it clearly:

> It is unlikely that we will deepen our relationship with God in a casual or haphazard manner. There will be a need for some intentional commitment and some reorganization in our own lives. But there is nothing that will enrich our lives more than a deeper and clearer perception of God's presence in the routine of daily living.[3]

It is not about adding more activities to stress you out or make you feel guilty, but about finding the rhythm that best fits your day, a way of "doing life with Jesus." When you wake up, invite the Holy Spirit to fill your life and be attuned to the presence of Jesus. Take some time each day for quieting your mind and reflecting on spiritual readings and prayers. During the day, invite Jesus into the situations of your life, going through your day aware that He is with you in everything. Receive all the fullness of vibrant living—love, forgiveness, joy, gratitude, peace, tranquility, and hope. Drive your car being mindful of Jesus; go to work aware of calling on Him for help, strength, and patience. When you come home, be aware of Jesus and the Spirit within you as you relate to those you live with, being loving and kind. Your life will become more focused, simpler, and quieter. You won't be as hurried and busy with things that don't matter. You won't waste time and deplete your energy. Unnecessary emotional and thought clutter will be cleared from your mind and lifestyle.

And when you fail, get disconnected, or block the flow? When you don't feel "righteous," when you are afraid, stuck in old patterns, or don't see positive fruit? When your brain goes down a negative path for a few seconds? Remember the promise and hope of flourishing. In every moment there is grace to get back into the streaming flow. Like the waves on the ocean, God keeps sending a constant rhythm of opportunity for you to reconnect to His grace. Be aware of how the flow is being blocked. Confess. Repent. Then take the next few minutes to get right back into the streaming flow again.

BECOME A BEAUTIFUL PERSON

This is a picture of "faith-based flourishing," living the life of shalom that God has created us for, and becoming the beautiful people we should be. When we are filled with the Holy Spirit, the emotions and traits of the Spirit flow out, reflecting who we are in our hearts. If this seems difficult, and if you don't feel like you are living up to it, it's because in your own natural, unredeemed self you can't. You can't exemplify the emotion virtues of the Spirit on your own, just by being a good person.

You may recycle, teach Sunday school, give back, and leave less of your carbon imprint on the earth. You may do random acts of kindness and eat only organic food. You may give to charity and even volunteer to help the poor. All these are helpful to your well-being, and it's good to be responsible to others and the earth. We are to do good, and enjoy and savor the good things in life. Yet none of our efforts alone, or what the modern world has to offer through products and activities, will ever alleviate the symptoms of soul languishing, providing the authentic love, joy, peace, and hope we long for.

All around we are offered shortcuts to being a beautiful person, such as self-help fads, infused products, retail therapy, and spa treatments. They come with promises of finding happiness and peace of mind. But becoming authentically beautiful and finding a soul sanctuary "requires a daily discipline, not just a spa treatment or a consumer product."[4]

It is only as we partner with the direct infusion of the Spirit of God in our hearts and daily lives that we can receive the gifts and fruits of the Spirit—the evidence of His life in us—love, joy, peace, patience, kindness, goodness, faithfulness, gentleness, self-control—and all the other spiritual emotions and virtues. (See Galatians 5:22–23; Colossians 3:12; 1 Corinthians 12; Romans 12.)

Practicing How to Flourish

Flourishing in God's way takes some initiative, some learning, and some practice. But so does everything else that is good for you! The fathers and mothers of the Christian faith have for centuries desired to cultivate more intimacy with God and abundant living. Their legacies and vast experiences clearly show that this is possible. When we intentionally arrange our lives around regular rhythms of positive habits and spiritual practices, we seed and cultivate our lives to flourish in spiritual emotions and character.

These pathways allow us to attend to God and respond to

His Word. It's what restores shalom in our lives. But please remember that healthy habits and spiritual practices in and of themselves don't change us. They are only methods to help us surrender to God, and to be transformed and conformed to live like Jesus.[5]

Martha Graham, one of the foremost pioneers of modern dance, reflected that the art of learning to live life was similar to learning to dance. "I believe that we learn by practice. Whether it means to learn to dance by practicing dancing or to learn to live by practicing living, the principles are the same . . . one becomes, in some area, an athlete of God. Practice means to perform over and over again in the face of obstacles, some act of vision, of faith, of desire."[6]

We are each living out our vision, faith, and desire to flourish, even during life's demanding challenges. We are learning the movements of the "flourishing dance" and training for our own unique dance of life. We do this while walking in step with Jesus. Some of us are learning to dance in the rain, and others are still stepping on feet. But wherever we are in our learning and practicing, Jesus invites us to dance with vision, faith, and desire, living freely and lightly with Him. And like learning an instrument, a dance, or a new habit, learning to flourish takes practice. We need to learn the basics and then learn to apply them until they become natural to us. As Aristotle once remarked, "We are what we repeatedly do."

The spiritual disciplines are the God-ordained ways we go about learning to live the fine art of the flourishing spiritual life. God is the one who teaches us, leads us, gives us His life, and causes growth in us to make it possible for us to flourish as dancers, singers, musicians, or "athletes for God." He is the great teacher, the great gardener, the master conductor, the Good Shepherd. We partner with Him to cultivate and nourish our souls, forming the masterpiece He has created us to be.

> *"One step forward in obedience is worth years of study about it."*
>
> —Oswald Chambers

TAKING INITIATIVE TO FLOURISH

The Orpheus Chamber Orchestra in New York is famous for the musical accomplishments of the twenty-seven permanent members and other musicians who fill in. This orchestra has won a Grammy Award and performs a broad repertoire of classical music. Mostly, Orpheus is famous for having a managing director but no conductor. Every member must take ownership and leadership for their skills and contribution.[7]

Some valuable observations have been made from studying this group that are relevant to our journey: Everyone takes initiative to practice their instrument and do their best in order to make beautiful music together.

In typical large systems, organizations, orchestras, or even churches, people tend to focus on the leader for direction and responsibility, and they stop paying as much attention to themselves and each other. They don't make as much effort in their own development and contribution. They rely on everyone else. Isn't that how we often approach life and our own growth? We especially tend to defer the nourishment and guidance for our soul and spiritual life to others.

However, in Orpheus, each member has to take more responsibility without someone else to defer to. They learn the skill of listening to each other. They are also more fully engaged, giving it their all, using their gifts, skills, and energy to benefit the group. Most people usually bring only about 20 percent of their talent and energy to life, relationships, and their jobs, leaving much of their full potential undiscovered. That is not enough to flourish. We were created for more, and like these musicians, we will rise to the best that God has for us if we intentionally take more initiative.

God is the "great conductor" of our lives, wanting to partner with us as we learn to play beautiful music for Him and with one another. There are so many little ways we can begin to take initiative in learning our part, taking responsibility to enhance our flourishing, and contributing in a positive way to be shalom bringers to others.

For instance, if we take initiative and intentionally focus our minds on the things that are good, we will have less worry and more peace. We can watch less TV and choose instead to read soul-nourishing literature. Daily, plant good seeds of thought in your mind. Infuse your life and others' with good works that will make your heart glad. Spend time in prayer; it will change you and others. Uplifting music will be medicine for your soul. Being grateful will increase your contentment and life satisfaction. Forgiveness will release you from cords that restrict and bind you.

It won't come easily at first. But as dancers and musicians of God, we must keep practicing, taking initiative, and arranging our lives intentionally to flourish in beautiful harmony.

Arrange Your Life to Flourish

Most of us live extremely busy lives. We are often spiritually careless and neglectful of our overall lifestyle and well-being, not able to implement the great aspirations we learn about, talk about, and long for. On a daily basis, we tend to get caught up in the stresses and demands of everyday necessities.

What do you live for? What are the desires and longings of your heart? How do you arrange your time and days for what your heart wants most and is most nourishing to your overall well-being? Thomas Merton expressed this well when he said, "Ask me not where I live or what I like to eat. . . . Ask me what I am living for and what I think is keeping me from living fully for that."

The plan for intentionally ordering your life around what your heart wants most and what you are fully living for was called a *rule of life* by early Christians. Life was centered around patterns and daily rhythms of three basic elements: prayer, work, and rest. These were intentional ways of staying connected with God and cultivating spiritual character growth in all of life—attitudes, behaviors, daily habits, and routine.[8]

The Greek word for *rule* means "trellis." The image is of a structure and support that holds the grapevine off the ground, giving it direction to grow upward and become more fruitful.[9] So our rule of life, or intentional plan, for developing a spiritual life is like a trellis that helps us stay connected to Christ and become more fruitful in abundant living. Like tomatoes need stakes, beans need suspended strings, and wisteria and rambling roses need archways and trellises, "we need structure in order to have enough space, air and light to flourish. Structure gives us the freedom to grow as we are meant to."[10]

The rule of life was later adapted to encompass the three great realms of life—love, work, and play—where we connect with others while pursuing meaning and genuine enjoyment.[11] The three realms of life are considered to be the criteria for positive mental health and necessary for human growth and successful living. When we are fully engaged and intentionally pursue and practice these daily in a balanced life, we enhance our ability to flourish in well-being.

There are many ways you can intentionally order your life to flourish. I've provided some of the realms for you to reflect on. As you look over this list (see pages 64–68), think of what you would start with or add. What season are you in now? What are the needs and longings of your soul and life to flourish? What are the hindrances and challenges that you have to overcome? Begin creating your own intentional rule of life that enables you to stay on the journey of growing in spiritual transformation. (Refer to appendix C.)

I have changed this list around many times according to my life journey and the season I am in. There are also many other life-enriching practices and habits that can be added or moved around. You don't have to check off everything on the list every day. What's important is that you discover an intentional regular rhythm, pace, and plan for your life—keeping in mind what you are fully living for in a balanced and healthy way, whatever season you are in.

Intentional Rhythms of Life

In the overall pace and rhythm of your life, pay attention to what you are feeling most attracted to, what your heart most wants, and what makes you feel most fully alive.

As you read through this list of options, what seems most life-giving to you at this time? These ideas have been helpful to many over the centuries. Consider this list as you begin intentionally arranging your life to include balanced practices and habits for your own personal renewal, learning, cultivated relationships, and purposeful living. Use appendix C in the back of the book to develop your own rule of life.

- **Pray—Connect with and love God**
  - Bible, devotional, inspirational, and spiritual reading
  - Christian meditation and Scripture memorization
  - Journaling
  - Silence and solitude
  - Daily prayers and spiritual listening (daily office)
  - Prayer walking
  - Music: praise and worship
  - Gratitude

- **Love and Relationships—Love and connect with yourself and others**

  Love yourself
  - Take care of yourself
  - Cultivate harmony and well-being as a whole person
  - Maintain a healthy mind and emotions

  Love others
  - Cultivate friendships and family connections
  - Connect with others in community, neighborhood, work, church
  - Connect with a small group
  - Practice hospitality
  - Practice altruism (Goodness. Kindness. Compassion.)
  - Maintain spiritual friendships, prayer partners, mentoring relationships

- **Work—Pursue meaningful service to God and others**
  - Study and learn
  - Focus on: Vision. Mission. Passion. Purpose. Goals. Calling. Vocation.
  - Discover and use your gifts and talents to serve others
  - Contribute in meaningful ways
  - Practice generativity, volunteering, and generosity
  - Care for the earth

- **Play and recreation—Delight in creativity and pure pleasure**
  - Exercise
  - Manage stress
  - Relax
  - Enjoy nature and beauty
  - Vacation
  - Celebrate
  - Cultivate creativity

- **Rest—Renewal. Restoration. Enjoyment.**
  - Practice simplicity
  - Unplug
  - Slow down
  - Sleep
  - Honor the Sabbath
  - Retreat

Arranging Your Life to Flourish

How do you practically and intentionally include healthy habits and spiritual practices in the pace and rhythm of your life? Arranging yo~ to flourish is a very personal thing, and it will develop a~ particular personality style, spiritual temperament, and Be realistic and flexible to what really works and is life ~

another list that you should feel pressured to check off, or a high standard you have to live up to. It is a way of remembering and being intentional to include a balance of prayer, love, work, play, and rest. Start with a few ideas, then continually reevaluate and update, considering what has been most meaningful to you and what you would like to add, then reevaluate according to the reality of your life season and circumstances.

Turn to appendix C and begin creating your own plan to flourish in the daily flow of your life. Here is an example of some of the ways I intend to arrange my life at this time.

Daily

- *Spiritual reading*. I use several devotional guides as options to read in the morning and at other times during the day.[12] The regular rhythm of praying and reading Scripture originates from Judaism and early Christianity and is known as liturgy of the hours, books of hours, fixed-hour prayer, or daily offices. I don't always read everything, and I may skip a day. But I always have these resources that I can turn to.[13]

- *Spiritual practices*. On most days I include some of the basic Christian spiritual practices that make me feel renewed and fully alive. The early morning and evening are natural times of silence and prayer for me. I often journal what I received in times of listening and prayer, or other meaningful things I want to remember.

- *Music*. I listen to uplifting music played on my laptop while I work, in the car while I drive, or on an iPod while working around the house, preparing meals in the kitchen, or exercising.

- *Paying attention*. I am trying to pay more attention to what God is doing in my life throughout the day, being more aware of His presence in all the practical things of life.[14]

- *Spirit-filled living*. I intentionally cultivate positive spiritual emotions and character traits in ways such as being kind to those I interact with, expressing gratitude to others and the Lord, being aware of chances to be generous and do good to others, and watching for automatic negative thoughts and challenging them.

- *Work*. Most days I do meaningful work using my talents that will benefit others.

- *Self-Care*. I try to take good care of myself. That means keeping up with medical checkups and being on top of the areas where I am vulnerable and need intervention (e.g., hormone balance, avoiding bone loss, lowering cholesterol, maintaining healthy weight, dental work). I generally eat frequent, nutritious, balanced meals; get exercise; get enough sleep; and manage stress. At the end of the day, I try to slow down and prepare for a good night's sleep.

- *Connect.* I can't spend daily quality time with all those closest to me, but on most days I usually have at least one meaningful interaction, being available as a flourisher.

Weekly

- *Church.* I usually attend a church worship service or gathering with believers at least once a week.

- *Sabbath rest.* I take one day of "Sabbath" rest, silence, solitude, restoration, reflection, and enjoyment. Lately, it's usually a Saturday. I spend time caring for my garden, replenishing bird feeders, being with family or friends, or just relaxing around the house alone.

- *Play and recreation.* I try to enjoy activities that are rejuvenating, like going to the farmers' market, bike riding, going to the beach, enjoying my hobbies, date night, and enjoying new adventures with my family.

- *Connect.* I stay connected with some of my most meaningful relationships through visits, phone calls, emails, or cards. At times, I gather weekly in a small group with people learning to live daily with Jesus and one another.

Monthly

- *Mini retreat.* Depending on my schedule, every few weeks I try to take a half-day retreat. I go to a botanical garden to enjoy the beauty of nature; go to the beach; have an extended leisurely time with a close friend; or occasionally go to the spa for a massage.

- *Giving.* There are several charitable causes that I donate to monthly that represent how I would like to make a difference in the world for the kingdom of God. I also give of my time and in other practical ways.

- *Creativity.* I try to nurture my inner well of creativity (right sensory brain) with free-flow creative writing, being out in nature, trying new things, and delighting in fun and playfulness.[15]

- *Connect.* I am involved with a small group that meets monthly for spiritual direction. I also try to show hospitality and invite others over for afternoon tea or a meal to share.

Annually

- *Making the most of celebrations.* The natural rhythm of the yearly calendar allows me to celebrate with others and cultivate emotion virtues. I make the most of all special occasions—birthdays, anniversaries, graduations. In January I celebrate friends and family, taking the opportunity of the New Year to evaluate my life and goals. On Valentine's Day I give cards and share gestures of love. Thanksgiving is a chance to express gratitude, and Christmas is for giving and enjoying the traditions of the season.

- *Retreat.* I go on a weekend retreat once or twice a year for an intentional time of renewal.

- *Take a vacation.* Even if it's a "stay-cation," I try to unplug and just get to a place of relaxing where I wake up and don't even have to know what day it is.

- *Volunteer.* This varies depending on the opportunity and my availability. I have served in homeless shelters and in child care at church during the holidays, traveled abroad to teach, and contributed in leadership and administrative capacities for organizations.

DISCERNING WHAT'S BEST FOR YOU

Growing and transforming to flourish are unique to each of us, depending on the instrument we are given to use, the tune we are playing, or the dance we are learning. Wherever you are on your unique spiritual formation journey, whatever road you are traveling, whatever season you are in, God will meet you specifically according to your personality, temperament, strengths, learning styles, and what makes you feel most spiritually alive and connected with Him and others. God desires for you to be redeemed and transformed into the most authentic, best you.

I recently discovered flowering teas and have been on a quest to find the prettiest and most pleasant flowering tea to my taste. I came across a shop called Bird Pick, where I found an interesting quote on their tea tin about the art and practice of cultivating tea. Reading it made me immediately aware of how analogous fine tea selection is to intentionally cultivating our souls through spiritual practices. This is what is on the tea tin:

> The name Bird Pick originates from an ancient practice of cultivating the finest tea leaves. Extraordinary birds with acute senses would pick out the best leaves for their own nourishment. We strive for the same standard by selecting the most aromatic leaves.

It struck me that we should be just as picky as we select the best and most nourishing resources for the well-being of our souls. This is how we become extraordinary and reflect the fragrance and abundance of the best life—the most excellent of what God has to offer us.

Be intentional to order your heart and arrange your life around what fits the desires and longings of your soul right now, and leave the rest. What nourishes and energizes you? You are able to do this more acutely when you are open and attuned to the Holy Spirit giving you discernment. The Holy Spirit shapes your life by helping you identify your desires and longings as you learn to discern whether the "aftertaste" of something is empty, satisfying, or fulfilling to your spirit and soul. Your part is to listen to that discernment and then choose to live it. The sidebars list various approaches to spiritual formation for you to consider.

Here is a general overview of the established Christian faith traditions that you can explore to enrich your spiritual growth:

STREAMS OF CHRISTIAN FAITH TRADITIONS[16]

1. **Contemplative**
   Discover the prayer-filled life devoted to God.
   —Spending time with God in prayer and meditation.

2. **Holiness**
   Discover the virtuous life—in thought, word, and action.
   —Having pure thoughts, words, and actions, and over-
   coming temptation.

3. **Charismatic**
   Discover the Spirit-empowered life.
   —Welcoming the Holy Spirit while nurturing and exercis-
   ing spiritual gifts.

4. **Social Justice**
   Discover the compassionate life.
   —Helping the less fortunate.

5. **Evangelical**
   Discover the Word-centered, good news–proclaiming life.
   —Sharing the gospel of Jesus Christ and reading the
   Scriptures.

6. **Incarnational**
   Discover harmony between faith and work.
   —Unifying the sacred and secular areas of life while show-
   ing God's presence.

EXPLORING PATHWAYS TO FLOURISH

Your maturity in Christian faith-based flourishing can be
enriched and nourished by a broad range of faith traditions and
spiritual practices. Let me share a little more about how this
has woven into my own journey. I grew up in South Africa in a
Baptist church and a Methodist school. In my early college years,
after coming to the United States, I became actively involved in
a Presbyterian young adult group. Then, in my early twenties,
I was given a copy of the book *The Way of the Heart* by Henri
Nouwen.[17] This started a deepening of my awareness of God's
presence and love for me. I then began to formally study theology,
spiritual formation, and psychology, which have broadened and
enriched my journey.

Along the way and through the seasons, my daily life has changed. I have struggled, wrestled, and felt close and alive in God in many different ways: being part of creative arts liturgical dance groups with Episcopalians, Catholics, and charismatics; celebrating with Messianic Jews; keeping the rhythm of daily corporate liturgy; enjoying traditional and contemporary worship; fellowshipping in huts in Africa; offering hospitality; doing deep study of the Word and teaching; and supporting the poor and women and children in need. I gather frequently with other women—"sacred soul sisters"—for retreats and group spiritual direction, where we share our stories and our lives, having a safe place to fall into and be nurtured.

In contrast, there have been seasons when I mostly sat in the back of church and felt as if I were looking in from outside, longing for more, longing to be closer to God again. When I was in graduate school full time, working, and had two small children, I just did what I could. And you might have seasons when you just do what you can, as well. In busier times, I have caught brief moments of quiet for a devotional, gone for a prayer meditation walk, played worship music throughout the day, listened to teachings, and stayed connected with my spiritual friends. I tried to be more aware of the presence

> *"We need to discipline our lives to an ordered regime. So many of us have found the idea of turning to Christ once every minute to be enormously helpful. It is a practice as old as Enoch, who walked with God. It is a way of living which nearly everybody knows and nearly everybody has ignored."*
>
> —Frank Laubach

of God in all the mundane of my life. As Teresa of Avila reminds us, "The Lord walks among the pots and pans. . . ." God's life-giving Spirit is present with us in all of life. Keep it real, and keep it simple.

Intentional Living to Flourish

Along my journey of the Lavender Jacket, I was impacted by what others had discovered on their journeys through self-assessment in the halftime of life. One of those was Frank Laubach, a successful missionary for years in the Philippines, who reached a place on his journey where he declared that besides all his achievements, "I was a rotting tree."[18] He was languishing. Frank "confessed he had learned nothing of surrender and joy in Christ."[19]

He was determined to do something about his miserable condition and decided to be more intentional about being in constant inner conversation with God for the rest of his life. How could he be more open and sensitive to God's presence, listening to the Spirit? He began experimenting with what he called "a game with minutes." He tried to be mindful of God at least one second of each minute, living moment by moment intentionally attentive to God's presence. Amazingly, Frank began experiencing remarkable change, and his life began to flourish with the joy of God. He was more productive and lived the second half of his life taking time to be with God, being honest about the condition of his heart and life, and trusting more that God loved him and desired to be in relationship with him.

Like Frank, I also discovered that there are many ways you can feel fully alive again in God and open your life to the infusion of the Holy Spirit. What matters is that you are more *intentional* in arranging your life around the life-giving habits, spiritual traditions, and practices that are most meaningful to you. God grows us each uniquely according to our individual personality and wiring. Discover what makes you feel most fully alive in God and draws you closer to Him. Create your own practices, methods, and "games." Then make this a priority in your life and do it. Transformation happens when you begin to change your old habits and ways of thinking, renewing your mind and lifestyle, and developing the habits of Jesus. Begin practicing the art of living an abundant life of flourishing.

In the rest of the book, you will discover more proven practices that you can begin integrating into your life as you partner with God to mature and grow in Christian emotion virtues of the Spirit— more love, joy, gratitude, peace, and hope. We will begin in the next chapter with learning about embracing God's love for us and through us toward others.

Prayer Practice Modeled After the Tabernacle[20]

Symbolic objects in the Tabernacle represent our new life in Christ as the dwelling place for His Spirit and glory as well as spiritual principles and prayer practices.

OUTER COURT: APPROACH THE LORD IN PRAYER

The gate: Enter with thanksgiving for what He has done.
Lord, I come to you in prayer, grateful for what you have done for me, such as . . .

The courtyard: Praise God for who He is.
I praise you, God, for the vastness and wonder of who you are. . . .

INNER COURT: CONFESSION, FORGIVENESS, CLEANSING, HEALING, SPIRIT WATERS

The Bronze Altar: Confession and repentance
Holy Spirit, reveal to me each day those thoughts, emotions, desires, and actions that are not of you. I confess these specific sins . . . giving them over to you, laying them down, knowing that I am forgiven. . . .

The Bronze Laver: The Living Word of God and Spirit cleansing and speaking to me
Lord, may the living water of your Spirit wash me and cleanse me, flow through me, bringing life to me. I come to

you and meditate, listening as you speak to me through your presence and your Word, cleansing, healing and transforming me. . . .

THE HOLY PLACE: PRESENCE OF THE SPIRIT OF THE LORD IN MY RENEWED HEART

The Golden Lampstand: Ministry, anointing, being a light in the world

Lord, I draw my life, light, and anointing from you, desiring your truth to radiate from me. I also pray for all those who minister and shine your light. . . .

The Table of Shewbread: Meditate on God's wisdom, His presence and provision.

Lord Jesus, I come into your presence knowing you are the "bread of my life," being nourished by your presence and your Word. I bring to you all the activities of my life and my personal needs, and pray for your Spirit to give me life, for daily wisdom and guidance. . . .

The Golden Altar of Incense: Most holy place of God's Spirit and intercession

Lord, I draw close to your Spirit, being infused with your new life. I send up the sweet fragrance of continual prayers of my heart for my family, friends, and even my enemies. . . .

The Holy of Holies: Worship the Lord.

I worship you, Lord, with a heart in tune with surrendering and resting in your presence. . . .

Reflective Questions and Flourish Practices

1. What instrument or dance of life are you metaphorically practicing and learning? What character trait or spiritual

emotional virtue do you need to be intentional about growing in?

2. What habits and practices would help you to intentionally pay attention to God in your ordinary, everyday busy life—even during your work? How could you be more "infused" with the streaming flow of the Spirit?

3. What gets in the way, hinders, or blocks the Spirit life flowing through you? What could be hindering the life flow of the Spirit now?

4. Create your own intentional rule of life. Write out the areas of your life and what you would pick to be most nourishing and life giving to you now. (See appendix C.)

5. What practices and "streams of faith" traditions are you most familiar with? Which ones have been most meaningful to you, and which new ones would you like to explore more?

6. How could you arrange your life—daily, weekly, monthly, yearly—to include the habits and practices that would keep you connected to God and growing in well-being to flourish? Create your personal intentional plan to flourish. (See appendix C.)

7. Do you know someone who has tried a new practice, or does someone's story inspire you to try a new practice or habit? What would that be? Begin finding practical ways to integrate this into the rhythm of your life.

PART 3

NURTURING LOVE
AND RELATIONSHIPS:
RELATIONSHIP ATTACHMENT
SYSTEM

*You flourish in the presence
of God's love and in relationship
attachment with others*

Embracing
God's Love

> Watch what God does, and then you do it. . . . Mostly what
> God does is love you. Keep company with him and learn a
> life of love. Observe how Christ loved us. His love was not
> cautious but extravagant.
>
> Ephesians 5:1–2 THE MESSAGE

The most important human need in order to flourish is to be
loved. Our relationship with God and others is what life and love
are all about. If we don't have love, we cannot thrive or flourish. We search for love throughout our lives, often looking in the
wrong places and trying to satisfy our deep longing for real love
and fulfillment with shallow substitutes, like food and sex. But
Proverbs 19:22 says it clearly: "What a man [or woman] desires
is unfailing love," lavish love, focused love, love we can count
on all the time.

People need connection with God and others. We are hardwired for it in every neuron in our brain. Biological systems predispose us to form and sustain enduring, nurturing relationships. We need to be loved and nurtured by one another, always.[1]

We are created to be relational, as God is relational, giving and receiving love to one another. In Genesis we read that God created us in His image, and this also includes being relational like Him. God said, "Let us [Father, Son, and Holy Spirit] make man in our image, in our likeness" (Genesis 1:26). Then He saw that it wasn't good for man to be alone, so He created a partner, and then a family. He let them rule the earth in relationship and community. The Father's heart is for us to experience His great love for us, which then becomes the template for how we are to love others.

God Loves You

God is love, and He wants us to love like Him. "Love comes from God," the apostle John tells us in 1 John 4:7. The reason you can love God, or love anybody else for that matter, is that God loved you first (1 John 4:19). He demonstrated that love by creating you, by providing everything you have in this life; it's all a gift of God's love. And He showed that love to the extent of sending Jesus Christ to earth to die for you. God longs for us to know how much He loves us. Paul prayed that we would realize God's love for us. "That you, being rooted and grounded in love, may be able to comprehend with all the saints what is the width and length and depth and height—to know the love of Christ which passes knowledge; that you may be filled with all the fullness of God" (Ephesians 3:17–19 NKJV).

What are we to do with this phenomenal experience of God's love? Jesus clearly commands us to live a life of love, and love others in a meaningful way. "This is My commandment, that you love one another as I have loved you" (John 15:12 NKJV).

God created and loved us in such a deep way so we can activate

His love in reaching out to others. Parents are created as God's image bearers for children, and other authority figures often play a similar role. This can be an overwhelming concept when we realize how imperfect we can be as parents, neighbors, teachers, and friends. However, God believes in the capacity of His created people to experience His love and then reflect His love to the world. Psychologists have found that children who receive adequate nurture and formation in their earlier lives get "filled up" enough to then be able to pass on some of these healthy relational patterns.[2]

However, let us remember that "all have sinned and fall short of the glory of God" (Romans 3:23), and this applies to our parents and caregivers, as well. Because of this, each of us grows up with some limitations in the way we have experienced love. God wants to be a healer of our hearts so that over time we can come to know how wide and deep and high His love is for us. As we truly experience this for ourselves, we can more authentically pass it on to others—as friends, parents, grandparents, teachers, and coaches.

If we don't have much love in our "love bank," or if we have a crippling view of love, we don't have much to give. In order to love others, we first need to understand and feel how much God loves us. We can talk about love, read about love, or discuss love, but nothing compares to experiencing the love and presence of God. We each long to reach a day when we finally, fully understand how God loves us completely and unconditionally. This is a healing journey as we become secure in our attachment with God and the truth that "Jesus loves me."

God Attachment System

Our created desire to attach to God and others helps us move toward relationships, get connected, stay connected, and repair our relationships when we are not connected. The way we attach to God is a combination of how we view and experience ourselves, others, and God. The psychology of religion and recent work by researchers who explore "attachment styles" is finding that the core beliefs about ourselves, as well as our previous relationship attachments, are significantly linked to how we attach ourselves to God.[3]

Attachment theory is a relationship model that outlines how we love and connect in relationships to others, and how we deal with difficulties that arise in our relationships. It was first conceptualized by psychologist/psychiatrist John Bowlby, and continues to be expanded on by other researchers today. I will present variations of this model briefly outlining attachment theory and how it profoundly informs us of how we love and are in relationship with one another and with God.

Safe Haven, Secure Base

In attachment theory, relationships are seen as attachment bonds. When two people are bonded, meaning that they are connected together in a meaningful way, they become significant to each other. This relationship bond becomes a source of comfort, called a *safe haven*. In this safe haven, as we get to know ourselves, we grow and we learn to improve our relationships. We turn to our safe haven in times of distress for comfort and care.

Our meaningful relationships also become a *secure base* from which we courageously venture out into the world, knowing that at any time we can return to our safe haven for love and support. It's not unlike knowing that there is a safe harbor close by when the seas get rough and your boat starts to leak.[4]

When we experience difficulties or hurts in our meaningful relationships, our relationship attachment system sounds an alarm and triggers our stress and fear systems. We then respond in certain ways in an attempt to be heard, to be understood, and to restore the relationship connection. The ways we respond either turn us toward our relationship, away from our relationship when we withdraw and shut down, or against our relationship when we fight back.[5]

Our early relationship experiences teach us about loving and connecting and repairing our hurts and our disconnections in relationship. These patterns become internal working models of our relationships. They are our maps—the guides that tell us where our safe haven is, what a safe haven looks like, and how to respond if that haven is not there for us. They also shape how we view ourselves and others in relationships.[6] They leave us feeling either secure, with a sense of "I can get the love I need and you will be there for me," or insecure: "I'm not sure I can get the love I need, and I doubt if you will be there for me." These ways of relating with others in our early life experiences shape not only how we view the lovability of ourselves and others, but also how we view our relationship with God. Our experiences influence our answers to these questions: Does God view me as lovable? Will He be there for me? Can I trust Him?[7]

The following table summarizes the major types of attachment styles that shape all our relationships. This is not permanent, as it is possible to change your attachment style.

The Major Attachment Styles[8]
To God and Others

Secure

- View self as lovable and valuable, able to reach out and get the love they long for

- View God as reliable, loving, and there; God cares and is available and responsive

- View others as trustworthy and caring; others will be available and responsive

- Secure way of being: comfortable giving and receiving love, understand and express core emotions, able to make sense of relationship disruptions and repair hurts when they arise

- *Life Experiences: loving, caring, love is reciprocal*

Anxious (Preoccupied)

- Low view of self; worry about their worthiness to get the love they long for
- High view of God: God is able to love them but is there for them based on their worthiness
- High view of others, but doubt the availability and responsiveness of others
- Anxious way of being: work hard to be seen and noticed and be deserving of love
- Long to be connected but worry others and God won't want to be close
- Can be emotional, often mixed emotions
- *Life Experiences: intrusive or inconsistent relationships*

Avoidant

- High view of self
- Low view of God: God does His part, they do their part; God is there but not necessarily involved; God desires obedience
- Low view of others: unsure others will be there for them
- Independent and self-sufficient way of being: substitute things and goals for love and comfort
- Uncomfortable with emotions
- *Life Experiences: rejecting, unsympathetic, dutiful*

Fearful (Avoidant)

- Low view of self: perceive themselves as unworthy of the love they long for
- Low view of God: if God really knew them He'd reject them; God is not available or supportive
- Low view of others: others won't be there; long for love but fear others will hurt and let them down
- A mixed way of being: I need you, come close, then I push away as I fear being hurt; give mixed emotional messages
- *Life Experiences: abused, neglected, hurt by caregivers*

If we grow up in a secure environment, where Mom and Dad are there for us and love us unconditionally, our attachment style is "secure." If our caregivers are not secure and our life growing up is full of tension and rejection, we develop a different way of attaching in our relationships. These three ways of being in relationship are known as Anxious, Avoidant, and Fearful. Refer to the preceding pages for an outline of how these styles influence our view of ourselves, others, and our attachment to God.

Our early childhood experiences can become internalized and therefore go through life with us. They also impact how we view our relationship with God. A person who feels insecure in human relationships is most likely to also feel this way about their relationship with God.

Along our life's journey, our image of God can be impacted by our early relationship experiences. They have the power to distort our beliefs and our attitudes toward God. For example, we may falsely believe the following distortions:

"The only way I can experience God's love is to make myself perfectly lovable."

"I can't really trust anyone. No one is safe."

"God will only be there if I never fall short. God is silent and too busy for me anyway."

"God just wants me to do the right thing; He doesn't really want a close relationship with me."

When we don't sense God as our safe haven, we are left feeling rejected, dejected, and disconnected deep within our hearts. God longs to be in a close, connected relationship with us, where we can build and foster a safe haven with Him.

GOD IS YOUR HAVEN OF SAFETY

God's design for us is to experience Him in a healthy relationship. God longs to be our ultimate safe haven; our source of comfort; a harbor to which we can turn when life's seas get rough; and a place where we can be loved, cared for, and protected. God longs to be our main rock, hiding place, shelter, and strong tower. In the Psalms, David declared, "But I am like an olive tree flourishing in the house of God; I trust in God's unfailing love forever and ever" (Psalm 52:8).

God longs to respond to our cares and needs by being a safe haven and secure base. When our attachment system sounds the alarm that danger is around us, or when we are ill, fatigued, or hurt, God longs for us to reach out to Him in prayer, get close to Him, and find encouragement, comfort, and help in times of need. And it's not because He is selfishly wanting our attention. It's because He knows that His comfort is more fulfilling than any other's. This is one of the reasons that we find the Psalms so comforting; they are filled with the ways that David went to God as his safe place. In Psalm 91:2, for example, David cries out, "God, you're my refuge. I trust in you and I'm safe!" (THE MESSAGE). He even seemed to feel secure enough with God to challenge Him. Being able to wrestle with God is as much a sign of security as being able to say the right thing to Him.

It is no wonder that during times of pain and struggle, through prayer we grow and flourish in our relationship with God more than at other times. Drawing closer to Him in our desperation helps us focus more keenly on what matters most in life.

GOD IS YOUR SECURE BASE

God is not only our safe haven, He is also our secure base. He provides a source of courage and confidence from which we can venture out into our daily living. Life is very complex. There are so many decisions to make, and we encounter major challenges almost daily. So we need both safety and security. We need to know that God is going before us, making a way and guiding us, and that He'll be there for us, available and supportive. The images of Psalm 23 are very helpful. We are the sheep of the Good Shepherd, safe in His fold. And when we venture out into the world with the visions and purposes that we feel called to and face the challenges of life, we can be sure that He "leads me . . . guides me . . . though

I walk through the valley of the shadow of death, . . . you are with me . . . comfort me . . . anoint [me]. . . . I will dwell in the house of the Lord forever."

But it's also good to know that He is watching over us, and when we stray, He will come and look for us and lead us back. When we need rest and refreshing, we can come back to Him and He will anoint us with oil for healing, protection, and enjoyment. He will restore our souls. When we are confident that as a caregiver, God will always be there, loving us, available to us whenever we need Him, then we can venture on our journey with hope and assurance that our life has purpose and meaning and we will always be taken care of.

YOUR IMAGE OF GOD

Let's pause and consider another important factor in our attachment to God: how we view Him. It's called our "image of God," and since we all have a slightly different image of Him, it helps if we ensure that our image is a healthy and true one.

Many biblical scholars, psychologists, and researchers have studied the phenomenon of how we imagine God. Some researchers talk about the "God concept"; others talk about "God representation" or "God images." These are terms used to refer to our deepest beliefs and experiences of God in our lives. It can be a caricature, a stereotype, or a hidden belief that influences the stance we take before God. It is intimately linked to our attitudes, our beliefs about life and others.[9]

Our image of God is also a reflection of our internalized relationship attachments with others, especially our early caregivers. Spiritual maturity does seem to be fundamentally relational and involves developing dependence on God. Finding and creating your internal representation of God is a lifelong journey.[10]

What kind of safe haven is God for you? Are you able to turn to Him and know He is there and He loves you and touches you in your daily life? Is He a *secure base* where in His presence you gain sustenance from Him and a sense of vision so that you then have more courage to live it out?

As you begin to understand how God longs to be and can be your safe haven, you may begin to experience yourself in a new way as someone who is lovable, someone He really cares about and wants to support.

Referring to the attachment styles list earlier in the chapter, which phrases fit your relationship with God (secure, anxious, avoidant, or fearful)?

God longs for you to have an accurate view of Him, not a scolding, unpredictable, inconsistent image. Consider who God truly is by pondering descriptions of His character and the meanings of His name. Which of the character traits and images of God in the list below are most meaningful and healing to you now?

Characteristics and Descriptive Names for God

Goodness. Holy. Merciful. Wise. Faithful. Full of grace. Comforter. Father. Mother. Shepherd. Judge. Defender. Nurturer. Rock. Fortress. Safe Hiding Place. Refuge. Tower. Shelter. Protector. Provider. Rose. Lily. Door. Vine. Potter. Dove. Light. Living Bread. Living Water. Love. Peace. Spirit. Healer. Friend. King. Teacher. Kindness. Mercy. Grace. Patience. All-Knowing. Creator of Heaven and Earth. Passover Lamb. Redeemer. Savior. Wisdom. Rescuer.

DISCOVERING YOUR IMAGE OF GOD

Regardless of all the possible character traits and images of God, what is important is how *you* see God. What is your image of Him? In discussing God images, I have found in my clinical practice that people have varying degrees of comfort and distress in approaching God the Father, Jesus the Son, and the Holy Spirit, even though they know they are all one. If you find it more comfortable to talk to Jesus rather than "Big God the Father," that's okay. However, as you explore this area of your spiritual life, you may want to consider whether there is some fear of a father that needs to be healed.

Some people also find it easier to approach a woman rather than a man, and some even have a greater attachment to Mary as nurturer than to God the Father or Jesus. As theologians and psychologists understand, God is beyond gender—the Bible talks of God in profoundly maternal as much as paternal ways. Which of our earthly parents—mother or father—has more influence on people's views of God? Curiously, researchers in this field have found that both parents have profound influences on our views of God. Even though God is referred to as the Father in the Bible, He is very much a mother *and* father to us in ways that go beyond human gender.

Consider whether the way you experience God deep in your heart looks like your mother or father. God probably looks like a combination of both of them, including traits of the most important friends, teachers, aunts, uncles, and grandparents. Researchers have found that our "preferred" parent or caretaker often has a bit more influence on our image of God because we tend to equate God with our picture of a good parent. However, people who have had very negative or abusive parenting experiences can have a distorted view of God. Thank heavens God and His kingdom shalom bearers are able to heal and redeem these difficult places in our hearts.

Whatever way you view God, if you find it works for you and makes you able to approach His throne, use that image as a starting point in your journey to know Him. Over time, your view and experience of God will expand and you may begin to see Him in other ways—as a mom, dad, friend, king, counselor, judge. These are all ways He relates to us. The broader our embrace of Him and our capacity to view and experience Him, the more true to His incredible character our relationship will become.

Cultivating a Loving God Attachment

The central theme of Jesus' personal life was His ongoing, growing intimacy, surrender, trust, and love for the Father. He loved fully and completely, ultimately giving His life. But how do we cultivate a loving God attachment? If you want to flourish, this will be important.

First, we must open our hearts and minds to who God really is—develop true images of Him. Ask yourself some revealing questions. *Who is God to me? How do I think of Him? How has my understanding of Him changed over the years? How true to biblical teaching is my understanding of Him? Who am I to God?* Our images of God are important because they affect our expectations and how we respond to Him. Our spiritual journey must include opening up to God, embracing His love, and attaching in a relationship. Distorted images will get in the way and impede our spiritual progress. To a large extent, our emotional, spiritual, and relational history can all influence the way we listen to and connect with God. Yet we each have other experiences that give us a taste—or huge gulp—of God's love and goodness. Let us consider the core characteristics of God's love and goodness for a moment.

GOD IS LOVE

"God is love, and he who abides in love abides in God, and God in him" (1 John 4:16 NKJV).

"One of the rich fruits of anchoring ourselves in the inexhaustible love of God is that God heals our image of who He is."[11] In the early stages of my Journey of the Lavender Jacket, I had to rediscover who God truly was to me in my situation, and how He was present with me on my journey. I rediscovered that love conquers our fears, our worries, our low-grade and sometimes severe anxiety. *What will happen? How will this all work out? Will I ever get through this? Can God ever help me get over these issues and find freedom? How could God or others ever truly love me for who I am?*

You may have wondered about God's love for you, or if you are even lovable. You may have turned to Him and been

90

disappointed. You may have been a part of something you are ashamed of. You don't think God would want you back. You may think you have ruined your life and are unlovable. But these are your fears, not how God really views you. We desperately need the assuring, unconditional love of God. Know that He is there with you, in all things, at all times. Let God love you just as you are, wherever you are. Let Him be your secure place and haven of safety.

GOD DOES LOVE US

In Isaiah 65:24, God says, "Before they call, I will answer." He loves us and knows exactly what we need.

One night a medical missionary in Africa, Dr. Helen Rose-veare, had worked hard to help a mother in the labor ward, but unfortunately she died, leaving a tiny premature baby and a crying two-year-old daughter. There was no incubator (and no electricity) and no special feeding facilities. The nights were often chilly with treacherous drafts. The only water bottle had broken, so they tried to put the baby as near the fire as was safe, keeping the baby warm.

The following noon, Helen had prayers with the orphanage children, telling them about the tiny baby, the problem about keeping the baby warm, and the two-year-old sister who was crying because her mother had died. A ten-year-old girl, Ruth, prayed with the usual blunt conciseness of African children: "Please, God," she prayed, "send us a water bottle. It'll be no good tomorrow, God, as the baby'll be dead, so please send it this afternoon."

While Helen gasped inwardly at the audacity of the prayer, the little girl added, "And while you are about it, would you please send a dolly for the little girl so she'll know you really love her?" Helen wondered if she could honestly say, "Amen" to such a prayer. Could God really do this? We know that He can do everything. The Bible says so. But there are limits, aren't there?

Halfway through the afternoon, a large twenty-two-pound parcel arrived! Helen felt tears pricking her eyes. She sent for the orphanage children and together they opened the package to find brightly colored, knitted jerseys. Eyes sparkled as they were handed out. Then there were the knitted bandages for the leprosy patients, and a box of mixed raisins and sultanas. Then, as Helen put her hand in again, she felt a brand-new rubber hot water bottle! She cried. "I had not asked God to send it; I had not truly believed that He could."

Little Ruth was in the front row of the children. She rushed forward, crying out, "If God has sent the bottle, He must have sent the dolly, too!" Rummaging down to the bottom of the box, she pulled out the small, beautifully dressed dolly. Her eyes shone! She had never doubted! Looking up, she asked, "Can I go over with you, Mummy, and give this dolly to that little girl, so she'll know that Jesus really loves her?"

That parcel had been on the way for five whole months! Packed up by Helen's former Sunday school class, whose leader had heard and obeyed God's prompting to send a hot water bottle, even to the equator. And one of the girls had put in a dolly for an African child—five months before— in answer to the believing prayer of a ten-year-old to bring it "that afternoon."[12]

We don't get all our prayers answered in such dramatic ways. But we can be assured that God still loves us and brings us exactly what we need, in His timing, in His way. How has God shown His love to you recently, in small and grand ways?

Don't try to come to Jesus and try to be intellectually stimulating to Him. Just come and love Him. He's looking for heartfelt sincerity, for visceral passion, for authentic relationship. He loves you. He enjoys all of us equally when we just love Him.[13]

Psalm 23—The Names of God

Consider the image of God that you hold in your heart.
Which aspect of God strengthens you on your journey at this time?

Jehovah-Rohi—my *Protector*

The Lord is my Shepherd,

Jehovah-Jireh—my *Provider*

I shall not want.

Jehovah-Adonai—my *Master,* my *Lord*

He makes me lie down in green pastures,

Jehovah-Shalom—my *Peace,* my *wholeness*

He leads me beside quiet waters,

Jehovah-Rophe—my *Healer*

He restores my soul.

Jehovah-Tsidkenu—my *Righteousness*

He guides me in paths of righteousness . . .

Jehovah-Shammah—my *Divine Presence*

Though I walk through the valley . . .

Jehovah-Tsebaoth—my *Warrior*

I will fear no evil, for you are with me;

Jehovah-El Elyon—my *Defender*

Your rod and your staff, they comfort me.

Jehovah-Nissi—my *Victory,* my *Encourager*

You prepare a table before me . . .

Jehovah-M'kaddesh—my *Sanctification*

You anoint my head with oil;

Jehovah-El Shaddai—my all-sufficient *Nourisher,* my *Blessings,* my *Fruitfulness*

My cup overflows.

Jehovah-El Elohim—my *Protector,* my *Strength*

Goodness and love will follow me . . .

Jehovah-El Olam—my *Eternity*

I will dwell in the house of the Lord forever.

GOD IS GOOD

After my friend Beth got the news of metastasized breast cancer, she just sat quietly in her living room into the night. Out of this shocking silence, a very strong impression came over her: *God is good*. It was a strange thought in some ways to have on the worst night of her life. And yet, somehow God gave her this firm impression to hold her through the coming storm.

In the midst of the devastating reality of advanced cancer, the everlasting truth and image of God that flooded her being was *God is good, all the time*. He has been so amazingly good to Beth over the last ten years, and blessed so many through observing and being part of that goodness. Sometimes we question that goodness and beat our fists toward God in the midst of hard times. That's okay. Jacob did, David did, Elijah did. God has broad shoulders. He wants us to make contact with Him—even if we are upset with Him. And through the wrestling as well as normal days, He wants you to remember that He is good and He loves you as His very special creation.

GOD IS CLOSE

There are many truths about God and His nature that will never change, no matter what we go through or how we feel. Isn't it good to know that God is as close as our breath, and is ever present in our lives, especially in times of trouble? We can connect with God any time—in times of struggle and times of celebration. He is as close as our breath and in our hearts. Sometimes He's as close as "under the bed," as the following story suggests.

Kelly Pinson Adkins writes that her brother Kevin thinks God lives under his bed. At least that is what she heard him saying one night. He was praying out loud in his dark bedroom, and she stopped to listen. "Are you there, God?" he said. "Where are you? Oh I see, under the bed . . ." Kevin was born mentally disabled, and although he's in his thirties and stands six feet two inches tall, he resembles an adult in few other ways. He lives a simple life, finding contentment in his daily rituals and weekend field trips. He is happy when he works, and does it diligently with his heart completely in it. He lives content in the now. "When it comes to Christ, he comes as a child. He trusts God. Kevin seems to know God—to really be

94

friends with Him in a way that is difficult for an educated person to grasp. God seems like his closest companion," Kelly says. It is with this open, uncomplicated, innocent simplicity of the heart that we are often more attuned to God's love and His presence.[14]

Drawing Close to God as Our Secure Base and Safe Haven

So how can we feel close to God when He is not present with us in actual physical form? We can feel attached in a psychological way—like when a child walks away from a parent to play but can still see or hear the parent and therefore feels a sense of security. This happens when we stay in touch with friends and family through letters, emails, or phone calls. These connections aren't physical, and yet the relationships are held in our hearts. Just knowing these relational attachments are available and accessible to us is comforting.

Psalm 139 reminds us of this connection we have to God, however far away He may seem. Even in our darkest moments, when it feels like no one "gets us" or sees our personal pain, God is there. "Where can I go from your Spirit? . . . If I say, 'Surely the darkness shall fall on me,' even the night shall be light about me; indeed, the darkness shall not hide from You" (vv. 7–12 NKJV). Even when we feel quite alone during the first weeks in a new place, during a loss, or in the midst of a private struggle—God is there.

The question is how can we hold on to Him, or allow Him to make His presence known to us, even at these times? We need to remember—like remembering God in the Passover. We need to gently request or boldly beg God to make His presence known to us clearly enough for us to keep going. Elijah did this when he was suicidal hours after a miraculous experience with God (1 Kings 19:4–14). If He can ask God for His presence in the best and worst of times, we can, too. As long as we perceive that God is readily accessible as well as responsive, we can have a sense of attachment to God. The way we can be assured of our connection with God is knowing that He is *omnipresent*, as Psalm 139 shows us. God is present everywhere. His life-giving presence is evident in all creation.

GOD IS JESUS

God is also present through Jesus, living in you, always walking with you. God knew it was hard for us to grasp Him, so He became human so we could literally touch and see and smell and hear Him. All images of God in the Bible harmonize with the character of Jesus. "Whoever has seen me has seen the Father" (John 14:9 NCV); "Christ is the visible likeness of the invisible God" (Colossians 1:15 NLT). How can you get to know what God is like? Get to know who Jesus is and become more like Him. Jesus reflects the character of His loving Father lived out in a person on earth.

GOD IS THE HOLY SPIRIT

God also shows us who He is through the Holy Spirit. When the disciples were devastated that this God who had become man had ascended back up to heaven, God made His presence known by sending His Holy Spirit. Jesus assured them that after He left, He would send the Spirit. Even though the Spirit doesn't have human arms, the gentleness and power of the Holy Spirit are accessible to us in amazing ways. Ask God now to make His presence known to you, as He did to the disciples, by breathing His life-giving Holy Spirit into you.

Spiritual Pathways to Connect With God[15]

How do you best relate to God, draw near to Him, express and receive love, and feel most fully alive in Him?

Naturalists: *Loving God in the beauty of nature outdoors*
• go for walks outside • create a garden sanctuary • go to places of beauty for times of prayer and being with God

Sensates: *Loving God with all the senses*
• light candles • reflect on images and art that express God *(visio divina)* • worship and sing praises • pray with prayer beads or a prayer shawl

Traditionalists: *Loving God through ritual and symbolism*
• attend liturgical services • read prayer and Scripture liturgy daily•
develop symbols you can place in your home, car, and office that celebrate the church calendar in meaningful ways • develop your own
personal rhythm and prayer rituals

Ascetics: *Loving God in solitude and simplicity*
• take retreats at monasteries • pray and study God's Word in quiet
each day • attend a night-watch service

Activists: *Loving God through justice, confrontation of evil, and change*
• get involved with a cause that makes a difference • volunteer for
a campaign • serve on a school board • attend meetings to improve
social programs

Caregivers: *Loving God by caring for and serving others*
• make meals for those who are in need • offer to help in practical
ways • volunteer where you see a need • visit someone who is sick •
listen and encourage someone who is going through a hard time

Enthusiasts: *Loving God with mystery and celebration*
• learn expressive ways of worship through music, dance, and the
arts • attend services where you expect God to move in mysterious
ways • spend extended time with God in worship, when your heart
soars and you can shout out His name

Contemplatives: *Loving God through adoration and heartfelt devotion*
• spend time in prayer and worship daily, resting in the presence of
the Lord • meditate and reflect on God's Word for transformation

Intellectuals: *Loving God with the mind*
• read the Bible reflectively and prayerfully *(lectio divina)* • read inspirational books • do Bible studies to learn more about God, faith, doctrine,
and His kingdom ways • respond to opportunities to lead a small group
or teach

Healing Our Images of God

The process of growing in our experience of God's love is one
that will envelop our whole lifetime. All of us have distortions—
all of us have sinned and all of the image bearers in our life have

sinned, as well. And yet God is a redemptive God; He wants to use people as well as His Spirit to heal and grow our images of himself. A lot of healing comes in wrestling with our negative views of God and working through the tough issues.

The first step to consider is becoming aware of the distortions you may have developed in your view of God. Research on views of God within the Christian community shows that even people with the same doctrines and in the same denominations can have varying views about who God is deep in their hearts. As a result, they might experience Him very differently. Some see Him as strict—a hard taskmaster—while others see Him as tender and tolerant.

The most important issue to consider is who you believe God to be in the core of your being. As you begin to face the realities and pains of your distortions of God, it is helpful to talk with family members, friends, mentors, or even a counselor or pastor. Whatever you do, be courageous and grow in your understanding of who God is.

It is also important to expand your spiritual contacts. Try to develop healthy relationships with new people, especially people of other denominations, who you see as godly, loving, and merciful—even fun. They will be agents of change in our transforming image of God. Pursuing a prayer partner, joining an authentic small group, or seeking spiritual direction may allow for new relationships that help heal your image of God.

Perhaps most important is pursuing a new way of relating to God. This includes acknowledging your doubts, fears, and insecurities and gently but courageously offering them to God. Ask Him to reveal His loving character to you. Create specific times of relational connection with God that are positive, enticing, and renewing rather than religious, obligatory, boring, or oppressive.

Go Deep in the Love of God

As we pursue becoming closer to God so we can flourish in the ways He intends us to, there will be seasons when we do not feel the closeness of God's presence. Don't panic and worry that you might be backsliding, or that God has abandoned you. This is a time when God wants you to develop perseverance. Most of the church fathers and mothers, as well as current followers of the Christian faith, have experienced dry, dark, and difficult times. This is normal. Don't give up. Hold on. Let God hold on to you and continue in daily spiritual practices whether you feel the presence of God or not.

St. John of the Cross spoke in profound ways about the "Dark Night of the Soul," a phase of spiritual loneliness and desolation. In current evangelical Christian life, often the opportunity to go deeper with God in the dark moments of life is missed, mainly because people too quickly run away from dark times and try to grab hold of surface joys and comforts. Spiritual depth is shaped by staying in our gardens of Gethsemane, not running away from them.[16]

Let God Love You

Some of us struggle to learn the art of letting others love us. So we might have to be a little more intentional in allowing God to love us in small and big ways, including through other people. Invite the presence of God into your everyday life. You may want to try this simple practice each morning as soon as you wake up or when you go to bed at night. Pray silently, with your heart. Just be still and surrender yourself to God, Jesus, or the Holy Spirit, whichever image is most comfortable to you, saying in your heart something like:

> *God, please be present with me now. Jesus, I surrender my life to you. Touch my life now with your love. Fill me with your presence, Holy Spirit.*

Give your love to the Lord. Let Him know that His love is the desire of your heart.

*I am here, God, and I love you. You are the center of all
creation and the center of my life. I worship you. I invite you
into my life. I enjoy being with you. Be with me now.*

Imagine that God is a shepherd on a hillside, holding you as
a lamb, or that you are in a safe place and He is being and doing
what you long for. Be filled with love, joy, and peace. Rest in this
connection.

Let Your God Love You

Be silent.
Be still.
Alone.
Empty
Before your God.
Say nothing.
Ask nothing.
Be silent.
Be still.
Let your God look upon you.
That is all.
God knows.
God understands.
God loves you
With an enormous love,
And only wants
To look upon you
With that love.
Quiet.
Still.
Be.
Let your God—
love you.[17]

—Edwina Gateley

Love God Back

Paul Tournier, a great Christian psychiatrist, said that life, in order to be life, must necessarily be *dialogue* with others and with God. Our attachment with God goes both ways. God created you and pursues you so He can love you, but also so you can pursue Him and love Him back.[18] We love God because He first loved us and restored us into a loving relationship connection with Him. "Christian spiritual formation and the experience of abundant living can only happen as we fall head over heels in love with God."[19] This is the key to enjoying the "heavenly emotions" of love, joy, gratitude, peace, and hope rather than being bogged down with stress, anxiety, anger, and depression. We each have to discover and cultivate our own journey of soul restoration and relationship connection with God that leads to the abundant life of Christ and the spiritual emotion virtues.

What is God's love language? How does He want us to show that we love Him? God wants us to have an ongoing love relationship conversation with Him. He wants us to love Him with our whole life—heart, mind, soul, and strength. (See Deuteronomy 6:5.) He also says that if we love Him, we will obey Him. (See John 14:15, 21, 23; 1 John 3:24; 5:3.) Find out what pleases God and do it. We love God back primarily by following His teachings and doing His will in our lives. That means seeking His will for us in each situation, listening to what He shows us, and then doing it. We must surrender our will, submit to Him, and trust. Throughout time, these have been the "secrets of a happy life."[20]

God also wants us to be thankful and grateful, taking all our concerns to him. This is His will for us and what pleases Him, showing that we love and appreciate all His goodness to us. (See 1 Thessalonians 4:18.)

We also love God by loving one another. God is love, and those who abide in love abide in God, and His Spirit of love will flow through them (1 John 4:7–21). When we are in loving union with God, we are "filled with all the fullness of God" (Ephesians 3:19 NKJV). This enables us to become our true self, with the presence of God flowing through us to love and serve others.[21] Loving others, especially in their time of need, is our love gift back to God. In the next chapter we'll discover more about how to flourish in love for others.

Prayer

Christ, I pray that you will live in my heart by faith and that my life will be strong in love and be built on love. I pray that I will have the power to understand the greatness of your love, which is greater than anyone can ever know. I pray that I will be able to know that love, so I can be filled with the fullness of God.

Adapted from Ephesians 3:14–19 NCV

Reflective Questions and Flourish Practices

1. Describe your mother and father, or two other significant people in your life.

2. Now describe your view of God. What three adjectives would you use? Why?

3. What images and names of God are you drawn to at this time on your journey?

4. Describe your relationship with God in three adjectives. How has your relationship with God changed over time? What has contributed to the change and growth?

5. Consider how the various people in your life have impacted your view of God for the better or for the worse.

6. If you asked God, what three adjectives do you think He would choose to describe you? How would God describe His relationship with you?

7. How do you think you can love God back with your life right now?

chapter 5

Strengthening Relationship Attachments

> Dear friends, let us continue to love one another, for love comes from God. Anyone who loves is a child of God and knows God.
>
> 1 John 4:7 NLT

Now that we understand the importance of attachment bonds, let's look at how we can strengthen our relationship attachments. Life is busy and there are many distractions. But when we don't love well, or when we fail to repair a damaged relationship quickly, we will suffer. It's not surprising that there is an epidemic of isolation, unhappiness, and other illness and health risks in our society. Our intimate relationship attachments are at the top of the list of predictors for happiness and well-being.

As emphasized in the last chapter, we are hardwired to connect with God and people. It's in our genes. We can't possibly flourish without healthy relationship attachments. God created us for love, so the nurture and love of one another is an essential ingredient in flourishing. Our relationships enrich every aspect of our lives. As we share our joys and tribulations together, we develop important buffers that can help us when we face stresses and struggles.

This process begins when we are infants and continues into marriage and throughout our lifespan. We need each other's love, nurturing comfort, and assurance as we discover ourselves, and also in finding and fulfilling God's purpose in our lives. When this happens, we won't merely exist; we will indeed flourish.

Flourishing in Life and Relationships

Love is the essential foundation for our social attachments, psychologically and spiritually. The Institute for Research on Unlimited Love, which "scientifically examines the power of unlimited love in human moral and spiritual experiences,"[1] focuses on the science of love, asserting that love is the crowning glory of every life, for it is the ultimate source of our meaning, dignity, and deep happiness.[2]

All the goodness of life is nurtured in the soil of love. Love comforts, heals, liberates, and elevates our lives in a way that is transformational. Successful human development involves absorbing love, sharing love, and giving love unselfishly away.[3]

Scientists and theologians alike tell us that we must each make daily choices to deeply embrace and live this love if we want to flourish. There is a lot of research and many stories to support this principle, and to help motivate you to give this a priority, allow me to cite some examples:

- Data from the University of Chicago's National Opinion Research Center reveal that people with five or more close friends (excluding family) are 50 percent more likely to describe themselves as "very happy."[4]
- The Masai tribe in Africa live in huts made out of dung. Ed

Diener found that the happiness of the poor Masai people is not substantially lower than that of billionaires. Happiness is clearly not about money or comfort, but rather it evolves from very strong, close family and social connections.[5]

- In the Report to the Nation from the Commission on Children at Risk, Janice K. Kiecolt-Glaser at the Ohio State University Medical Center did a series of studies and found there is a link between relationship/intimacy and better health/stronger immune systems.[6]

- Children and teens from families who are emotionally attuned and connected have better physical health, score higher academically, and are able to regulate their emotions, allowing children to get along better with friends and have fewer negative reactions at school. When these children are sad, angry, or scared, they are able to react in more emotionally healthy ways such as making sense of the situation and soothing themselves, then bouncing back and completing school work.[7]

The evidence is overwhelming that we flourish in the presence of secure love attachments—in our family, marriage, friendships, community, church, small group connections, school, and workplace.

There is value in friendship. Two really are better than one. We are better together. The support of others can ease devastation or disappointment, and it opens up the possibility for

"One becomes a truly loving person by opening oneself to love and goodness. True love is calm, confident and self-possessed: it presupposes the liberating experience of having been loved. This wonderful and irresistible power of love is the ultimate treasure in human life. In order to receive it, one must be open to the gift that is in life: one must look for flowers and drink in their beauty: one must count blessings and dismiss woes."

—Demetrius Dumm, OSB

healing, growth, and flourishing. To pursue happiness and a flour-ishing life is to pursue healthy relationship connections—to love people and be loved.

Loving Relationships Can Change Your Life

Little baby Jessica was born addicted to heroine, morphine, and cocaine. She was given only about eight hours to live due to the severity of the drugs in her little body. But she managed to survive. For two weeks she was in intensive care. My friends Cecelia and Jeff received this sweet girl into their home when she was eight months old, and they began taking her to pediatric specialists. She had cystic lesions on the right frontal lobe of her brain, which resulted in partial paralysis on the left side of her body. She couldn't crawl.

Cecelia and Jeff believed that God would heal Jessica, so they continued with all the medical specialists and the treatment advice along with daily exercises. Every day they prayed and spoke over her when she went to bed and when she got up. They prayed, "Thank you, Jesus, that Jessica is being healed." After two years of persistent care, every cystic lesion in Jessica's brain was resolved. The neurologi-cal specialist declared, "Jessica is a medical miracle. I have never seen a healing like this! The love connection is what healed Jessica."

Love has the power to heal physical, mental, and emotional problems. Today Jessica is in college and is flourishing. She loves Jesus and is continuing to live out a promising, thriving life.

How to Foster a Loving, Caring Relationship
That Can Provide a Safe Haven[8]

1. **Be trustworthy.**
   Be not only dependable, but emotionally reliable and predictable.

2. **Be emotionally available.**
   Be fully present and attuned to the person you are caring for.

3. **Be physically available.**

   Be willing to show up and give the gift of your time.

4. **Be considerate when responding.**

   Choose to respond in the best interest of the person and your relationship.

5. **Be willing to repair conflict.**

   Be quick to apologize and quick to forgive.

6. **Be willing to grow as a person so you can grow in loving others.**

   Trust is built when those around you know you are willing to self-reflect, learn, and change.

Love Is Who You Are

Watching little Jessica flourish in the loving embrace of Jeff and Cecelia, and through the support of their church community, I became more and more convinced of how powerful the impact of love and healing can be in our lives. I have seen the healing power of God's love flowing through the lives of my daughters, my sisters, and my friends. Jesus calls us to reflect Him, to allow His life and Spirit of love to flow through us, providing life-giving nourishment to our souls and to others, like a stream or a rose in the desert.

The world desperately needs to see God's love shine from those who genuinely and accurately reflect Christ's likeness. We were created to live our lives practically, reflecting Christ, with love for God and others.

When we flourish in shalom, we naturally respond to the command of Christ to love the Lord with all our heart, mind, and soul, and to love our neighbor as ourself. When we invite true shalom into our lives, we take it out to the world that so desperately needs love, joy, peace, justice, and the opportunity to flourish in well-being.[9]

Be a Loving Person

There will be so many situations in life and relationships when things get messy and you just won't know what to do. You may feel stuck by people or situations. As a psychotherapist and life coach, I hear the question "What should I do?" over and over again. And honestly, there are times I don't know what to say. During these times—and times in my own life when I don't know what to do—I've found that the most helpful question to ask is, "Lord, who do you want me to be right now?" In these moments of desperation, all I can be is a person who reflects the love of God, and try to express the positive spiritual emotions that God has taught me.

Even if you are trapped in a troubling situation without any clear direction or solution, you can always at least be loving—humble, patient, kind, and unselfish. Be filled with the Spirit of God. The doing will come out of the being. A good tree will always bear good fruit. A loving person will always do kind things. A person walking with God will be able to discern the mind of Christ. A good relationship is the result of loving well. So for each relationship in your life, ask yourself this question: "Who do I want to be in this relationship?"

A sure way to test if you are living a lifestyle of love is to put your name as a substitute for the word *love* in the passage on love in 1 Corinthians 13: (Your name) is patient, kind, not jealous, doesn't brag, isn't proud, not rude, not selfish, doesn't get upset with others, doesn't count up wrongs, isn't happy with evil but is happy with the truth. (Your name) patiently accepts all things, always trusts, always hopes, and always remains strong. Does this ring true for you?

Create a To-Be List

Who do you want to be like? What character traits are you aspiring to? Consider the loving character traits of God the Father, Jesus, and the Holy Spirit.

Love Is Unconditional

Unconditional love creates a safe place for us to be transformed and become authentic. The greatest need and yearning for each of us is to be fully known and yet still deeply loved. When we know that we are loved unconditionally, we are more willing to be honest about who we are.

Franklin Graham tells of how, as a teenager, he pulled up to his dad's office on a Harley motorcycle one day and burst into his father's board meeting to ask for some money. Franklin was dressed in leather, all dusty and bearded. But without hesitation, Billy proudly introduced him as his son to his prestigious board. He didn't apologize for his son or show any shame or embarrassment. Franklin tells of how the love and respect his father gave him that day never left him, even during his rebellious years. Billy Graham modeled the unconditional love of God toward him. He loved him just as God loved him.

It is this supernatural power of the unconditional love of God that changes people's lives.

Love Is a Choice

Those of you who aren't feeling loving right now will be encouraged to know that love isn't a fanciful state of blissful feelings. Love is mostly a decision about who we will be. Don't confuse it with romantic love. Mature, true love is unselfish and is transformational. The media has distorted our perceptions of love with some crazy myths. Love doesn't strike you with an arrow, or slay you, rendering you uncontrollable. You don't fall in love like you would fall into a ditch and not be able to get up again. Mature love in a broader sense is a form of closeness, a decision and a commitment to be and act in a certain way.

Being loving isn't always easy. Sometimes loving can be very difficult. At some point you will be challenged to love the unlovable—people who don't love you back, who even irritate you. We have to choose to love people who are unkind, ungrateful, and even hurtful. Doesn't that sound like some of the people you have to live with—a spouse, a child, a family member, a friend, a co-worker? Often, the people closest to us end up being the ones who are difficult, irritating, demanding, and disappointing. It's so much easier to love those nice people we connect with only occasionally.

Without God's love in you, you can't possibly have this mature kind of love. It won't necessarily come naturally. Your fearful emotional brain system will hijack you down the low road, causing you to act defensively and protect yourself from perceived harm. Your defenses will tell you to take care of yourself and be selfish. Your stress response system will either put up a fight, run away, or shut down. Your tongue will give some lashings to put the person who hurt you in his or her place (which you will later regret). In the moment, fighting back will feel good. Your behavior will be controlling to match your obsessive, fearful, negative thinking. Overall, if you just give in to these automatic unloving ways, you will eventually feel lousy.

Loving others starts with our response to God's love. It is up to us to choose to reciprocate His love by loving Him back and then loving others. He won't force us, but you can choose to direct, lead, and open your heart toward the best, most loving way. This is the key to lasting, fulfilling relationships, and ultimately your happiness.

Love Can Be Cultivated

"Dear friends, let us continue to love one another, for love comes from God. Anyone who loves is a child of God and knows God" (1 John 4:7 NLT). If love is who God is in us, then we can learn to access and release more love. The more you choose to be loving and do loving things, the better you will become. "Practice these things; be committed to them, so that your progress may be evident to all" (1 Timothy 4:15 HCSB). Continue choosing to love others. Let the Spirit flow through you, and God's love will come more naturally.

You will have to rely on the love of God in you. It will take a conscious effort to battle against doing what comes naturally in all your human systems. You will have to tell your brain how to think so it can direct your actions and feelings. Love as a mind-set, a daily way of being, becomes part of your intentional lifestyle, a habit and regular life practice. And it starts with a decision.

When you learn to love imperfect people with God's unconditional love flowing through you, lives will change and you will change. If you will commit to this, you will experience God's transforming love, which is filled with abundant, vibrant joy, peace, and hope. I pray that "your love will grow more and more; that you will have knowledge and understanding with your love" (Philippians 1:9 NCV).

God's love in us is built on a few pillars: patience, kindness, and unselfishness.

BE PATIENT

"Be completely humble and gentle; be patient, bearing with one another in love" (Ephesians 4:2). Becoming a patient person is important because it helps you respond in a positive way to a negative situation. No one likes to be around an impatient, emotionally reactive person. It doesn't bring out our best flourishing self. Patience uses self-control to manage the emotional brain when confronted with difficult emotions like anger. When we have reactive outbursts, we always regret it, and it never makes anything better. Patience helps you control your emotions and your tongue, rather than having them control you. When we practice patience, we bring internal calm during an external storm. We can learn to be still, wait patiently, and foster peace and quiet within and without. With patience, we can persevere during hard times along our journey, in our relationships, and resting in our hope and trust in God.

111

BE KIND AND COMPASSIONATE

"Let no one ever come to you without leaving better and happier. Be the living expression of God's kindness: kindness in your face, kindness in your eyes, kindness in your smile."

—Mother Teresa

"Be kind to one another, tenderhearted, forgiving one another, just as God in Christ forgave you" (Ephesians 4:32 NKJV). This is the way we should live; it's who we are called to be and what we should do—be kind, loving, and forgiving. Kindness is love in action. "Dear children, let's not merely say that we love each other; let us show the truth by our actions" (1 John 3:18 NLT). If patience is *how love reacts* in order to minimize a negative circumstance, kindness is *how love acts* to maximize a positive circumstance. Love expressed in kindness is what you do, how you behave. Patience avoids causing more of a problem, and kindness creates a blessing. "Love makes you kind. And kindness makes you likable."[10] When you are kind, people want to be around you. They see you as being good to them and for them.

Every small gesture of goodness and kindness can make a world of difference to our own well-being and to others'. Kindness writes notes of appreciation, listens, and is considerate. Research has shown that a single act of kindness can strengthen our immune system and increase the levels of serotonin (which makes us feel happy and at ease) in both the recipient of the kindness and the one being kind. Those who witness an act of kindness are affected in the same way. Kindness is essential to good relationships: a happy marriage, a loving family, and satisfying friendships.

Compassion and Kindness Can Be Costly but Rewarding

It had been one of those really full, busy days, and the family was waiting at home for me to bring some dinner. I quickly stopped off at the store and picked up the very last cooked rotisserie chicken they had. As I started the car, I noticed a man rummaging in the trash can. I was strangely filled with compassion, so I got out, approached him, and said, "Hello, I was wondering if I could buy you something to eat." Surprised, he straightened up, and I could tell his mind was scrambling for a choice response. "Wow—well . . . that would be very nice. Um, well, let's see, um . . . what I would really like . . . I think . . . is . . . one of those . . . cooked chickens."

No, not the chicken! I thought. *It's the last one.* "Would you like a sandwich, or a hot meal from the food bar?" I tried to get him to change his mind. "No, no," he replied, "I really would be quite happy with the cooked chicken." It was all just too bizarre. He had to choose the thing that would cost me the most.

It took me a few seconds to process my thoughts. "I don't want to be a bother," he said. It was then that I realized I needed to just give him the chicken. "I would be glad to give you a chicken. In fact, I have one here in my car. Let me get it for you."

Gratefully, he took the chicken, and I drove off with a "helper's high." I felt a sense of meaning, buoyancy, and warmth, which research has shown are some of the benefits of doing good unto others. Although I now had no dinner for my family, I still felt a sense of joy and fulfillment in having responded to the prompting of the Holy Spirit to give up my chicken in a somewhat random but intentional act of kindness.

Each day we face the challenge of listening to the voice of the Spirit of God leading us to give up our time, our expectations, our selfish ways and our stuff. Jesus modeled this for us. He was always in tune with the voice of the Father—to the extent of giving up His life for us. How are you being stretched to show kindness and compassion to someone in your life? What is it costing you?

BE UNSELFISH

Some women give, serve, and nurture others to the point of self-depletion. When they try to take care of themselves, they feel like they are being selfish. Others act selfishly out of pain, neglect, and fear of not being provided for. Women who were raised in indulgent or neglectful families often feel entitled and can tend to be selfish.

The world tells us to watch out for ourselves and put others second. But it's not that you come second, and others first. I believe that we need to be more balanced—not holding on too much, but also not giving away so much that we are truly depleted and damaged. We love others as we love ourselves. Healthy self-care is a spiritual practice in flourishing. When you put the well-being of others before your own in a healthy, balanced way, you actually experience more love within yourself, and that leads to inner joy. Fulfillment comes when we are unselfish. In a marriage, when you relinquish your rights for the sake of meeting your mate halfway, you get a chance to lose yourself to the greater purpose of marriage. Any time we give of ourselves to a meaningful purpose greater than ourselves, we are cultivating fruitfulness and the fulfillment of a life worth living.

Serve

Serve others by loving God. Love God by serving others. When we choose to serve others, our relationships flourish. Serving is the way to conquer self-centeredness. Jesus came to serve. To serve means to do something good for a person, to perform an act of love. Love looks for what is good and puts itself out to do that. When we live with an attitude of servanthood with our whole lives, we can still take care of the needs of our own soul while we live as servants. When we find this healthy balance, our lives bear fruit.

New research verifies that when you discover your gifts and strengths and use them to serve in your relationships and activities each day, you will be happier and more fulfilled in life.[11] Discover your gifts and strengths, and use them to serve.[12]

Be Altruistic and Volunteer

According to Stephen Post, president of the Institute for Research on Unlimited Love and coauthor of *Why Good Things Happen to Good People*, there is a definite link between doing good to others and living a happier, healthier, longer life. When we serve others with our gifts and strengths without any anticipated payoff, there is a definite benefit to our own well-being.[13] Giving altruistically to others has proved to be one of the most consistent elements of happiness in people across the world. Teens who volunteer and get involved in altruistic projects have a lower chance of high-risk behaviors, and they continue these positive behaviors into adulthood, reaping continued benefits to their well being.

Purposeful Giving and Generosity

"Giving is one kind of love you can count on, because you can always choose it: it's always within your power to give. Giving will protect you your whole life long."[14]

As we recognize how much we are blessed in so many ways, we naturally respond with generosity. Realizing that all we have is entrusted to us by a loving God, our hearts are then moved to share.

In *Gift from the Sea*, Anne Morrow Lindbergh talks about how women instinctively want to give, yet resent giving themselves away in small pieces, purposelessly. They fear that their energy expended is just going down the drain. "Purposeful giving is not as apt to deplete one's resources; it belongs to that natural order of giving that seems to renew itself even in the act of depletion. The more one gives, the more one has to give—like milk in the breast."[15]

Purposeful giving has balance and boundaries. A woman can give to the point of depletion unless she also cares for herself and receives from others. Receiving is often harder than giving but is just as important. When we receive from others, we reveal to them the gifts they have to offer. It is in our receiving that others discover their gifts.

Be a Cheerful Giver

One of thirteen children, Michael Oher grew up in a rough section of northern Memphis, Tennessee, bouncing between life in foster care and on the streets. He was left to fend for himself by a drug-addled mother until one cold night when Leigh Anne and Sean Tuohy invited him into their home.[16]

"It's great to write a check . . . but it's more important to give up your time, and yourself, your talents," Leigh Anne Tuohy says. "Michael's life wouldn't have been changed if we just wrote a check. He needed our time and our attention and that's what kids need."[17]

Money is not the only way you can give. Sometimes a kind smile, a friendly hello, or encouraging words may be just the pick-me-up someone needs for that day. You can also give of yourself to serve in a practical way, or give someone an opportunity.

"If there is one meaning we'd like you to take from our story, it's this: The person you just walked past is the one who could change your life," the Tuohys wrote. "So, every once in a while, stop and turn around."[18]

We can learn from this family about being cheerful givers. I like Sean Tuohy's Popcorn Theory about noticing others: "You can't help everyone. But you can try to help the hot ones who pop up right in front of your face."[19] The Tuohys didn't plan on adopting Oher. He was an opportunity that came their way, and they responded. The Tuohys show us wholesome compassion and cheerful giving by word and deed. When you notice how you can become a *flourisher* to the people you come in contact with, you become a sacred shalom bringer.

Stop and thank God for His goodness to you, and then ask Him how you can reach out to someone in need.

Share Good News and Joy Enthusiastically

Respond positively to daily good events in others' lives. Share in their joys. *What do you do when things go right?* We don't usually think that this makes much difference, but it does. Tell your family and friends about the good news and events in your life. Research done by psychology professor Dr. Shelly Gable and her colleagues at UCLA found that telling others good news about positive events in our life—sharing our joys—is associated with positive benefits such as more love, joy, happiness, and well-being. Another benefit, increased relationship satisfaction and intimacy, is even greater when the person we tell responds enthusiastically to our good news. This is known as *active/constructive responding.*[20] Be just as excited if not more than they are. Ask a lot of questions and show genuine happiness about the good events in others' lives. Be present and engaged; maintain eye contact; and show genuine interest, enjoyment, and excitement. This gives such a wonderful picture of how God delights in us and all the goodness He shares with us, and He wants us to celebrate this together.

Repair Relationships

All this goodness, kindness, and love is nurtured in a complicated system that involves all we are. Naturally, we aren't going to get it right all the time. You will be hurt, let down, and offended by people, either intentionally or unintentionally. You will be wronged and taken advantage of, and this isn't fair. The way you handle these offenses will impact your peace and happiness systems. The research shows that when you have hurt someone, let them down, and not been their safe haven, how you come together and make sense of it, listen to each other, and show empathy is what is most powerful. Often it is not that we have the argument that matters, but whether we are able to come back and repair the hurt from the argument.[21]

In all relationships, the ability to repair an argument, a disagreement, or an offense is essential to powerful healing. When we ignore repair attempts we not only continue the hurt, but we reinjure the person. We build upon previous hurts. Failed repair attempts cause you to lose hope in the relationship. Your fears arise and you begin to think, *We will never get along. We shouldn't be in a relationship. I knew you would reject me. I'm never understood by anybody.*

John Gottman, researcher and expert in the study of marriage, found that couples who argued in negative ways using criticism, contempt, defenses, and stonewalling were heading toward unhappy marriages and divorce. However, if a couple is able to make small repair attempts in these negative interactions, the conflict is deescalated. This has a profound impact on a couple's ability to bounce back from arguments.[22]

Forgive and Let Go of Grudges

When our friends let us down, our spouse criticizes, our children don't appreciate us, or our boss is holding us back, we are often filled with perceived and real injustices. We are left to decide: Do we hold a grudge or begin the process of forgiving?

One of the main benefits of forgiveness is for ourselves, not the person who has wronged us. When we hold on to anger and resentment, it leads to ruminating on our offenses. We build a case, adding to the emotion and negativity. What was once manageable is now overwhelming and unforgivable. What could have been repaired now feels like a deep, unforgivable offense. Bitterness and resentment take root and create a grudge. We entertain and obsess on vengeful fantasies that distort our perceptions of others and life. Holding a grudge poisons all your life systems, causes you to languish, and can even make you sick. That is because it increases the level of stress hormones, blood pressure, hostility, and the chance of depression along with the desire to numb and soothe your pain with shopping, food, and substances. Holding a grudge causes you to redefine a part of your life by how you have been hurt.

So you have to decide if you will spend the rest of life with the pain you didn't deserve in the first place, or if you will get freed from it and get on with your life. Letting go of grudges releases all your life systems from excessive stress hormones and frees you to greater spiritual and psychological well-being. Forgiveness is the only way to heal yourself and free and repair relationships. When you let go of grudges, you have more freedom, health, happiness, and well-being. My father, Dr. Archibald Hart, says that forgiveness is giving up your right to hurt someone back.

Research on forgiveness done for decades by Everett Worthington Jr. highlights the importance and complexity of forgiveness. There are two different types of forgiveness. Decisional forgiveness is when we decide to forgive. Emotional forgiveness is when we experience other positive emotions in place of negative unforgiving emotions. For example, you may make a decision to forgive a drunk driver who causes someone to be paralyzed, but you may not feel warm toward the person.[23]

Dr. Lewis Smedes, another well-known writer on the topic of forgiveness, shares a few simple things about forgiving that can be helpful. Forgivers are not doormats; they do not have to tolerate the bad things that they forgive. We don't have to wait until the other person repents before we forgive him or her and heal ourselves. We don't have to instantly feel peace about it. Forgiving is a decision, and it is a journey. It takes time, so be patient and don't get discouraged. If you make a mistake, you have another chance to do it over again.[24]

Letting Go of Grudges Exercise[25]

1. Begin with being committed to the process of forgiveness and change.
   - Be intentional about shifting your focus from the pain of grudges to gratitude. Use gratitude to loosen the grip of grudges on your life. Focusing on negative emotions causes your brain to have tunnel vision and keeps your view narrow, constricted, and negative.

   - When you intentionally make your brain think of a positive emotion like gratitude, another part of your brain is accessed, and this allows you to have a broader perspective. You then have the ability to more accurately make sense of the situation, have empathy, hold the other person's perspective, and journey out of the clutches of the negative impact of the grudge.

2. Is there a person or a situation you have a grudge against?
3. Draw a circle in the center of a page and write a few words that catch the essence of your grudge.
4. On the rest of the page, write words or phrases that describe how

God is using this situation, and other positive things and perspectives about the person or situation. What are you grateful for?
5. Now hold this out at arm's length and take a look at the situation from another perspective.

Flourish in Relationships

As we approach enriching our relationships, we usually want to know how to improve our skills to make them better. How to love our spouse, how to parent, how to be a better friend. As we have explored in this chapter, healthy love attachments are based on who you are and who you are becoming. God uses our relationships to help us grow and become more mature in our character. Your relationships are God's crucible for your transformation and for Him to reveal himself to you. With His Spirit of love in us, He shows us how to practice the fine art of loving—how to be patient, kind, and unselfish.

We learn these spiritual character traits while in close relationships with friends and through the process of growing in a marriage or as a parent. These relationships are opportunities to refine our souls, to enrich our lives, and to become shalom bringers to each other. Loving others is a primary pathway to letting God love you; worship God and love Him back. Loving others begins in our most intimate relationships: family attachments, meaningful friends, and community connections.

FAMILY

Virginia Satir, American psychologist and educator, taught about the value of love beginning in our primary attachment relationships with our parents and families. She states that "feelings of worth can flourish only in an atmosphere where individual differences are appreciated, mistakes are tolerated, communication is open, and rules are flexible—the kind of atmosphere that is found in a nurturing family."[26] The power of unconditional love, acceptance, and nurture transforms us. It starts when we are children and continues throughout our lifespan.

While researching for my book *Is Your Teen Stressed or Depressed?*[27] I came across a PBS special on the teen brain. In its conclusion, despite all the new scientific research, experts said that the most beneficial thing for teenagers and the development of their brain is a good relationship with their parents. The advice they gave parents was to spend quality time with their children, loving them.

Some of you may not have a "safe haven" family. You can choose others outside your family, who then serve as your attachment objects. What a blessing it is that we have the "Family of God"—where we are all brothers, sisters, and parents to one another. Spiritual mentors, spiritual directors, and other people of wisdom become our spiritual parents. Sacred-soul-sister-friends nurture and mother one another. Our closest friends and our church community can become our family of choice.

CLOSE FRIENDSHIPS

Friendships nurture and nourish us in times of joy and sorrow. Friends listen to our heartaches without blaming us for having problems. We find out who our true friends are when they are happy with us for our successes and sad for our failures. True friends are companions, not competitors. Friends give us wise counsel to keep us from making foolish choices. We run the spiritual race better when we do it alongside others. When accompanied by close friends on the journey of life, we are more likely to take risks, pursue goals, follow through on commitments, and endure trials if someone goes through it with us. Who do you "do life" with?

> *"Friendship is a basket of bread from which to eat for years to come. Good loaves fragrant and warm miraculously multiplied; the basket never empty and the bread never stale."*
>
> —Catherine de Vinck

In the Bible we read that Peter had James and John. Paul had Silas and Barnabas. Moses had Aaron and Miriam. David had Jonathan. Elijah had Elisha. Mary had Martha. Which friends have you chosen carefully to journey with you? (See Proverbs 12:26.)

People with social support live longer and are healthier. Friends who help you flourish influence you to be the most authentic, best self that God intends you to be. They replenish you when you are depleted. They give you permission to be fully human and fully alive in God. My very best friends and soul companions are those who are also friends with God and who strengthen my faith journey and relationship with Him.

Spiritual friends share a kindred desire to intentionally pursue and be open to the things of God. They help pay attention to the work God is doing in each other's lives and help each other respond. They are a safe place we can fall into, where we can be undone, where we can become authentic. They spur us on to grow in the abundant life God has for us. They reflect to us the best of who God has us to be. Find ways to connect with friends and ways that you can nurture one another.

COMMUNITY CONNECTION

"Each friend represents a world in us, a world possibly not born until they arrive, and it is only by this meeting that a new world is born."

—Anais Nin

In addition to friends, we also need to be connected to communities. "Those who are planted in the house of the Lord shall flourish in the courts of our God" (Psalm 92:13 NKJV). Christian life flourishes in community connection. In following Jesus together, we are to encourage one another to outbursts of love and good deeds. (See Hebrews 10:24–25.) Gathering together for times of worship, liturgy, music, teaching, and sharing in meals and fun times provides nurture and sustenance to our souls.

I have experienced these profound benefits in the Strength for the Journey retreats that I co-lead, and in the quarterly gatherings of women I host in my home. We partner in leadership as we gather together to be encouraged and strengthened in the presence of God and one another. We share our stories, listening and praying with each other. God is always present with us, and our lives are enriched and changed for the better.

Being together increases our happiness, hope, health, and longevity, and lowers stress, fear, anxiety, and depression. It is in the company of God and one another that we are transformed, becoming our best, most authentic selves, flourishing in God's love flowing to us. So throw a block party, host a potluck, join a team, invite someone along with you when you venture out and do something fun.

Cherish the Love in Your Life

A healthy attachment doesn't just happen. Each relationship is like a garden of its own, needing tending and cultivation to grow. Without proper nurture and attention, relationships wilt and can become stagnant. Conflicts and disrepair can be like weeds crowding and choking out all good growth. So don't neglect or waste the love systems in your life.

Research on love by Dr. Vaillant describes how the notion of love does not live in the rational part of the brain. Rather, love, like spirituality and grief, is a system that exists in the limbic "olfactory" brain, where scents, caretaking, and memory all come together. He explains that we assimilate the people we love by suffusing them with positive emotion so we can take them inside and metabolize them.[28] It is then that transformation happens and we are changed forever. Our attachment system is more than feelings of love. Our attachments become our internal working models, a part of us, changing our lives.

Love is who we are, the way we live, the way we act. It is a system that is centered in our hearts and our brain. So when you are with your spouse, friends, family, and community, savor and cherish your time together so that you can enjoy the connection benefits of positive emotions and experiences you have together.

I am passionate about the value of creating meaningful attachments. Fostering opportunities to build relationships and close supportive connections is the key to helping us flourish. This is how we experience the love of God flowing through one another. When we show true hospitality, offer a listening ear or a helping hand, and come together to be strengthened in the presence of God and one another—we flourish.

Prayer of Saint Francis

Lord, make me an instrument of your peace;
where there is hatred, let me sow love;
where there is injury, pardon;
where there is doubt, faith;
where there is despair, hope;
where there is darkness, light;
where there is sadness, joy.
O divine Master,
grant that I may not so much seek to be consoled as to
    console;
to be understood, as to understand;
to be loved, as to love;
for it is in giving that we receive,
it is in pardoning that we are pardoned,
and it is in dying that we are born to eternal life.
Amen.

Reflective Questions and Flourish Practices

1. Who do you "do life" with? Who are the closest five relationship attachments that help you flourish?

2. As you reflect on these relationships and others who are close to you, ask yourself: "Who do I want to become in this relationship?" Make note of your response next to each name.

3. What will a self-care plan look like for you to care for yourself before you care for others?

4. Consider how you can include these practical, researched ways of connecting:
   • Stay connected to extended family.
   • Do connecting activities with your immediate family or those you are close to every day, such as eating dinner together.
   • Celebrate special occasions with family and friends. Laugh and share humor.
   • Get to know your family history and introduce your children to it.
   • Make regular dates to see friends weekly.
   • Show hospitality. Invite people into your home and your life.
   • Try to get to know your neighbors. Be friendly and open to meeting new people.
   • Have a pet if you can; people who do feel happier and healthier.
   • Be part of a church community. Attend worship services. Join a small group.
   • Serve others with your time, strengths, talents, and gifts.
   • Listen. Offer deep, attentive presence toward others.
   • Nurture a relationship with God through daily times of prayer, silence, and reading the Word.

5. Think of a few ways you can be helpful to those closest to you, and serve others or volunteer using your gifts and strengths.

6. Who has shared an accomplishment or good news or is celebrating a special occasion where you can share in showing joy and active/constructive responding?

7. Is there any relationship interaction you have had recently that needs repairing, or an offense that needs forgiving? Consider how you could resolve this in a healthy way.

PART 4

RESTORING A HEART OF JOY: JOY AND PLEASURE SYSTEM

You flourish when facing challenging emotions with a heart open to joy and gratitude

chapter 6

Aiming
for Joy

In your presence is fullness of joy; at your right hand are pleasures forevermore.

Psalm 16:11 NKJV

Joy is a net of love by which you can catch souls. A joyful heart is the inevitable result of a heart burning with love.

Mother Teresa

The longing to flourish is often expressed in wanting to be happy, to "live in a happy life," as the little Zambian girl, Sharon, expressed in chapter 1. Most polls indicate that what people want is to be happy in life and relationships, and they want the same for family, children, and friends.

It used to be that sex sells, but now, it appears, so does happiness. Over five thousand books were published on happiness in just the last few years. The media, secular voices, false prophets, and self-help half-truths offer all sorts of ways to transform yourself. They promise the secrets to love, peace, joy, fulfillment, and, of course, happiness. We now have to sort through all these new fad soul diets and propaganda. Huge Coke ads around the world invite you to "open happiness." A lid of yogurt promises you'll "find happiness naturally here." Most of what is promoted as happiness, joy, and pleasure is not just confusing, but shallow and unsatisfying. Fad products may have made a lot of people rich, but they're not directly responsible for making people truly happy. Despite all this, the pursuit continues and the epidemic of unhappiness and languishing is still on the rise.

> *"Happiness . . . is not a destination: it is a manner of traveling. Happiness is not an end in itself. It is a by-product of working, playing, loving and living."*
>
> —Haim Ginott

Right now, one in four adults say they are unhappy.

I saw a poster recently that showed a picture of a long road with a sign on the side depicting an arrow pointing ahead to Happy. Underneath, the caption read: "Happiness is just at the end of the road. Then again, look how long it is. Yeah, I wouldn't even try. . . ." The confusion about flourishing in true joy and happiness only leads to more despair and unhappiness.

But this is not all life has to offer us. God has called us to discover how to flourish and live fully in the light of His grace and abundant generosity. Discover how to choose this life, traveling with daily joy on the flourishing pilgrim's way.

Flourish in Joy and Happiness

The terms *happiness* and *joy* are often used interchangeably and can mean many things, including contentment, pleasure, gladness, cheerfulness, delight, enjoyment, and exhilaration. Typically, *happiness* is when happy things happen and we experience some elation and feel uplifted. Lasting happiness, sometimes called "enduring happiness," is closer to joy, and not tied so closely to events in your life. The term *joy* is more reflective of a spiritual emotion virtue beyond circumstantial happiness. Joy is a deeper experience and appreciation for life. Our faith in God brings joy because we can see life as being so much bigger than ourselves. Joy can move us outside of ourselves and our circumstances. We live in a body with a brain that is designed to experience happiness.[1]

In John 15:11 Jesus says, "These things I have spoken to you, that My joy may remain in you, and that your joy may be full" (NKJV). We are offered this gift of an abundant life of joy, peace, and all the gifts and traits of the Spirit. The faith-based flourishing journey is also about the full joy of living. We are designed for all the simple, pure pleasures of delight in life: joy, happiness, love, laughter, gratitude, and serenity. God desires us to be full of joy, using all our senses to appreciate and enjoy His good gifts. (See Philippians 4:4 and John 15:11.) This powerful joy and pleasure system enriches our spiritual experience, nourishes our relationships, and enhances our enjoyment of the simple things in life. This can make us happy—enduringly happy.

The term *joy* is mentioned in the Bible about two hundred times, and the term *rejoice* is also used frequently. Joy can also be translated as "delight." So God was also saying that He wants His delight to be in us and He wants our delight to be full. Happy, glad, and cheerful people are mentioned throughout the Bible. The primary objective of the teachings of Jesus was for us to experience His abundant life, with the fullness of His joy. When God tells us to "always be joyful," it is because this is His will for us (1 Thessalonians 5:16 NCV).

A faith-based view of flourishing and happiness is the way of our ancient fathers and mothers of the faith, like Moses, Solomon, Ruth, Mary, Esther, Paul, John, and many others. Classical flourishing in happiness is a life lived well, a life of virtue and character, a life that manifests wisdom, kindness, and goodness.[2]

Psychology associates flourishing with mental and emotional

health and well-being. Those who flourish have the capacity for positive emotions, including happiness and joy. They generally are able to be in good spirits and are cheerful, calm, and peaceful.[3]

Sovereign Joy Is From the Holy Spirit

But flourishing goes beyond just feeling good, being happy in the moment, or being satisfied with your life. It is living life to the fullest. Although you may experience grief, frustrations, and sadness, your emotional life is primarily reflective of spiritual emotions like love, joy, gratitude, and peace. You are able to face challenges and adversity with hope and optimism. Flourishing in a happy life blossoms with possibility and shows remarkable resilience to hard times. It is not escaping pain. The complete palette of our feelings keeps us growing and changing. There is a season for everything. Challenges are important to strengthen us, and build good character traits like gratitude, hope, and empathy. As Peter writes: "Be truly glad. There is wonderful joy ahead!" (1 Peter 1:6 NLT).

Can you experience this joy of the Lord even in adversity?

There is a sovereign joy that God's Spirit graces us with that is deeper than basic life happiness. Divine joy can transcend outward circumstances or other people; it is more like quiet contentment and assurance. God says He gives us His joy through His Holy Spirit and His presence when we surrender our lives and trust Him. Let's begin here, and then we will explore how we can cultivate more joy and a healthy pleasure system.

My sister Sharon's husband was killed in a terrible car accident in 1995. We were all devastated as we gathered at the graveside, and she was, naturally, absolutely distraught, not knowing how she would ever be happy again. In a moment of feeling overwhelmed, she gazed out over the cemetery, and something caught her attention. For a moment she was distracted. My toddler daughter had wandered away from the funeral gathering and taken off her dress. While we were grieving at the graveside she was having a lovely time playing hopscotch on the adjacent graves—dancing and sing-ing to herself.

A burst of "sovereign joy" (as Sharon described it later) flowed over my sister's heart. "There still is life to be lived," she felt the Lord saying to her. In this divine moment she caught my other sis-ter's and my attention, and we were all struck with this "sovereign joy." I confess that in that solemn moment there was a brief burst of inappropriate laughter. Yes, these are moments of sovereign joy, bringing hope and renewal.

Longing for Joy

How can we tap in to this sovereign joy, a joy that goes beyond sadness and the reality of life's struggles? When we really listen to our hearts, we often get in touch with a holy discontent. Much of the disappointment and sadness deep down is knowing that we aren't flourishing in shalom, fully alive in the fullness of God the way it should be. So we have to arrange our lives so that the redemption of shalom, God's design for us originally from the garden of Eden, can take over. I am not suggesting it is easy. In a sense we have to convince our brains that God's redemption is working, that with God's help we will overcome and all will be well.

Our soul may not be well with God. Relationships may be in conflict, loved ones may be ill, and our children may not be on the path of life we want them to be. But we must patiently wait for the redemption of shalom to become a reality in our lives. We may long for things to be different and better, but we must not give in to despair. No matter how hard the going, we must stay on the road to flourishing.

It is in this longing void created by disappointment and sadness that we aim for cultivating more positive, heartfelt emotion virtues, compared to the negative experiences we endure. Dr. Barbara L. Fredrickson has discovered what she calls a positivity ratio of three to one.[4] That is, we need to have three times more positive moments and emotions than negative ones. This is the "tipping point" that moves us toward flourishing.

Positive emotions are so important that getting your ratio to three to one and beyond will improve your overall well-being and your positive influence on others, and it will even add ten years to your life. This doesn't mean you have to live like a Pollyanna, getting rid of all negative emotions. Negative emotions, such as normal anxiety and genuine anger, are also necessary for you to be fully human and flourish. But the ratio of heartfelt positive to negative emotions and experiences determines whether you flourish.

The New Science of Happiness

Scientists have made tremendous progress in discovering what makes us happy and what role the brain plays in and looks like on joy. These discoveries are helping us find ways to cultivate a healthy and more fulfilling experience of real joy.[5]

"Every human being can say yes to more positive emotion. All of us can say yes to more engagement. Every human being can say yes to more meaning and purpose in life. Every human being can say yes to better relationships." This is the conclusion that Dr. Martin Seligman, a renowned psychologist and pioneer of the new positive psychology movement, has arrived at after many studies he and others are doing.[6]

Research also shows, however, that we are often misguided in pursuing happiness. We often look for joy and fulfilling pleasure in all the wrong places. As it turns out, we aren't very good at predicting what will make us happy in the future and in understanding how our joy system works.[7]

This is not surprising. Most humans know this from personal experience, but it is comforting to have it confirmed by research. Have you ever wanted something really bad, and then got it, and realized it didn't make you as happy as you had hoped? That new outfit, a new job, moving to a new location, better people to live with, having more money, being famous . . . Typically, people think of external possessions and circumstances as the primary bringers of fulfillment and happiness. But research shows clearly that these things don't provide lasting happiness. Once you have what you need to live comfortably, more cash doesn't boost your happiness.

So how do you become happier? What brings you true joy? There are no quick fixes or easy steps. That's not how real life works. But some biblical principles and new science show that joy comes from the Spirit of God, from within and from without, and you can make choices and live intentionally to cultivate more.

Changing Your Happiness Set Point

Your joy system is more than a feeling. It is a state of being that encompasses all of your brain, mind, and heart, and even the very cells in your body. All these systems of your life are inter-related and involved. The heart, body, and brain are all designed to thrive on positive emotions and your overall well-being. Facial expressions and the way you breathe, talk, move, and even rest affect the release of feel-good hormones.

Some of us seem to have more "happy hormones" than others. There is a fixed range of happiness that we can raise intentionally, but we usually return to the set point after less happy times. While our genetic makeup plays a role in this process, the good news is that just as with our weight, our happiness set point can be changed. To lose weight we know that we must boost our metabolism and control our calories. You can boost your happiness and joy system by changing what you feed it, also. You aren't helpless against your genetics or circumstances. You can intentionally cultivate more joy.[8]

Our biological set point or *genetics* is responsible for 50 percent of how we usually feel when something happens to us. Yet these genetics don't have to control our lives. Brain imaging shows how positive emotions like joy and gratitude can change the brain. There are five major mood areas of the brain: the prefrontal cortex, the cingulate gyrus, the deep limbic system, the basal ganglia, and the temporal lobe. Several neurotransmitters are also involved in determining mood: endorphins, seratonin, oxytocin, and dopamine. And while it is reassuring to know that science has clearly identified the neurology of happiness, we don't have to know all the intricate processes that work to make us happy. We only have to live out the flourishing life God has promised us.

When your brain is healthy and happy and the key areas of the brain are functioning well in harmony, they will accomplish what they were designed to do. However, if these brain systems and transmitters don't work well, happiness and joy are more elusive. Depression, panic anxiety, attention deficit disorder (ADD), obsessive rumination, negative thinking, fear, worry, and a host of other experiences can interfere with our happiness systems.[9] If we want to be joyful, we have to deal with these basic disrupters.

Protect Your Pleasure System

For starters, in order to experience fullness of joy and pure pleasure, we especially have to guard the area of the brain designed for joy. It's called the "nucleus accumbens"—commonly known as the brain's pleasure center. All positive experiences and emotions go through this system. If you block or flood this pathway to the pleasure center, you literally rob the brain of its ability to give you that good feeling of pleasure. When you feel like a "joyless working machine,"[10] what is the main culprit? Our highly stressed, overstimulated world, which has caused an epidemic of what is known as *anhedonia*.

Anhedonia is "the inability to experience pleasure in the little things of life."[11] And if you cannot experience real, healthy, pure joy and pleasure, you are not going to be able to flourish in well-being and harmony. The world we live in is pushing the brain's pleasure system button too fast and too often. We need it louder, faster, more intense, and more stimulating. In fact, anything that gives too much excitement, such as stimulating behaviors and substances (even caffeine), can cause anhedonia and depression. Overindulging yourself in what may seem temporarily pleasurable can lead to unhappiness.

We don't have to reject everything of this earth and feel guilty for wanting to be happy and enjoy good things. Instead, we must learn to protect and not abuse our natural pleasure centers. God's plan for us is to discover authentic joy and pure, good pleasures.[12]

Seven Pathways to Restoring Your Pleasure Center[13]

* Pursue pure, natural pleasure.

    Pursue pleasures that lower your stress hormones, provide deeply satisfying enjoyment, and bring true happiness. Get enough sleep. Practice good self-care. Eat healthy food for the right reasons. Enjoy healthy connections with others.

* Find joy in the simple things.

    What simple joys do you remember as a child? What have you recently found pure pleasure in? Recapture and recall past joys and heighten your memory by being thankful for the simple pleasures of life you recall.

* Control your adrenaline.

    Limit your excitement and sensation-seeking. Change your attitude about needing high stimulation in order to be happy. Lower your stress hormone levels. Develop healthy habits of slowing down and changing the pace of your lifestyle.

* Use humor to boost your happiness.

    A good laugh is healing to your mind, emotions, and body. Lighten up and brighten up. Notice the humor in yourself and life around you. Get a daily laughter workout.

* Be grateful and appreciative.

    Gratitude and appreciation will help you feel happier and more emotionally stable. Pay attention to the goodness around you each day, and before going to bed each night count your blessings. Be thankful and show appreciation to those around you.

- Practice relaxation and meditation.

  Learn how to take time to calm your body and mind through relaxation and Christian contemplative meditation, prayer, and practicing the presence of God.

- Be intentional about what matters most.

  Make space in the pace of your daily life for God and spiritual priorities, friendships, family, and letting go of grudges as well as cultivating hope and learning from failure and disappointment.

Train Your Brain for More Joy

Our brains can change and we can transform our minds because of something called "neural plasticity." The brain's neurons are flexible and can change. It's happening all the time. It is neural plasticity that helps us learn to play the piano or throw or kick a ball. Every time we learn something, neural plasticity is at work. Even though you may have been born with a disposition toward gloominess or anxiety, you can learn and train your brain and direct it toward a happier and more joyful outlook. This also applies to other problems, like anxiety, fear, and phobias. If you have gone down a pathway that has blocked your joy and pleasure system, know that learning and memory are the result of all sorts of experiences, and the brain can change in response to new experiences and intentional living.

This happens in several ways, but mainly through intentional practices, habits, and skills like the following:

- *Enrich your outer world*—through a stimulating environment, what you read, what you do, and the people you are around.

- *Enrich your inner world*—nourish your soul, think healthy great thoughts, learn and try new things. Change and be transformed by the renewing of habitual patterns of thinking and feeling. (See Romans 12:2.)

- *Enrich your body/mind connection* through healthy nutrition, supplements, exercise, sleep, and rest.[14]

Steps to Greater Joy

As we discovered earlier in this chapter, research has found that 50 percent of our initial happiness seems to be determined by our natural happiness set point. In addition, the way we think, life conditions, and circumstances can determine 10 percent of our happiness. The remaining 40 percent determining our happiness has to do with the voluntary thinking, attitudes, intentional lifestyle activities, and practices we choose. We can help all our systems function well and light up with joy, happiness, and gratitude, calming fear and anxiety. Just as the Bible promises and science is proving, joy can be learned. Let's discover how.

1. PRAYER

Research in psychological science and religion shows that people of faith are not only happier and healthier, but they recover better from traumas.[15] We benefit from the social support of the fellowship of kindred spirits. Our relationship with God is clearly a haven of safety and a source of comfort in troubled times. Having hope—knowing God is good and has a purpose in everything—gives us meaning. The practice of prayer is a primary source of being in God's presence, finding joy in our faith and caring for others.

> *"God is most glorified in me when I am most satisfied in him."*
>
> —John Piper

One of my favorite studies is with nuns while they were in meditative centering or contemplative prayer, not just silent, but also using words. When their brain imaging patterns were observed, they lit up on the left front region of the brain, the area associated with clarity and happiness. The lower back part of the brain, the "reptilian brain," which is involved in fear memory and the stress response, was more subdued. This shows that while in prayer, meditation, and worship, we are able to let go of our fears and worries, relax, and experience a deeper sense of well-being, joy, and peace. This sense of serenity and joy even carries into the rest of our day.[16]

2. CONNECT WITH OTHERS

New science proves that our love connections trump all for happiness and joy. Healthy relationship attachments with mutual love will bring more joy, and happy people enjoy better relationships. When comparing extremely happy people to average-happy people, the one characteristic that made the difference is meaningful, lasting relationship attachments. Those who have a broad range of social connections, with generations of families living close together, have the highest happiness. The more healthy connections, the higher your chances of happiness.

Conflict in relationships, on the other hand, is a primary hindrance to our happiness—whether in a marriage or with children, a roommate, or difficult people at work. We never really adapt to interpersonal conflict without repair. It causes us to ruminate and become anxious and depressed, destroying our daily joy. The neurobiology of attachments explains that healthy relationship connections stimulate the brain activity that helps to create systems that lead to our developing empathy and enjoyment of positive interactions, and managing stress that goes with negative interactions.[17]

3. BECOME A "JOY SPREADER"

"Pleasant words are like a honeycomb, sweetness to the soul and health to the bones" (Proverbs 16:24 NKJV). Did you know that you can actually spread and catch the emotions of the people around you, like you can catch a cold? Recent research studies have validated that happy, joyful people can pass on their good cheer to others around them. According to Daniel Goleman, the author of *Emotional Intelligence* and *Social Intelligence*, emotions spread as an emotional or social *contagion*.[18] This is when you transmit an idea or emotion from one person to another. The stronger you feel something, and the more you consistently stay with it, the more likely you will "infect" others with the positive emotion or state. In fact, happiness spreads outward by three degrees, to the friends of friends of friends.

Our happiness and joy has a biochemical effect on our brains and bodies. When we experience a joyful interaction, our brains flood our cells with happy hormones. When you are around someone who is kind, affirming, and supportive, doesn't it just draw that out in you? When being served by someone in the store who is always friendly and smiles, wouldn't you rather wait in her line?

If you are going through a hard time, it's difficult to be around unhappy, angry, miserable, or anxious people. It floods us with stressful and harmful chemicals. Surround yourself with people who will uplift, nourish, and help you flourish. "A cheerful look brings joy to the heart, and good news gives health to the bones" (Proverbs 15:30). Become a joy spreader. Let's get a joy epidemic spreading.

4. HEALTHY HABITS OF THE MIND

Set your mind on having positive thoughts. There are many hindrances of joy to be aware of, such as depression, discontent, selfishness, and ingratitude, but the greatest is fear. We combat these negative patterns of thinking by developing healthy habits of the mind:

Optimism

Focus on the positive. See the good in life and in others. You can't always control what happens to you, but you can always take responsibility for how you respond. Optimism can be learned.

Research shows that in as little as one sixteen-hour training work-shop we can learn how to dispute chronic negative thoughts and become more optimistic. This is referred to as "learned optimism."[19] In biblical terms, optimism stems from true hope. Cultivate hope in your heart to become more optimistic.

Count your blessings

Be aware of and attuned to savoring the simple, enjoyable things in life. Gratitude and appreciation lead to infusing daily life with more meaning and more joy (25 percent more), as you will discover in the next chapter. When you pray, also be thankful, grateful, and appreciative. Start your day by being attuned to what you have to be thankful for, noticing God's goodness in all of your life. Before you go to bed at night, write down a few things you were most grateful for that day.

Dispute negative thinking

Automatic Negative Thoughts (ANTs) are a big challenge to our joy and peace. Don't believe everything you think. Learn to question your thoughts, considering alternative, often more real-istic, positive ways of thinking and viewing life situations. We will explore this more in chapter 9. Using Scriptures, God's promises, and inspirational affirmations, you can learn to seed your think-ing with more optimistic, positive thoughts to cultivate positive emotion.

Cultivate positive emotion

When you cultivate positive emotion, it broadens and builds your ideas and opens your awareness to a wider range of expansive thinking. Joy spurs you to be creative and playful. Serenity ignites the urge to savor the moment. This opens our hearts and minds to be more creative and more receptive to each other. We are then open to learning new skills, making new connections, and having greater clarity and insight. This helps us become our best.[20]

5. MUSIC

Music changes your brain

Listening to music is one of the easiest ways to improve your mood; it has immediate positive effects. In the Bible we read that David playing music with his harp was the only way Saul's inner turmoil was calmed (1 Samuel 16). Praise and worship always bring hope, joy, and breakthrough (See Numbers 21:16–17; 2 Chronicles 20:18–22; Isaiah 61:3.) If we are cheerful, we are to sing. (See James 5:13.) When we are filled with the Spirit, we

> *"Happy are those who reside in your house,*
>
> *Who praise you continually."*
>
> —Psalm 84:4 HCSB

are to sing together and continually have a song in our heart toward the Lord. (See Psalm 144:9; Ephesians 5:18–19.) And new songs are always being sung in heaven (Revelation 5:9).

Music has a powerful impact on our lives. Research on music shows that tones that boost brain activity can improve our mood, learning, and memory.[21] Brain wave vibration activity in the four primary zones has been researched to effectively achieve states of relaxation and sleep. Music that uses natural, easy-flowing, steady rhythms and relaxing sounds can raise the expectation of relaxation and reduce stress. Research shows that stress hormone levels drop while listening to relaxing music. Music with vibrations around 40 to 68 Hz can have a positive effect on depression and anxiety. Factors that boost immunity increase, making the mind more receptive to positive thinking and emotions.[22]

Music changes your heart

Music actually changes the functioning of your heart as well as the state of your brain. Dr. Mike Miller, a research cardiologist at the University of Maryland Medical Center in Baltimore, has been studying the effects of "things that make people happy."[23] "Turns out music may be one of the best de-stressors—either by playing or even listening to music," said Miller. As people listened to music they like, "The inner lining of the blood vessel relaxed, opened up and produced chemicals that are protective to the heart," he said. Music can counter the effects of stress and bring more joy. "It gives us an overall feeling of good, well-being—a sense of euphoria in some cases," Miller said. But hearing the same song repeatedly didn't have the same effect. "You need to vary your songs, so when you hear the song fresh, it brings back the sense of joy and opens up the system." So sing a new song, choose some new music, and boost your brain and heart with joy.

6. JOY BOOSTERS

All the daily habits of natural joy boosters in this chapter will build your resilience to resist and be able to deal with the negative stresses and challenges in life. They act like an immunization we would give to our bodies against viruses and diseases. Like a buffer, they help us to recover more quickly from life's challenges.

Live with meaning and purpose

You flourish when your life has meaning and purpose and you routinely experience emotion virtues such as love, joy, gratitude, peace, and hope. Deep joy and meaningful fulfillment come from being aware of how we are connected to the larger story of humanity, from our spirituality and our faith. We have meaning when we know we are making a positive impact on the lives of others around us through our work and legacy. Our sense of purpose in life is what defines our role in the world, in our family and our work, and what we believe in and stand for. What brings meaning and purpose to your life?

Buy experiences for more happiness

Studies done by Thomas Gilovich of Cornell University reveal that people are more enduringly happy after spending money on experiences rather than material things. So, money can buy you some happiness, if you spend it wisely. Satisfaction with "experiential purchases" starts high and increases over time. A massage, a retreat, a vacation with friends or family, a Broadway show, a subscription, season tickets, a pass to a place of beauty—all live on in the stories we tell and our memories.

In contrast, spending money on material things may feel good at first, but actually makes people less happy in the long run, says Dr. Gilovich. If you do buy something, like a bike or a flat-screen TV, research found that how people view a purchase—for exercise, enjoyable music, or making memories, also influenced their level of satisfaction. Remember this when buying gifts for others (or suggesting gift ideas for yourself). Choose something that can continue on with enjoyment and good memories.[24]

Discover your gifts and strengths and use them to work and serve

We flourish in meaning and purpose when we serve others with our unique gifts. American writer and theologian Frederick Buechner says that the place you ought to serve is where your greatest joy meets the world's greatest need. What are your greatest joys and passions? How could you use your gifts and talents to serve others in all areas of your everyday life, increasing your happiness?

Set goals and visualize the future

Taking action toward your goals and values makes you happier than directly trying to make yourself happy. Our brains light up when we are being creative, when we are working toward something new and exciting, anticipating achieving our goal. When we work hard toward a positive goal, making progress to the point of expecting a goal to be realized, we don't just activate positive feelings—we also suppress negative emotions such as fear and depression.[25] What are some of your goals right now?

Be generous and kind

Flourishing is also about doing good, adding value to the world. Out of a deep sense of gratitude for the abundance in our lives, we

145

are motivated to share with others. Giving brings us joy as well as contributes to the flourishing and joy of others and the community around us. When you flourish, you connect with your friends, family, work, and community. You aren't just about making yourself happy. You want to make a difference, be a shalom bringer and joy spreader. When you flourish, you desire to become your best possible self, going beyond self-interest, sharing goodness and celebrating goodness in others.

Share goodness

"Anxiety in the heart causes depression, but a good word makes it glad" (Proverbs 12:25 NKJV). Doing good and saying good things makes you and others happier. When you do good, you will feel good. When you live well, you will feel better about yourself; you will have better self-esteem and a greater vision of yourself being a healthy and moral person. This will result in feeling more fulfilled and happier.

Laughter and humor

Laughter and a happy heart are good medicine. (See Proverbs 17:22.) When you laugh, your body releases biochemicals known as endorphins which elevate mood and a sense of well-being. Laughing even when you don't feel happy will give you the benefit of an endorphin boost. So have a good laugh about life with a friend, find the humor in life around you, rent a comedy, and laugh.[26]

Enjoy time in nature and beauty

Bring the beauty of nature into your life. New research shows that the smell and sight of flowers can change your brain chemistry and lift your mood. In a study by Haviland-Jones, women who received flowers unexpectedly showed an improved mood that lasted for up to three days.[27] Turn your home or workplace into a sanctuary with beautiful blossoms. You will stress less and be more creative, and others will enjoy the benefits as well.

Get out and appreciate the beauty of nature as much as you

can. Taking a twenty-minute walk surrounded by nature will refresh you. Being out in the sun will give the added benefits of vitamin D. If you can't get out, studies show that looking at pictures of natural beauty can have the same effect to calm your brain and uplift your outlook.[28] Have beautiful picture books around the house, a nature screen saver, or a digital photo frame that rotates meaningful photos. Watch movies of pleasant places, travel, and beauty.

Aromatherapy

In *Aromatherapy for Everyone*, P. J. Person and Mary Shipley write that smell hits the limbic system (the mood center of the brain) first, surpassing the other senses.[29] Have you ever gone down memory lane in an instant when just one quick smell brought back memories? For me it is fresh-baked bread. Reminds me of the bread truck that I used to wait for as a child, and also of the first time I saw bread being baked while I was on a field trip to a monastery in South Africa. Certain smells directly stimulate or calm the brain. You'll find pleasant aromas in candles, body wash, soaps, essential oils, or just natural plants and foods.

Keep reading, learning, and growing

Reading and learning new information causes neural growth in the brain, nourishing our souls and inspiring our minds. Self-help and inspirational reading, known as bibliotherapy, is being prescribed by some British doctors to help decrease symptoms of mild to moderate depression and anxiety. Reading about and learning new skills and practices that can be applied to your life can help cultivate a lifestyle that brings more joy.[30]

What have you always wanted to do or learn? A new recipe, a new hobby? Give it a try. Have you been curious about a topic, how something works? Learn about it. Be creative. Invent or make something new from scratch. Get immersed in the flow of a task you enjoy, a hobby, or the joy of learning so much that you lose track of time. The love of learning and growing does the brain and soul good.

Take good care of your body/brain connection

Exercise is good for everything, especially to boost your mood. We will explore this more in the chapters on peace and tranquility. But for now, get out and move your body as best you can for at least ten thousand steps, or up to one hour most days for health and brain-boosting benefits. Get at least eight to nine hours of sleep a night. Take twenty-minute naps if you can. Observe the Sabbath: one day of rest, relaxation, and recreation a week. And be aware of the mood/food connection. Eat small, healthy meals every three to four hours. Avoid processed foods and what I call "white trash"—white flour, white sugar, white starches, and fatty fried foods. Also avoid "pseudo-stressors"—the stimulant products we reach to for a pick-me-up—which actually end up stressing us out and letting us down. Caffeine is the main culprit!

Celebrate

Celebrations keep us attuned to what fills our heart with deep gladness and gratitude. These are opportunities to delight in God, people, and experiences that enrich life with thankfulness and joy. Celebrations help us remember the beauty, goodness, and abundance in life. We remember positive connections with the past, enjoy the fullness of living in the moment, and anticipate the future. As we savor the laughter, music, dancing, symbolism, worship, or sharing during these times, we cultivate more positive spiritual emotions and experiences that enrich our lives to flourish.[31]

Celebrate as many occasions as possible. Make them meaningful and memorable. Take photos to savor and recall the positive emotions during those times. Celebrate firsts, birthdays, weddings, anniversaries, graduations, family traditions, funerals, Mother's Day, Father's Day, vacations, and church calendar events. Go all out to make the most of the meaning of the New Year, Valentine's Day, Lent, Easter, Thanksgiving, Advent, and Christmas. Be there to celebrate with others.

7. SAVOR GOODNESS AND APPRECIATE LIFE'S SIMPLE JOYS AND PLEASURES

We tend to overlook the good, focusing in on the most pressing or distracting items on our minds. Slow down; be attentive and savor life's simple pleasures and joys. Savor goodness in the here and now. All we truly have is the moment to make the most of. Enjoy savoring the taste of your food, the beautiful sights around you, the smells and enjoyable times with people. Make the most of the moment, using your senses to capture all aspects of the experience in your memory. Take photos and videos, and bring home symbolic mementos to savor these good times later. Your brain and senses will record these in your memory to be recalled and relived.

Gratitude Opens Us to Joy

There are stresses, challenges, and struggles we have to overcome in life. But there is also so much abundant beauty and blessing around us to enjoy and be grateful for. Every day notice, savor, and appreciate all the bountiful goodness in your life. Say thank-you regularly to God and those around you. When you do, you make joy grow and invite more goodness into your life.

Gratitude elevates, energizes, inspires, and transforms—as you will discover in the next chapter.

Prayer

God, you have been wonderful to me; I am one happy person.
And now, God, do it again—
Bring rains to my drought-stricken life
So when I plant my crops in despair
I will shout hurrahs at the harvest,
So when I go off with a heavy heart
I will come home laughing, with armloads of blessing.

Adapted from Psalm 126:3–6 THE MESSAGE

Reflective Questions and Flourish Practices

1. What makes you happy and brings you joy? Is there a place that makes you feel content and fully alive? Remember as many of the sensory details as possible. The sights, sounds, smells, feeling, taste. Enrich your experience by savoring these experiences now.

2. What is your greatest joy and passion in life? How is it meeting the world's greatest need?

3. What are some of the simple, pure pleasures that you can delight in, using your senses and natural desires? (For example, watching the sunrise and sunset, enjoying the company of loved ones, listening to uplifting music, and being surrounded by fragrant candles.)

4. What hobbies and creative experiences do you enjoy? What can you do to grow and cultivate these interests and talents to bring more enjoyment and delight in your life? (For example, music, gardening, dancing, visiting places of culture and beauty, photography, scrapbooking, cooking, knitting, tennis, golfing, making jewelry.)

5. Consider rearranging your day around what brings you joy, to savor life's simple pleasures, moving toward your goals and what matters most.

6. What occasions or traditions do you celebrate? How could you become more intentional to practice joy by celebrating special occasions and holidays?

7. Having read through this chapter, what new choices can you make in order for your life to be more joyful?

chapter 7

Developing Gratitude

It is a good and delightful thing to give thanks to the Lord,
to sing praises to Your name, O Most High; To show forth
Your loving-kindness in the morning and Your faithfulness
by night.

Psalm 92:1–2 AMP

It has been my practice for many years now to start the new
year praying for a theme to reflect on and live intentionally all
year. This last year I have focused on gratitude. As I write this
chapter, it is the Thanksgiving season, so I am fully immersed
in gratitude and appreciation. I am especially excited about this
chapter, because you will discover how the feeling and practice
of gratitude is the single strongest predictor of life satisfaction.
Gratitude can impact every aspect of our lives for the better. I have
learned this through personal experience and verified research.
Nurturing a grateful heart leads to a healthier body, a happier

mind, and relationships that flourish. The practice of gratitude can actually change the state of your brain, right down to your neurons. If you want your brain to light up and flourish in a more vibrant, fulfilled, happier life, learn to live in a state of gratitude and appreciation.[1]

God Encourages Us to Be Grateful

Throughout Scripture, God encourages us to be thankful and have an attitude of gratitude. For example, 1 Thessalonians 5:16–18 tells us to "Always be joyful. Pray continually, and give thanks whatever happens. That is what God wants for you in Christ Jesus" (NCV). Yes, at times this may seem somewhat impossible. The "whatever happens" part is the most challenging. We have to constantly remind ourselves that all good things are from God; they are gifts we must be thankful for. Being joyful and grateful is evidence of being filled with the Spirit of God.[2]

Even difficult times can be considered a gift of sorts. They could be wake-up calls or opportunities to grow closer to God or stronger in our character, faith, trust, and hope. In the deep places of our heart and mind, we can turn our fears into trust, our worries and confusion into calm and stillness. Our loneliness can be transformed into a sense of belonging and love, and our despair can be turned to hope.

Our American forefathers understood the value of this virtue of gratitude—acknowledging the importance of honoring God—and the benefit for ourselves as well as the nation. After a devastating war of tremendous struggle, George Washington made a proclamation in 1789. He declared a day of thanksgiving and prayer, a day to acknowledge with grateful hearts the many blessings that God provided in the midst of hardship. It is so good that we continue to uphold this annual tradition for giving thanks, because we need to be reminded to be grateful. We tend to forget, get distracted, and lose perspective with the business and cares of everyday living.

This diminishes our capacity for joy. While Thanksgiving is just one day of the year, we would do well to embrace a powerful lifestyle of gratitude all year.

Gratitude Can Be Learned

Keeping the practice of gratitude in your life will not only give you great benefits personally, but it shows love and respect toward God and others. Like manners, gratitude doesn't come naturally. It has to be learned.

No doubt some of us have to work a little harder at discovering, learning, and practicing this habit of counting our blessings rather than our troubles. During challenging and stressful times, we tend to be more negative and miss out on opportunities of expressing gratitude. Being aware of and thankful for the most fundamental things in life is especially difficult for those who tend to be pessimistic. Those who struggle with depression will find it particularly difficult seeing the glass half full. When facing challenges, there is a tendency to put a negative spin on things—comparing, contrasting, and complaining. Good news can be dampened with the dread of it being short-lived, waiting for the bad to come crashing in. One can rationalize this perspective by saying they are just being a realist.

Unfortunately, a lack of gratitude will make you miserable. God's intent for you is to be joyful. He longs for you to flourish in every way. When you are ungrateful, you deplete your capacity for joy. And when you are miserable, having no joy, you make other people miserable. It only takes one person in a relationship, a situation, a group, a family, or the workplace to put a damper on things for everyone else. This "downer" attitude will cause you to lose your joy and the potential for enjoyable relationships. It will keep you from all God intends you to be. Is practicing gratitude a part of your daily life?

How are you doing at being grateful?

Take this quick quiz to assess your level of gratitude awareness. It is not a test, so there is no right or wrong answer for each question. The scale merely gives you some sense of how much you value and practice being grateful in your life.

Select one of the following ratings and enter it alongside each of the ten questions:

1 = None of the time; 2 = Some of the time; 3 = Most of the time

___ 1. I am aware of having much to be grateful for in my life.
___ 2. When I wake up in the morning, I feel especially blessed by God.
___ 3. When I pray, I thank God for His goodness to me as well as share my requests.
___ 4. Not a day goes by that I don't reflect back and give thanks for something.
___ 5. I show appreciation to the people in my life I am grateful for.
___ 6. I don't feel resentful toward people who say life is great for them.
___ 7. I don't feel envious of people who seem to be more successful than I am.
___ 8. I feel appreciated by others.
___ 9. I feel that people really care about me.
___ 10. As I get older my feelings of gratitude get stronger.
___ **TOTAL**

SCORING: Add up your score for all 10 questions. Your maximum score can be 30.

Score: 25 to 30—You are living with an attitude of gratitude.
Score: 20 to 24—You are a grateful person most of the time.
Score: 15 to 19—Your gratitude attitude can do with some improving.
Score: Below 15—Be more intentional to practice gratitude.

The Pathway Back to Gratitude

The good news is that if you have learned bad habits or have unhealthy patterns of thinking, you can unlearn them by replacing them with new ways to see the world. You can become more alert, attuned, and intentional, being aware of the good things in life. You can change your choices and the pathways in your brain.

According to studies on happiness, only part of our positive emotions are determined by genetics; part is due to life circumstances, and the rest can be controlled by our thinking and behavior.[3]

Research has found that positive emotions such as joy and gratitude can be increased with practice, and they can provide similar benefits to physical exercise. By practicing gratitude exercises daily, you can become more alert, attuned, and intentional in your gratitude habits. Nourish your soul with new habits of grateful thinking and behavior.

Gratitude Elevates, Energizes, Inspires, and Transforms

Gratitude and appreciation provide tremendous benefits to our own well-being as well as to those around us. The Bible and faith practices emphasize this. Remember the hymn that goes "Count your blessings, name them one by one"?[4] Well, now science is proving the benefits of counting your blessings.[5]

Modern psychology has only discovered the value of gratitude in recent years. Earlier textbooks on psychiatry and psychology seldom made mention of the mental health benefits of gratitude, but today, science-based psychology is putting a lot of effort—and money—into researching positive emotions and virtues such as gratitude.

Discoveries from many years of research conducted by Dr. Robert Emmons, also known as the "gratitude doctor," confirm that those who regularly practice gratitude will see improvements in areas such as relationships, energy level, academics, and even dealing with tragedy.[6]

Gratitude leads to infusing daily life with happier moods (25 percent more), more optimism, better sleep, lower levels of chronic stress, fewer physical symptoms of illness and pain, and the ability to avoid emotions that cultivate bitterness, envy, stress, and depression when facing life challenges. Gratitude and positive emotional vitality expand our mental ability, creativity, and problem-solving skills. They build physical health and good relationships, which support us through challenges. Dr. Emmons states that "the benefits from counting blessings are tangible both emotionally and physically."[7]

Gratitude Changes Your Brain

When we are focusing on what is wrong in life, our amygdala alerts us that danger lies ahead. The amygdala is the brain's warning system. It sounds an alarm and primes us to face danger whenever anything threatens us. To this end, stress hormones flow through our bloodstream, priming our body to fight, flee, or freeze in the face of perceived danger. We also begin to feel anger, fear, and anxiety. When we keep focusing on the negatives of life, we keep our bodies flowing with stress hormones, and our hearts feel anxious.

When we expand our focus and begin to think about what we are grateful for, our amygdala senses that the perceived danger is not so dangerous. Our inner alarms stop sounding, stress hormones are flushed out of our body, and hormones that promote a sense of well-being, harmony, happiness, and joy begin to flow through our blood vessels. It is understandable, from our bodies' perspective, that focusing on what we are grateful for in the midst of trials will have a powerful impact on reducing an overall sense of fear and anxiety about life and circumstances.

Here is why this new research on what is basically a biblical mandate is so compelling. Gratitude brings alive what is good in life and may be even more valuable in hard times. This is clear from what is often referred to as God's peace prescription: "Don't worry about anything; instead, pray about everything. Tell God what you need, and thank him for all he has done. Then you will experience God's peace, which exceeds anything we can understand.

156

His peace will guard your hearts and minds as you live in Christ Jesus" (Philippians 4:6–7 NLT). Being thankful for what God is doing and preparing (although you don't see it) will open up and release the unfolding of His promise and blessing. As we take everything to Him in prayer—being thankful—thinking on the good—we will have peace.

Let's light up our brains right now. What three things are you grateful for today?

Gratitude in the Midst of Difficulty

But gratitude not only benefits our emotions, helping us to be happier and more content. Grateful people report higher levels of vitality and positive emotions even when experiencing difficult emotions or negative experiences. Those who report feeling positive emotions like love and gratitude—along with negative emotions of suffering and loss—show better psychological and physical functioning in the short and long term.[8]

Hard times tend to override the brain to focus on fear, losses, and anxieties. That is why in the darkest times you need to be the most grateful. Heighten your awareness of what there is to be grateful for along with your hardships. Gratitude is often as small as the light of a firefly, but it sparks hope in a dreary situation.

There are times we may have a longer list of things we are not grateful for—the desolations, disappointments, and stresses—but slogging through difficult times forces us to keep our thoughts turned toward the good and positive things we can be grateful for.

The begging bowl

There is a story about a group of monks in earlier times who would go begging daily for their food. Each morning they would go with their "begging bowls" out into the streets. Some days when they returned to the monastery, their bowls would be filled to overflowing and they would be grateful. Other days there would be a meager amount, but they would still be grateful.

The begging bowl for us can be a symbol of being open to receiving what the Lord provides each day, and being grateful for what we get. I am learning about what it means to be grateful. My ability to be grateful is dependent on how I am experiencing God's grace in my life. When I see how much of God's grace I have experienced in my life I can't help but practice gratitude. Grace and gratitude always work hand in hand. During a Strength for the Journey Retreat, we each received a symbolic blue "begging bowl" as a reminder. I eat my breakfast out of it each morning. I lift it up and ask God to give me what I need for that day. I remember, like the monks, to be grateful in times of abundance and in times of struggle. Then I thank Him for whatever He provides through His divine will for me. Consider getting your own "begging bowl" as a reminder.[9]

—Dr. Sylvia Hart Frejd

Be Surprised by Gratitude

After a conference session on the topic of gratitude, a woman shared that she had been a victim of a racial crime and was so filled with anger and hatred that it was destroying her life, literally. She shared how the Lord began to show her that she needed to shift her focus away from what made her feel sad and depleted, and balance her life out by starting to be grateful and give thanks for the good in her life. She said, "Just that one shift in my perspective changed my heart and set me free from all the cords of bitterness and hatred."

This is not an isolated situation. I have seen these dramatic benefits over and over again in my own life and as I counsel and coach others going through challenging times. Regardless of our circumstances, we can keep the perspective of seeing God in everything. Be aware that He is present in all things and wastes nothing in our life. All things work out for His purpose to those who love Him (see Romans 8:28). So get an attitude adjustment. You will be surprised by what you discover.

We will all face stresses, challenges, and adversity. How we react to these events will determine the joy and happiness in our lives.

COUNT YOUR BLESSINGS—
NAME THEM ONE BY ONE

After my friend Dr. Gary Oliver lost his son, then two months later his wife, then shortly after his sister, he experienced a new awakening of the power of gratitude. This is what he discovered: "Gratitude unlocks the fullness of life. It turns what we have into enough, and more than enough. It turns denial into acceptance, chaos into order, confusion into clarity. Gratitude turns problems into gifts, it turns failures into success, the unexpected into perfect timing, and mistakes into important events. Gratitude makes sense of our past, brings peace for today, and creates a new vision for tomorrow."[10]

During tough times, do you spend too much time feeling sorry for yourself, or can you, with gratitude, learn how to dance in the rain? It is so much easier to count our deficits, our problems, and our shortcomings, isn't it? We take so many little things for granted and don't give God and others thanks for them. On default setting, we are so much more aware of our struggles, our pains, and our concerns rather than our blessings.

It is easy to be grateful for the good things in life, but it requires more intentional spiritual work to be grateful for sorrow and failures. When we can be thankful for all that has brought us to this moment, we are truly grateful.

Make an Ebenezer Altar of Gratitude

As a family, in a small group, or on your own, take a few stones or pennies and make a little gratitude altar pile, like Samuel did in the Old Testament. He took a large stone and set it up between the towns of Mizpah and Jeshanah. He named it Ebenezer—which means "the stone of help"—saying "God, you have done such a marvelous work here, and there, and in this situation." (See 1 Samuel 7:12.) Lay down a rock or something symbolic for what you are thankful for. "Lord, thank you for my friends; that I am clothed (fortunately for others); that I have food and a car that works; an opportunity—all the good in my life." You may want to write a word or sentence on the rock in permanent marker as a reminder.

Gratitude Inspires Generosity

The level of your giving shows the level of your gratitude. When you are grateful, you are more generous and more likely to pay it forward and give back to others. Be generous, kind, and loving toward others, giving and sharing in all you have and are. Even small acts of kindness reveal a grateful, generous spirit.

As I write, I am on a plane flying to New York with my family. I noticed a lady across from me was separated from her husband— he was sitting a few rows back. So I offered my seat across the aisle and moved the few rows back so they could travel together. It wasn't much of a sacrifice, and I was hoping for an opportunity to do some act of kindness on this flight, as an expression of my gratitude and generosity.

BEING GENEROUS CAN BE INCONVENIENT

Now, lest you think more of me than you ought, a spontaneous thought comes to mind that I am compelled to confess. Not too long ago I was on another flight going to speak somewhere, and I was asked if I would give up my seat. Understand my dilemma: I had a nice aisle seat on an exit row, which I had made quite an effort to get. I was planning to get some last-minute prep time in and relax and focus for the event. When I found out that the exchange was a middle seat in the very last row, I wanted to say, "No, I don't think so. I am going to speak on how to flourish in positive spiritual emotions, and I can't be put out."

But it was a mother wanting to be closer to a child. Honestly, it was an intense battle within. I could empathize with the mother/ child dilemma, but I desperately wanted to hold on to my seat and not be so inconvenienced.

I eventually said the right thing, "Sure," but I reluctantly trekked all the way to the back with quite an attitude inside. As I sat with my back straight up against the wall, squashed between two very large men, I started doing my deep breathing relaxation exercises. "Breathe in the good, and let go of the bad." It was then I was struck with another spontaneous thought. *It's okay to make a sacrifice. There will be other times when you get the nice seat. You will make it. Besides, talk about having to be inconvenienced while being generous. This is what Jesus would have done.* With that thought, I snapped right out of it. God used the whole experience to inspire me to feel very grateful and quite humbled at my minuscule, reluctant generosity.

Pay Attention to Goodness and Abundance

Feeling and practicing gratitude is the single strongest predictor of satisfaction with life. Gratitude and appreciation can be increased in your life through many small practices. Repeat them daily until they become regular habits. Throughout your day, be attentive to God's goodness and blessings, to the "kisses of God." Notice the small things around you as well as the grand. Look for signs and symbols of His presence through people and situations. Following are some ways you can begin to practice gratitude.

"COUNT YOUR BLESSINGS" GRATITUDE JOURNAL

Count your abundant blessings by recording them in a gratitude journal. Every night before going to bed, reflect on and write down at least three good things that happened during the day that you are grateful for. Then you might reflect on why you think these good things happened. "The benefits from counting blessings are tangible, emotionally and physically," says Dr. Emmons. "People are 25 percent happier, and more energetic if they keep gratitude journals, have 20 percent less envy and resentment, sleep 10 percent longer each night and wake up 15 percent more refreshed, exercise 33 percent more and show a 10 percent drop in blood pressure compared to persons who are not keeping gratitude journals."[11] A gratitude journal is different from a lengthier writing journal. It could be a little journal you keep next to your bed or in your purse where you just jot down words and phrases. It may be a more creative, artistically enjoyable journal or a scrapbook-type journal that includes photos, cards, poems, your own psalms, quotes, collages, reminders of nature, and other symbolic ways of remembering and expressing gratitude.

THE PRAYER OF THE EXAMEN

This is a rich and meaningful prayer based on the St. Ignatian Examination of Conscious. It is a way of experiencing and finding God in all things of your life. After doing this practice regularly, you will feel more relaxed in times of stress. As Socrates said, "The unexamined life is not worth living." Looking back and reflecting over the day will keep you aware. At the end of the day, reflect on where you found God in the events of your life. Replay the day like a DVD. Where was Christ in your day? Are you becoming more of the person you want to be? What lenses were you wearing—anger, fear, stress, sadness? How have you grown in these areas during the day? What were the opportunities? Was there someone who needed help or a kind word you missed? Now put the whole day in the hands of the Lord. Reflect in His presence and plan how you can live the next day. Be prepared to find God tomorrow where you didn't see Him today.

What grace do you need to see God fulfill these longings in you? Enter prayer with an attitude of gratitude, realizing anew that all you have and are comes as a gift from God.

PRAYING EXAMINATION OF CONSCIENCE[12]

1. Thanksgiving
   Lord, I realize that all, even myself, is a gift from you.
   Today, for what things am I most grateful?

2. Intention
   Lord, open my eyes and ears to be more honest with myself.
   Today, what do I really want for myself?
3. Examination
   Lord, show me what has been happening to me and in me this day. Today, in what ways have I experienced your love?
4. Contrition
   Lord, I am still learning to grow in your love. Today, what choices have been inadequate responses to your love?
5. Hope
   Lord, let me look with longing toward the future. Today, how will I let you lead me to a brighter tomorrow?

Rick Warren shares how life is not a series of hilltops and valleys. It is more like a railroad track, with two tracks going next to each other at the same time. We will always have something to be grateful for and something we are struggling through.

Here is another way to daily practice the examen.[13] At the end of the day, light a candle and take a few minutes to reflect on what was most life-giving for you (flourishing) and what was most draining and depleting (languishing):

Consolation

What moments was I most grateful for? What moments was I least grateful for?

Where did I experience God's life-giving presence the most today—with others and my most authentic best self in God?

When did I feel right with the world, freely open to love and the Spirit of God, even during moments of pain and struggle?

Desolation

Where did I experience God's presence and the Spirit flowing through me the least today?

What am I least grateful for—the stresses, pressures, worries, struggles, or pain?

In what ways did I feel out of touch with God, others, and my most authentic self?

In what ways did I feel inner turmoil, un-centered, confused, or disconnected?

These may be significant events or just subtle daily happenings. Don't judge them. Just pay attention to what you can discover, learn, and surrender, cultivating more of what is life-giving and less of what is depleting. Then, when you wake in the morning, anticipate the Lord blessing you, and pay attention to the small and big ways He is present in your life.

Show Appreciation

What people want more than anything else is to be loved, valued, and appreciated. One of the greatest human desires is the desire to feel important. We crave sincere, honest appreciation. I know I do. Don't you? Appreciation is the best gift we can give each other, especially on special occasions. Savor and value the people and the blessings in your life. Tell your loved ones how much you love and appreciate them. Point out strengths and virtues you appreciate. Act grateful. Say thank you. Write notes and perform gestures of thankfulness.

Let people know how much they really mean to you. What do you value about them? During a birthday celebration, gather everyone and go around the room, sharing memories and ways you love, value, and appreciate the birthday person. Have everyone write their thoughts on a three-by-five card as a memory to be read and enjoyed over and over again.

Make Christmas and other special occasions more memorable with gestures of love and appreciation. Rather than just buying something, ask people what would make them feel valued and appreciated. Consider making a list of a few important people, and offer to give the gift of time and help with a project.

In expressing your gratefulness, where appropriate, show others your appreciation toward God. God is good, and all blessings come from Him. By telling others how good He is to you, you will give hope and inspire spiritual renewal, as well. We are not only called to "share each other's burdens" (Galatians 6:2 NLT), but to share our joys, blessings, and gratefulness, as well.

APPRECIATION FROM THE HEART

Appreciation enhances the value of your life. Applied sincerely and consistently, appreciation can help transform your attitude, shift perceptions, and improve your mind, health, and quality of life.

Scientists tell us that positive spiritual emotions also have measurable physiological states. Appreciation is one of the most powerful core emotions for lowering the heart rate and increasing a relaxed mental and physiological state.

Different emotions are reflected in different heart rhythm patterns. When you are angry, frustrated, or upset, your heart pattern will be jagged and heart rhythms will be erratic and incoherent. If there is an orderly wave pattern, it is known as *coherence*. When you experience love, appreciation, or gratitude, your heart rhythms are smooth and even—there is coherence.

When the physiological state of coherence is generated during sustained positive emotions like appreciation, there is a link with beneficial health and other positive outcomes like stress reduction.

The appreciative heart practice engages the heart to help reduce stress and low-grade anxiety, producing sustained states of this heart coherence.

The Appreciative Heart[14]

Take some time to sit quietly and disengage from your thoughts and feelings—especially stressful ones.

Shift your attention to the area around your heart—and for a few minutes breathe deeply and gently for twelve inhalations and exhalations.

Make a sincere effort to activate a positive feeling of appreciation for someone, someplace, or something in your life. Quietly sense any change in perception or feeling.

Make a sincere effort to sustain these feelings of appreciation, care, or love while radiating them to yourself and others.

When you catch your mind wandering, gently focus back on your breathing, reconnecting with feelings of appreciation.

If you are in touch with any stress, ask yourself what would be an efficient, effective attitude or action that would balance and de-stress your system. Then, refocus on appreciation in your heart.

Appreciation and Gratitude Letter

Recall any acts of love or kindness directed toward you in the last week by friends, family, co-workers, or strangers. Recall and feel how you felt at the time. Allow your feelings of appreciation to form. If possible, write a brief thank-you letter or journal entry expressing your appreciation and gratitude to someone who was kind and helpful to you.

Think of others who have been kind and helpful to you but have not heard your personal expression of thanks and gratitude. Consider parents, teachers, coaches, friends, and relatives, all those who might be expected to be kind and helpful because of the relationship or their job. Pick one of these people and write them a gratitude letter including why you are grateful in specific and concrete terms. If at all possible, deliver it personally and ask the person to read the letter in your presence. If personal delivery is not possible, mail or email the letter and follow up with a phone call.

Express Gratitude Regularly

The wisdom of Solomon in Proverbs 16:24 (NKJV), "Pleasant words are like honeycomb, sweetness to the soul and health to the bones," reminds us that when we share good, encouraging words to others, we can actually help contribute to their well-being and health. Reflect to others their value and virtue and how you are grateful for their impact on your life.

Here are some phrases to prompt your good, positive, inspiring words:

> *"What I love and appreciate about you . . ."*
> *"Thank you for . . ."*
> *"A blessing or 'good word' for you is . . ."*

Verbalize and be practical in your expression of gratitude to God and others. Be creative in expressing your gratitude. What new ways can you explore being thankful? Here are some ideas: praise and worship; prayers of thanksgiving; the gift of time; giving thoughtful presents; creative, expressive writing; thank-you letters, notes, emails, texts, or cards; a gratitude journal or scrapbook; hosting a party. When you pray and praise God, you become more aware of His presence. Singing praise and saying prayers of thankfulness lifts your spirits and will build gratitude in your heart, increasing your feelings of peace and joy. (See Philippians 4:4–7.)

CULTIVATE CONTENTMENT

Be aware of not comparing, contrasting, and competing, which result in corruption, compromise, dissatisfaction, or entitlement. Refrain from negative comparative statements. Instead, be thankful for your unique strengths and abilities, your journey with God. Be the tree or flower you were created to be. Think great, grateful thoughts. When you fill your mind with the good things in life, it builds more joy, peace, and tranquility (see Philippians 4:8–9), as you will discover in the next chapter.

> I will give thanks to you, Lord, for you are good. Your love endures forever.
>
> Adapted from Psalm 118:28–29

Prayer

O God,
Let something essential and joyful happen in me now,
Something like the blooming of hope and faith,
Like a grateful heart,
Like a surge of awareness of how precious each
    moment is . . .

—Ted Loder[15]

Reflective Questions and Flourish Practices

1. Consider the questions in the Examen exercise, but instead of examining your day, review the past season of your life. What are you most grateful for? Have you seen God's hand in your life? What have been the most difficult aspects of this season?

2. In the midst of your current season of life, which of the gratitude practices below would you like to do? Is there another that comes to mind? *Count your blessings; keep a gratitude journal; develop an appreciative heart; write gratitude letters; pay attention to goodness; express gratitude; show appreciation; cultivate contentment.*

3. What situation in your life has made it most difficult to

keep the seed of gratitude alive? What is one thing to be grateful about in the midst of this difficulty?

4. Out of a heart of gratitude, how can you practically be more kind and generous, pay it forward, or give back?

5. During the next holiday season of Thanksgiving and Christmas, create your own Twelve Ways of Gratitude and Twelve Days of Giving. Be creative with ideas to include with friends and family to share together.

6. Take a thirty-day kindness challenge, doing one act of kindness for someone every day for thirty days. Notice how this impacts your life.

7. Instead of just giving "stuff" as gifts for special occasions and holidays, consider something more meaningful, loving, and appreciative. Ask loved ones what they would like. Offer the gift of your time, talent, and service. Let them know how much they are loved and appreciated with a custom, hand-written card.

PART 5

RENEWING PEACE:
PEACE AND
TRANQUILITY SYSTEM

*You flourish when
your mind, soul, and body
are at peace and tranquil*

chapter 8

Calming Stress in Your
Mind and Body

A plain and simple life is a full life.

Proverbs 13:7 THE MESSAGE

As I've already mentioned, every New Year I choose a theme for
the year. A few years ago, the theme I chose was *peace*. I had been
reflecting on Psalm 23 at that time, and the verse that stood out
for me was "He makes me lie down in green pastures, he leads
me beside quiet waters" (v. 2). It was exactly what I needed. Some
rest and refreshing. So I began reading all I could get my hands on
that expanded on the themes of Psalm 23.

I started off with great anticipation of some quality time of
tranquil and enjoyable peace and quiet. But it wasn't too long
before I discovered a whole new meaning to "He *makes* me lie
down"—to take time to rest, find peace, and recover. On about
day four, I was awakened at three a.m. with such vicious spinning in my head that I felt I had to hold on to the side of my bed

to keep from falling out. This went on for days. I couldn't move my head without tremendous motion sickness. The diagnosis was "positional vertigo."

So there I lay—still and quiet—for days on end. Not what I had in mind for starting out the year of peace. But, as the hours and days went by, I discovered that there were great treasures to be found in experiencing true rest, peace, and tranquility. I have practiced contemplative spirituality and stress management for years, but this level of extended quietness is really hard to do. It goes against the grain of our modern accelerated lifestyle. It reveals just how far off we can get from the way we were designed.

We don't all have to lie still for days, but we desperately need to daily create a peaceful soul sanctuary—a place of quiet and recovery, restoring and renewing of our weary souls and minds. We need to allow the redeeming shalom to be cultivated in our lives.

He Makes Me Lie Down in Green Pastures

Over the years since then, I have discovered some very helpful insights into Psalm 23. One of those insights is how King David, the author of the psalm, sees the analogy between sheep and God's people from the shepherd's perspective. We are like the sheep and God is the Good Shepherd.

Since most of us haven't been on a sheep farm and know little about raising sheep, some facts about sheepherding might be illuminating. For starters, they tend to eat too much. Their digestive system is similar to a cow's in that they continue to eat while digesting, but sheep will overindulge themselves until bloated, even coming close to death. They don't stop of their own accord. So a good shepherd *makes* them lie down, because if they don't, sheep will keep standing and eating. They won't eat when they lie down. And in some respects, this is how we can be. Not just in our eating, but our living. If we don't monitor ourselves very well, we will consume too much of life and just keep going, trying to push beyond our limits. We are vulnerable to never being satisfied, to overdoing and overachieving. If we are not careful, we will suffer for it in increased and devastating stress. Helplessness and hopelessness can set in. Our bodies pay the price, as we lose our vitality. So sometimes God has to "make us lie down." This is not His punishment, but the care of a Good Shepherd who wants to pull us back from languishing and give us His peace.

The Gift of God's Peace

God offers the gift of His peace not only in the extraordinary moments of our lives, but in our ordinary, humdrum daily living. In John 14:26–27, where Jesus is preparing His disciples for His departure one day, He tells them, "The Friend, the Holy Spirit . . . will make everything plain to you. . . . I'm leaving you well and whole. That's my parting gift to you. Peace" (THE MESSAGE). Then in John 15:11–12, Jesus continues to reveal His love and joy when He says, "I've told you these things for a purpose: that my joy might be your joy, and your joy wholly mature. This is my command: Love one another the way I loved you" (THE MESSAGE). Clearly, Jesus connects love, joy, and peace—they are all bound together.

What are the "things" He has told us? In summary, it is that "*If* you live by my ways, stay connected to me, abide in my love, and love others, *then* you will have my joy and peace." (See John 15:5–10.) It is the Holy Spirit that makes this possible. And "the harvest is sure to be abundant" (John 15:5 THE MESSAGE). This is the way of the heart, the Jesus way of abundant, vibrant living, the way of the Spirit. It is how we become who Jesus wants us to be, living lives that cultivate joy and peace. This is our right, our inheritance. We must learn to manage our lives to cultivate this peace. Our lives can be like pots and pans with holes. The inevitable stress and struggles of life can cause holes that leak out the joy and peace of the Spirit.

Beware of Peace Pilferers

So what is stealing your peace? What drives your life, hindering true joy and peace? What challenges are you facing that are wilting you? In this chapter I will focus primarily on the stress-related challenges that most of us face, and the importance of recovery for peace. In the next chapter I will focus on worry and tranquility, because they are somewhat related.

Stress is a major hindrance to flourishing, no matter what you are going through. I have experienced this myself, and it is a common concern with those I coach, counsel, and lead in retreats. Stress has a more significant effect on our health and coping behaviors than ever before in history.

Women in particular are suffering. They put too many expectations on themselves, stretching to the limit with multitasking and multiple roles, and rarely taking time to relax.[1] There was a time when life moved at the easy pace of a camel. However, many of us are now propelled into a breathless rush, needing to slow down, simplify, open our lives, and rearrange our days to receive the gift of God's peace. Others of us need to find "a holy soul sanctuary," a place of refuge, "a sacred place" where we can go for protection and refreshing for our souls.[2]

The Problem of Stress

There are two factors that characterize modern-day stress and set it apart from stress in previous generations. First, it is the result of the dramatic increase in the pace of life. We move faster, think faster, and function faster than ever before. Second, we are robbing ourselves of adequate recovery time. The stress system in the body is very limited in its resources and is designed to deal with stress that is short lived. Most important of all, the stress system needs repairing. And to repair our stress systems, we need rest—down time. Today, we do not give a high priority to rest. Four out of five people are sleep deprived, and stress-related disorders are epidemic.[3]

The stress I am referring to does not come only from the bad things of life, but from what can appear to be good things, as well. Stress is anything that pushes up and prolongs our natural excitement and emergency response system, which triggers stress hormones (adrenaline and cortisol), causing stress-related disorders.

The purpose of the stress system is to protect and warn us of dangerous and life-threatening situations. However, today's accelerated lifestyle and internal stress turmoil propel us to live outside the boundaries of God's design. Increased levels of stimulation, even in our spirituality, can have consequences. All prolonged excitement and stress ultimately become damaging, hindering us from peace and tranquility.

In a study by the American Psychological Association, more people reported physical and emotional symptoms due to stress in 2008 than they did in 2007, and nearly half (47 percent) of adults reported that their stress had increased in the past year, and it was still rising. The paradox is that many said they were "handling their stress well."[4] How can this be when people report more physical and emotional symptoms? The answer is simple: Stress doesn't always feel bad, so we aren't aware and monitoring it well. Adrenaline stimulation can actually feel good, which is why it can lead to forms of addiction. There is unanimous consensus in the scientific world that if Americans continue to experience these high levels of stress for prolonged periods of time, they are at risk for developing serious illnesses. This has devastating implications for the next generation. And the most important effect of all is a diminished capacity to experience God's peace in a flourishing life of shalom.

Understanding the Stress Response System

After two years and, needless to say, many stresses and setbacks, Ed Stafford and Cho Sanchez Rivera finished walking 4,000 miles along the Amazon river. Now that's a *journey*!

There are two types of stress experienced on a trip like this and that we deal with every day: *acute* and *chronic*.

Along the way, Ed and Cho encountered arrows pointed at their chests. Cho suffered a severe machete cut. Ed got a skin disease and had to have a botfly removed from his skull.

Although everyone would expect these acute stresses to be the hardest things for them to encounter on the journey, they weren't. Ed said that the adrenaline kicks in, enabling you to deal with exciting, potentially dangerous moments like that. It triggers the fight-or-flight response just as when we are in a car accident, relationship conflict, or other difficult challenges.

"It's been the mundane that has really challenged me," he said. It was the weight of the rucksack, eating the same old basic food, the unending mosquito bites, and constant thorns. The things that wouldn't be such a stressful bother on a two-day expedition are what become the most challenging on a longer journey. The chronic, long-term stresses are what wear down your body, mind, emotions, and spirit. Things like dealing with illness, extended caregiving, loss of a loved one, or other ongoing challenges.[5]

THE BRAIN

Stress affects your brain and other life systems, interfering with your ability to experience positive emotions like joy, happiness, and peace. You can't be stressed out and peaceful and tranquil at the same time. There are two primary parts of the brain that work together like an alarm circuit in response to stress, the amygdala and the hippocampus. The amygdala, also known as the emotional brain, sends signals to the other parts of the brain about whether an experience is threatening or not. The main job of the hippocampus is to register the context of our experience and to keep the amygdala quiet.

The problem with chronic stress is that it sensitizes the amygdala, which is most helpful if you are trying to survive a difficult or dangerous situation. The more ongoing stress you experience, the more this system stays on alert. And the longer it stays alert, the less time it has for recovery.

THE AUTONOMIC NERVOUS SYSTEM

When your stress brain circuits are triggered, the *sympathetic system* causes the other systems in your body and brain to be on heightened alert: It limits relaxation and positive emotions and experience. The *parasympathetic nervous system*, on the other hand, allows you to be calm and opens you up to peace, beauty, and other positive emotions. This is the system you want to intentionally enhance in order to calm stress and increase the state of peace and tranquility.

STRESS HORMONES

The stress response system releases fifty-seven hormones, but the most damaging are *adrenaline* and *cortisol.*[6] When danger is perceived, these hormones are released and trigger the fight-or-flight response. It could be in response to a snake, a bear, or a car accident; while studying for an important test; or in a conflict when someone is hurting your feelings. The primary purpose of this system is to deal with threats and dangers, but it also raises the demands and challenges of life. We need this system to keep us protected and motivated, and intrinsically it isn't harmful to us. But when it becomes a lifestyle, addicting or chronic, it becomes just as threatening as facing a lion in the jungle.

STAGES OF THE STRESS RESPONSE

1. Alarm stage

This is when the body prepares for the flight-or-fight response. Adrenaline goes up to prepare you to respond to whatever you perceive as dangerous, threatening, or demanding.

2. Resistance stage

This is when the body tries to adjust to chronic stress by releasing the stress hormone cortisol. Cortisol blocks the tranquility and joy system while in alert mode, causing disruption that over time leads to anxiety and depression. This is where many of us are vulnerable to falling into exhaustion.

3. Exhaustion stage

This is when the stress hormones of adrenaline and cortisol take their toll, and all other life systems get worn down and deplete our well-being. Stress lowers the immune system, damages brain cells, and leads to anxiety and depression.

For an expanded list of stressors, symptoms of excessive stress, and negative effects of stress, please refer to the chapter on stress, anxiety, and depression in my book *A Woman's Guide to Overcoming Depression.*[7]

Creating a Peaceful Soul Sanctuary

We now come to what we can do to create a place where our bodies and minds can find refuge. Flourishing in peace in your life begins with paying attention to the state of your heart and soul. Discern the consequences of unresolved issues, emotional strain, relationship conflict, or modern-day stress in your life. Discover practices for resolving conflict, calming your stress response system, lowering your stress hormones, and recovering daily. Here are a few proven pathways you can begin integrating into your lifestyle today.

Listen to Your Life

1. *What are the strains, struggles, and stressors in your life?* Pay attention to the state of your soul. If you have inner turmoil, what could be the cause? Are you being challenged with illness, relationship conflict, job or family changes, caregiving? Is your life out of balance as a whole person? Are you feeling chaotic and depleted?

Are you too busy producing and consuming, driven by misguided natural desires and longings? There may be unresolved bad habits, emotional wounds, and worries. Women especially tend to push themselves beyond their natural limits.

2. *What are the symptoms you are struggling with?* How are you responding to the stress in your life? Are you driven to some unhealthy habits and patterns? All the systems of your life will give you signals that you are stretching yourself too far or depleting your mind, body, spirit, or relationships. Listen to your soul and body while they are still in the alarm stage. Pay attention to symptoms before you get into the resistance stage, where cortisol does all the damage. Consider getting a complete medical checkup to assess if your symptoms are related to stress or something else. The neurocircuitry of your emotional and social pain is closely connected to the neurocircuitry of physical pain, so you may feel genuine pains when stressed, lonely, or in relationship conflict.[8]

LISTEN TO YOUR LONGINGS

If you have no joy in your spiritual journey, that is telling you something. All these systems will signal to you when you are restless, tired, unhappy, anxious, or stressed. Are you constantly looking for something? Do you need to always find excitement and stimulation? Can you sit still and be quiet for a while? Recognize these symptoms. Here is an important clue.

Whenever you try to unwind, the symptoms of stress will appear. While you are under stress, your body is still trying to maximize, cope, and respond. When the busyness stops, you finally slow down, and it is quiet, you will have an adrenaline letdown. You may get a headache or feel low, bored, and empty. The longings of your heart will become evident. You'll have thoughts like, *What do I really desire and want in life? How do I really feel?* When these come to the surface, it can be scary. Embracing our longings and desires might set us up for disappointment. Lean in.

LISTEN TO YOUR HEART

Feelings of stress and peace are reflected in your body. The body may tell you something is wrong through pain. Or it may not be that obvious. If you are having a hard time discerning the stress in your life, get a medical checkup to measure your cholesterol, hormone levels, thyroid, and sugar levels. One way scientists measure stress is through *heart rate variability*. Emotions and stressful states are reflected through heart rhythm patterns. When you are angry, stressed, frustrated, or upset, your heart rhythms become incoherent or erratic. If you experience positive emotions and states like joy, gratitude, and peace, your heart rhythms are smooth and even. As we discovered in chapter 7, this is known as *coherence*, the harmonious, peaceful state you want your heart to be in. There are instruments available to help you learn how to get your heart in a peaceful state of coherence.[9]

ELIMINATE BUSYNESS AND HURRY

Many like to keep busy and choose a lifestyle full of activities and overcommitment because it feels good. And this is what adrenaline does. It provides an enhanced feeling of well-being so we can cope with whatever stress we are facing. The problem is that we can become addicted to this enhanced feeling and then refuse to give it up.

Busyness, which usually includes hurriedness, has a status attached to it. We wear it as a badge of honor because it makes us sound and feel important. When we talk with people and they ask, "How are you doing?" we reply, "Oh, I'm so busy." This gives the illusion that you must be an important person of value, doing things and going places. But most of us fill our lives with things that could be eliminated, that aren't necessarily assignments of fruitfulness from the Lord. They just clog up the flow of the Spirit in our lives and, like weeds, crowd out the good seed.

We are compelled to participate in complex technological social networking—emailing, Facebooking, and tweeting valuable time away. The new spiritual practice to combat this is to unplug from all this stimulating technology and media that drives our lives and interferes with the well-being of our souls. Other essential practices are slowing and quieting our souls from the noise and frenzy of everyday life. All this increased stimulation of the stress response system and pursuing excitement is our most dangerous drug and poison to our well-being.

"If you want to last over the long haul . . . you have to learn how to recharge yourself spiritually, emotionally, physically, and mentally. Here's an easy formula to remember: Divert daily, withdraw weekly, abandon annually. Know what relaxes you and what recharges you—and do it."

—Rick Warren

When you find yourself saying, "I'm so busy," take some time for self-examination and reflection to consider: What can I eliminate from my life and time commitments that is wasteful, cluttering, or contaminating? What drives my life? What attitudes, thought patterns, resentments, and unforgiveness must I let go of? How can I prioritize what matters most? What are the more important ways I can focus my time and energy to allow for more peace? The next time someone asks you how you've been, what would it be like to be able to respond with something like, "Things are really balanced and slow for me right now"?

Slow Down and Simplify

Most of us try to do too much in as little time as possible. I know, because I have done it. Even then, too much of a good thing isn't good enough. The antidote, therefore, is to slow down, simplify your life, and do less rather than more. The mere act of slowing down lowers adrenaline and facilitates stress healing. Learn to set boundaries and prioritize so you can say no to less important things and say yes to the more important things. Commit to a simpler, more intentionally focused lifestyle. Spend more time on enriching, relaxing events and people. As Stephen Covey says, "The main thing is to keep the main thing the main thing."[10]

Don't keep pushing yourself. You don't always have to be busy. Take some time-outs. There are times when we are necessarily busy, like when we're moving or having a baby or finishing a project with a deadline. So it is even more important during these times to relax and have some down time instead of always doing something. Research shows that if you take time off work and literally slow down, unplug, rest, and recover, your productivity and levels of creativity will go up. Have you noticed that some of your best ideas come when you are simply doing nothing, like taking a shower, driving in the car, or walking?

Here are some ways you can practice slowing down and pacing yourself: Leave a little early so you aren't rushing; drive in the slow lane; eat your food slowly, chewing each bite completely; allow enough time each day to read a few pages of a book; spend time in prayer and meditation, simply being with God.

Our minds are usually running at a fast pace, multitasking and going several different directions at once. This is known as *polyphasic thinking*. Slow your mind down. Try to have only one stream of thought at a time. The brain functions best when you think and stay focused on one theme or stream of thought at a time.

Calm Your Stress Response System

Your body can't be calm and stressed at the same time. If you regularly lower your stress response system to a place of rest and relaxation using some of the following ideas, you will recuperate from stress damage. Learn how to relax, lower your stress response hormones, and keep a calm emotional brain. This will open your life to more peace.

TEND AND BEFRIEND

During the 4,000-mile hike along the Amazon, what were the greatest pleasures of the journey? Ed Stafford said it was the warmth of the people and the village children who frequently welcomed them and offered them home-cooked meals. People and our relationships are the most valuable in times of stress.

There is a specific stress in women that focuses around the neuropeptide *oxytocin*. This hormone is essential to the bonding of mothers to their children and for cultivating friendships, couples' relationships, and other meaningful attachments. It is the "we are better together" chemical that proves the importance of how supportive relationship connections are essential for our optimal health and well-being. Recent research by Shelley Taylor and her colleagues at UCLA shows that oxytocin is instrumental in protecting us against stress, anxiety, and depression.[11]

Besides the fight-or-flight response, people demonstrate "tending and befriending" responses. During stressful times, women especially seek positive social relationships, because they provide safety. An increased level of oxytocin in our system motivates us to seek out positive social contact, which decreases the stress hormone cortisol. This brings a sense of calm. Blood pressure, heart rate, and levels of stress, anxiety, and depression go down. This helps us be more positive in communicating and increases trust, empathy, and altruistic feelings in relationships.

In times of stress, it makes sense if you have the urge to share lunch with a friend. It is de-stressing and restoring to make a phone call to chat; clean up and organize your house (your "nest"); bake some healthy, comforting food to share; or reach out to care for your children or someone who needs you.

185

REACH OUT AND TOUCH SOMEONE

Oxytocin is also released when we hug, hold hands, cuddle on the couch, or walk arm in arm. Touch is the wordless expression of love. Even micro-touches count, like stroking a hand, resting your hand on a shoulder, a kiss on the forehead, a pat on the back, or a rub on the arm. These are true gestures of comfort, consolation, and encouragement. These moments of healing touch are truly sacred.

Studies show that a simple act like holding hands can reduce stress.[12] "For I, the Lord your God, will hold your right hand, Saying to you, 'Fear not, I will help you' " (Isaiah 41:13 NKJV). The Lord knows the value of having our hand held to reduce fear and stress. Research done at the University of Virginia found that when happily married couples held hands during stressful times, their brain scans looked calmer than when not holding hands.[13] This agrees with what we know are the benefits of social connection and the importance of close emotional relationships, as well as supportive touch.

Healthy, Proven Ways to De-Stress
What works for you?

Slow down • Unplug • Breathe deeply • Take a warm bath with candles and aromatherapy • Get a massage • Get eight hours of sleep • Take a nap • Take a time-out • Calm your mind • Stop and think things through • Relax your body • Stretch and move your body • Go for a brisk walk • Get outside and enjoy nature • Pray and meditate • Watch a funny video • Breathe deeply • Drink some relaxing herbal tea • Get out and enjoy sunlight • Journal and write it out • Share your concerns • Reach out • Talk with a friend • Spend time with someone who makes you laugh • Get professional help • Do something good and creative • Prioritize • Make a to-do list • Simplify • Create your own sanctuary • Listen to relaxing music • Begin and end each day with some quiet • Do simple relaxation exercises • Write out what you are grateful for • Read an inspiring book or magazine • Claim the promises in Scripture • Don't catastrophize life • Don't contaminate the good times • Take some quiet time • Plan time for self-care • Take a stay-cation • Just say no or "Let me get back to you on that"

• Eat nutritious, balanced meals • Avoid going for the quick fix—caffeine or high-fat, processed foods • Call and talk to a friend • Help someone • Clean and organize • Buy fresh flowers • Streamline and simplify your life • Manage your time • Take a walk in the beauty of nature

PHYSICAL SELF-CARE

See yourself as a whole person in your daily life. You can't separate out bits and pieces of yourself; they are all interrelated. Your body is the vessel for your heart, soul, and spirit. When your body is stressed out, your brain isn't functioning well, and your lifestyle habits are depleting, you will be peace-challenged. Eat healthy, balanced nutritious meals; exercise; get enough sleep; and observe the Sabbath for rest, renewal, and restoration.

Can we still flourish if our bodies aren't fully functioning right—if we are ill or have cancer or other physical limitations? Absolutely. My friends with cancer or other health challenges are some of the most flourishing, inspiring people I know. Dr. Bernie Siegel has worked for years studying and writing about the remarkable factors that contribute to surviving cancer. In his book *Faith, Hope and Healing*, he tells many stories of how people have battled cancer with more success by thinking like a winner, choosing happiness, letting go, giving love, and receiving prayers and support in return. Even during times of physical illness, our spirit, mind, heart, and soul can work together to provide an environment to flourish in well-being.

Active Recovery Through Exercise

"In a way," John Ratey states, "exercise can be thought of as a psychiatrist's dream treatment. It works on anxiety, on panic disorder, and on stress in general, which has a lot to do with depression. And it generates the release of neurotransmitters . . . that are very similar to our most important psychiatric medicines. Having a bout of exercise is like taking a little bit of Prozac and a

187

little bit of Ritalin, right where it is supposed to go" (with positive side effects).[14] Exercise is good for just about everything: recovering from stress, elevating mood, reducing the risk of diseases, and helping us stay trim. It is an essential rhythm to our lives. There is so much new, convincing research being done in the new umbrella field of Positive Health Psychology.

Dr. Tal Ben-Shahar, professor at Harvard, observes that the best way to interpret this is not that exercising is like taking an antidepressant. Instead, not exercising is like taking a depressant.[15] We were created with a need for physical exercise to benefit our overall well-being. If we deprive ourselves of water, oxygen, and basic nutrients, we will face consequences. Likewise, if we don't exercise regularly, we will be depleted in all areas of life. So, to be spiritually alive and emotionally healthy, get up and move your body regularly.

Passive Recovery Through Relaxation and Restoration

RESTORE A SENSE OF CONTROL

Lack of a sense of control turns bad stress into severe stress. Feeling helpless leads to hopelessness, which leads to depression. That's why having hope is so important.

It's not the mountains we climb that do us in, it's the sand in our shoes. We need challenges to build character and psychological immunity. It is the ongoing stress that we feel out of control about that shortens our lives. It's not the CEO, carrying all the high-end decisions, but the janitor with fewer options and choices, who has more stress. Dealing with stress is about having a sense of control. You may not have much control over your outer world, but you have most of the influence in your inner world. The Spirit of God in you can transform the way you think—your beliefs, attitude, and perceptions.

Building your faith and hope through spiritual practices can restore a sense of control. You can pray. You can build a sense of meaning and purpose. You can have confidence that God is there with you, fostering hope. Spiritual practices are key to managing stress. Knowing God is in control, quieting your mind and soul to see His perspective, gives you a sense of knowing you are not helpless.

SLEEP. PRAY. FLOURISH.

"A significant proportion of all ethnic groups are experiencing sleepiness that impacts their day to day living," says Thomas J. Balkin, PhD, chairman of the National Sleep Foundation. "Sleepiness impacts every aspect of our lives, so for those people who are not getting a good night's sleep, getting better sleep will make you sharper in the boardroom, give you a better quality of life, and [make] the sun seem a whole lot brighter."[16]

What you do before you go to bed also makes a big difference. If you watch TV, surf the Internet, or engage in other stimulating activities, you won't sleep as well as those who pray and do relaxing rituals. People with busy schedules often cut back on sleep to make time for other things. However, sleep should be nonnegotiable; it is as important as diet and exercise to our overall well-being. Most adults need about eight hours of sleep, but if you can get nine you will do even better.[17]

DEEP BREATHING

Deep breathing helps you strengthen and activate the parasympathetic and autonomic system to lower stress. When life gets busy and we are stressed, we unconsciously switch from natural, deep diaphragm breathing to shallow chest breathing. Life is in the breath. Deep breathing is important for more energy, relaxation and a healthy body. Take a few deep breaths now. Inhale slowly from deep in your chest, expanding your belly, then slowly exhale out. Deliberately relax your body. Do this ten times and then return to a regular rhythm of breathing.

As you breathe in and out, remind yourself to breathe in the Holy Spirit. It may begin with a prayer, a word, or a phrase. Eventually it may become a simple contemplation in a quiet sanctuary or humming a song.[18]

Solitude and Silence

"We need to find God, and He cannot be found in noise and restlessness. God is the friend of silence. See how nature—trees, flowers, grass—grow in silence; see the stars, the moon and the sun, how they move in silence . . . Jesus always waits for us in silence. In silence He listens to us; in silence He speaks to our souls. In silence we are granted the privilege of listening to His voice."

—Mother Teresa

In studies on the most effective ways of achieving lasting personal change, "quieting the mind" was on top of the list.[19] We need places and times to be silent and still, to rest awhile free from distractions and noise, to find solitude of the heart, an inner heart sanctuary. It's not just about being quiet and being alone. Richard Foster says that "the purpose of solitude and silence is to see and hear."[20] This is how you learn deep centeredness and control of your inner being.

Sitting still in silence really frightens people. It surfaces anxiety, worry, and fear, but it also opens our heart to hear from our real, authentic selves and be better able to listen to God. The regular practice of doing nothing keeps us from having an inflated view of our importance.

Blaise Pascal, a scientist and theologian, identified way back in 1670 that "all the unhappiness of men [we can add women to this] arises from one single fact, that they cannot stay quietly in their own room."[21]

SOLITUDE

In solitude we nourish the longing for God in our hearts, we find ourselves, that place in our being that is known by God and is "centered" inside. When we have experienced this solitude of the heart, we can always carry this portable sanctuary of the heart through our coming and going and being around people.

Henri Nouwen says that "simplicity and regularity . . . allow us to make the discipline of solitude as much a part of our daily lives as eating and sleeping. When that happens, our noisy worries will slowly lose their power over us and the renewing activity of God's Spirit will slowly make its presence known."[22]

Finding Sanctuary

Where are your places of quiet sanctuary? David found that God was his hope, trust, and hiding place in times of storms. God is our "sanctuary" that we can resort to continually. Where do you go to find release, comfort, and peace? We can find refuge and peace when we run to Him, be still, and wait in the presence of the Lord.

How can you create a sanctuary in your environment, inside and outside? Find a place that allows you to be still and quiet, a sacred place where you can just be in the presence of the Lord. It may be a corner in your house, your garden, a place of beauty outside, or a chapel. Use everyday activities to get solitude and create mini-spa moments.

SILENCE

We are each on a journey, discovering how to flourish. Fortunately, we don't have to hike the Amazon or jet set around the globe like Elizabeth Gilbert did in *Eat, Pray, Love* to capture the experience. Instead, your journey can start right where you are, with an internal conversation with yourself and God.

Find time and space in your daily life where you can be quiet and begin asking powerful questions, listening to the Spirit of God speak to you. *Who am I? Who is God in me? What is my life purpose? What is my "dance" or my "song"? Where am I going?*

I must admit, finding time to quiet the mind and turn to God each day can be difficult. Most of us have busy lives that are filled with the necessary, the mundane, children, and others who demand our time. But the spiritual journey to flourish begins with just doing what you can do, even if it starts with ten minutes a day of focused silence or spiritual reading.

It is only in the silence that we can get some space for our souls to quiet down and to hear the voice of God. "To tune in to God's voice, we must tune out this world's noise."[23] In silence, we are less likely to be able to hide from our problems and be spiritually careless. We nurture our listening skills and are better able to be attuned to and hear the quiet voice of God. We can also identify the distractions in our head and the noise in our heart. To work toward purity of heart, we must have times of silence.

The main benefit of silence is to listen to God and our true, most authentic self. This is essential to our peace of mind. It is when we have inner silence that the inner life can flourish. The soul is like a garden. When you enter into silence, you will first notice the weeds—the distractions inside yourself. You pull them up, but they quickly grow back. But you need to keep weeding so the flowers—the Spirit and Word of God in you—can blossom and grow.

Practical Ways of Silence, Sabbath, and Retreat in Your Daily Life

Have time when you don't listen to music in the car. Keep the TV off. Just let there be silence for a while. Be more thoughtfully reflective, and notice the presence of God in your life. Enjoy the early morning and nighttime as natural times for silence. Create a sanctuary in your home or garden where you can regularly go for silence. Even in a day filled with noise and voices, you can experience silence and solitude within your heart if you are centered and seeing the presence of God in everything around you.

Keep a regular rhythm of quiet time in the morning and evening. Turn your heart and mind toward God, read His Word, pray and give all your cares and concerns to Him. Before going to bed, reflect on what you feel stressed about and what you are grateful for. As you focus on your blessings, you will have a better night's sleep. On one day a week, take a Sabbath rest, doing activities that are relaxing, enjoyable, and rejuvenating.[24] Enjoy the beauty outdoors, your hobbies, visiting with friends and family, taking a nap, or just doing nothing.

When you are able to take the extra time, allow for a half day, a day, a weekend, or a week for a retreat. Create your own spiritual retreat.[25] Plan for some rest, reading, journaling, and time for silence.

Relaxation for Body and Mind

Now that you have an understanding of the stress system and how important it is to keep stress low and remain calm in order to have peace, there is nothing like just doing it. Take a few minutes at any time during your day to do a brief stress reduction and relaxation exercise. You can do this in silence or listen to relaxing instrumental music.

A complete version of this relaxation for body and mind exercise can be downloaded from *www.howtoflourish.com.*

Get in a comfortable position either sitting in a chair or lying down. Begin to relax. Take a few cleansing deep breaths way down in your belly. Breathe in for three slow counts, and breathe out for three slow counts. Keep breathing slowly and deeply, each breath leaving you more and more relaxed. Each breath purifies and relaxes your whole body and mind. Breathe in and breathe out.

Now, imagine in your next breath that clean, pure white air is coming in through the soles of your feet, or in as you breathe. See this clean white air as the Holy Spirit spread throughout your whole body, collecting the debris of tension and stress.

As you breathe in, this air gets darker as it collects the stress and tension from your body. Then as you breathe out, see the dark air exiting your whole body and being, leaving you clean, fresh, and relaxed. Keep breathing in and out.

Take another deep breath and feel it cleansing your whole body of stress and tension, worry and fear. See these all leaving your body with each breath out.

With each breath in see the presence of this light, filling you more and more with the positive, spiritual presence of peace and calm. Feel more relaxed and enjoy this feeling of peace and calm that is spreading throughout your body and being with each cleansing breath. Keep breathing naturally and comfortably in this state for as long as possible.

Now imagine carrying this feeling into the rest of your everyday life. See yourself as confident, relaxed, and calm. See yourself smiling to those around you. As you move into your day, you will live from this centered, cleansed state of calm. Be aware of the cleansing, pure white presence of the Holy Spirit flowing throughout your whole being. You will draw from that strength and rest in that confidence. Say to yourself: Relax. Trust. Calm. Peace.

The Priestly Blessing

Lord, please bless me, keep me, and guard me.
Lord, make your face shine upon me
And be gracious to me.
Lord, lift up your face and presence upon me
And give me your peace.

Adapted from Numbers 6:24–26 NKJV

Reflective Questions and Flourish Practices

1. Pause for a moment and be aware of the Holy Spirit of peace, present now with you, coming to give light and life. You may be so caught up in your own feelings or busyness that you have forgotten the special presence of God or the gifts of His guiding Spirit. Take a minute, and welcome that light and peace into your life.

2. What do you feel now, knowing that God is present with you and always has been? Express what you feel: words of sadness, trust, or thanks.

3. What would you say is stealing your peace? What are some of the strains, struggles, and stressors in your life?

4. What are the most effective, healthy de-stressors for you? How could you incorporate some of the de-stressors into your daily life?

5. List ways that you can connect with others as a powerful stress reliever.

6. How can you create a sanctuary in your home, garden, or other meaningful place for regular quiet and spiritual practices?

7. Consider how you could incorporate mini-retreats into your day; go on an annual spiritual retreat to reduce your stress and calm your mind and body.

chapter 9

Creating a Tranquil
Soul Sanctuary

I am leaving you with a gift—peace of mind and heart. And
the peace I give is a gift the world cannot give. So don't be
troubled or afraid.

John 14:27 NLT

Along my Journey of the Lavender Jacket, I entered a competition
for a big spa retreat makeover. It seemed just what I needed to
celebrate my birthday and help restore my soul. So I prepared the
three-by-five entry card artistically laid out with a convincing sob
story of why I should be picked. Then as I waited, I began fanta-
sizing about what clothes I would pack, what I would share with
the group, how my TV interview would go, and how this event
would transform my life. We could all do with a spa makeover,
couldn't we? Even if it isn't extreme, we could do with a touch-up
here and there, or just some time of pure relaxation.

Of the forty thousand entries for the spa competition,

undoubtedly some women needed it more than I did. When they announced the winners, they summarized the needs represented. There were women suffering multiple layers of losses, like husbands leaving their marriages, battles with cancer, natural disasters, and violent crimes. Others were burnt out from extended caregiving to family members. There were women struggling with life transitions, retirement, menopause, accumulated disappointments of midlife, or turning fifty. Most of the women entering the spa makeover longed for a way to deal with the adversities in their lives—the strain and worries, the depletion of joy and peace. The antidote was deep recuperation and renewal, and they hoped that a spa massage or two would also give restoration for the soul.

He Leads Me by Still Waters.
He Restores My Soul.

And it's no wonder. Studies are showing that due to increased stress and anxiety, men and women are yearning to find renewal, peace, serenity, and tranquility. We are desperately looking for ways to meet this deep need within that we can take home and blend into our everyday lives. Again I turned to Psalm 23, and the Lord helped me realize that I don't have to win a spa makeover for soul restoration and transformation. God has a custom plan for each of us that will meet our needs and deep longings for soul nourishing and peace. The Good Shepherd knows His sheep. He is our protector, provider, healer, guide, nurturer, and peacemaker. He calls each one of us by name. He sees our thoughts and our deep heart longings. He hears us when we call and He sees each tear that falls. Our part is to listen, turn to Him, and follow His beckoning. (See John 10:1–10.)

The Good Shepherd knows that we need protection and refuge. We need a safe haven to run to, where we can be nurtured, nourished, and restored. That's why He goes ahead of us and finds

197

just the right "green pastures" where we can rest, recuperate, and be renewed from the stress and strain of everyday life.

He also leads us by calm, peaceful, still waters. He has to lead because His sheep are naturally fearful. They don't like fast-moving water and will only drink from a serene pool. They will run away from rushing water and not get the refreshing they need. He knows our limitations, weaknesses, fears, and worries. He calms our fearful, anxious hearts and refreshes our thirsty souls. The Lord encourages us in the Scriptures to "not worry," "fear not," and "don't be anxious" more than anything else. He wants us to learn to trust Him when we feel weak and afraid. The presence of the Spirit of God is like the refreshing, restoring waters we need to flourish. He moves us away from a worry-filled life to an abundant life of peace, serenity, and tranquility in the Spirit.

Still Waters Reflection

Listen to the sound of running water—a fountain, stream, or the ocean if possible. Or simply imagine a scene with quiet waters.

1. Sit or lie relaxed. Begin with a few deep breaths.
2. Imagine a scene of quiet water. Maybe a lake surrounded by trees, a cool spring on a hillside, a calm sea with gently rippling waves.
3. Then, along with this clear image, repeat to yourself, "He leads me by still waters. He restores my soul."
4. Imagine your heart feeling appreciation and gratitude. Feel your soul move toward surrender and trust.
5. Rest awhile in this place, knowing confidently that your Good Shepherd is providing refreshment and restoration for your soul.

Finding Peace and Tranquility

Our peace and tranquility was a high priority in our original created design. There is a fantastic tranquility system within our brain, so our natural brain state is peace and tranquility. When tranquilizers were first introduced (Librium was the first, in 1958), we didn't really know why or how they worked. Much later, it was discovered that they worked because the brain itself produces its own tranquilizers. There is a biology of tranquility that works alongside our spiritual and psychological experiences of tranquility, but they are all dependent on this special system in our brains.

Flourishing in tranquility is all about helping our spirit, soul, brain, and body work together to generate natural tranquilizers in our brain. Tranquility is the antidote for anxiety and brings biological harmony to the brain. Other systems of stress and the emotional brain can trigger fear. While designed to protect us, it can sometimes get out of control and rob us of our natural tranquilizers. Of course, when we lower our stress and cope with our fears, we are restored to a state of peace and tranquility. Fortunately, we are now discovering that there are many psychological and spiritual pathways that can help us flourish in our tranquility. How do you know if your tranquility system is functioning properly? Your heart will have peace. Your brain, mind, and heart will be at rest, serene and tranquil, not stressed or anxious.

Negative Thinking and Worry

The battle for peace and tranquility is primarily in the emotional brain and the mind. The negative thoughts and worry that go through our minds steal our peace and mess with our tranquility system. The human default setting for these systems tends toward the negative. We have to intentionally develop healthier thinking patterns; otherwise, we will be disposed toward fearful and negative feelings, which can potentially lead us to unhappiness and languishing. The emotional brain continually intrudes into our present experience with negative thinking, reminders of past pains, and worries about the future. We have to learn how to control these intrusions.

Some of us are hardwired with a little more tendency toward worry. Women especially do it well. It can start early in life and

199

be learned from our parents. My dad tells of how his mother was always nervous and worried. She would ask him before he went to school if he had clean underpants on—in case something terrible happened to him. So as a young child he would leave home afraid and worry all day that something bad would happen.

Fear, on the other hand, is different. It is our protector. We are designed to deal with fear, not worry. Fear is centered in the emotional brain and our stress response system, warning us of real danger. If fear is not addressed properly, it can lead to worry. We must not let our fears overtake us. Jesus said so many times, "Do not be afraid," and, "Do not worry" (e.g., Matthew 6:25; 10:26; Mark 13:11; Luke 12:4, 29; John 14:27). He knows that our emotional brains can wreak havoc on us. We will experience emotions like fear, anxiety, anger, depression, sadness, or envy, but we must deal with them rather than let them dominate our thinking.

GETTING RID OF ANTS

According to research by Mark George, MD, and his colleagues at the National Institutes of Health, happy, hopeful thoughts have an overall calming effect on the worrying brain, while negative thoughts impact the brain toward fear, anxiety, and depression. What you think really matters.

Dr. Amen, brain imaging specialist, uses the metaphor of killing the ANTs that invade your mind. ANT stands for automatic negative thoughts. Here again, this is our default system. If our ANTs are not dealt with, Dr. Amen says, "they can ruin your whole day, maybe even your life." These thoughts can be so habitual that you hardly recognize them. Dr. Amen has identified nine different kinds of ANT species, or ways our thoughts can distort what we perceive, causing a downward spiral of negativity and lack of tranquility.[1] See if you recognize any of these:

Mind-reading. Predicting someone is thinking negatively about you.
I think you don't like me. I think I am going to get fired. I think they are staring at me.

Fortune-telling. Predicting a bad outcome to a situation before it has occurred.
This new job isn't going to work out. I know something bad will happen.

Overgeneralizations. Always, never, every time, everyone. Not true.
You never listen to me. It always turns out like this. Everyone else always wins.

Guilt beatings. Obsessing on past failures or problems: "Shoulda, coulda, woulda."
I should have done much better. I'm not good enough, a failure. If only I could have . . .

Focusing on the negative. Seeing the glass half full, even if things go well.
Just because the stock market went up doesn't mean I will make up for what I lost.

Thinking with your feelings. Allowing your feelings to convince you of reality.
I feel disconnected and neglected, so you must not love me anymore.

Labeling. Generalizing with broad assumptions.
You were late for the meeting, so you must be lazy, a procrastinator, and not care.

Personalization. Misinterpreting things, taking them personally.
You forgot our anniversary date, so you must not love me enough to care.

Blame. Avoiding responsibility and putting the blame on others.
I am not at fault, it's all your fault. I am a helpless victim and not responsible.

Other negative ways of thinking you might recognize include demand for approval, helplessness, avoidance, perfectionism, all-or-nothing thinking, catastrophizing, jumping to conclusions, and unrealistic comparing. These negative ways of thinking hijack the brain onto the road to worry, which can lead to anxiety. No matter what we are going through, this is the most common struggle we all have. The Anxiety Disorders Association of America reports that anxiety disorders affect at least 40 million adults in the United States, or about 18 percent of the total U.S. population.[2] I'm not able to address the full spectrum of anxiety disorders in this chapter; we will focus primarily on worry and our thoughts. The good news is that anxiety disorders are treatable, and if you are struggling with more severe anxiety, there are great resources and professional help available.[3] The following are some strategies you can use to deal with worry.

YOU CAN'T BELIEVE EVERYTHING YOU THINK

Just because you think something, doesn't mean it is true. Does a thought help you or hurt you? Check your thoughts against reality to see if they are true. If you don't, your mind will believe it and your brain will follow through with a reaction and behavioral action. Don't just automatically believe all thoughts as reality.

CHALLENGE NEGATIVE THOUGHTS. DISPUTE AND TALK BACK.

"Just as a gardener cultivates her plot, keeping it free from weeds, and growing the flowers and fruits which she requires, so may a woman tend the garden of her mind, weeding out all the wrong, useless, and impure thoughts, and cultivating toward perfection and flowers and fruits of right, useful and pure thoughts."[4]

One way to deal with worry and negative thinking is to notice thoughts, challenge them, and get rid of them. Tune in to what you are saying to yourself. At times, our emotional brain can trigger anxiety and fear from a previous experience, even from childhood. Something can happen that will take you to a place you don't want to go again. You may be reminded of when one of your parents left, or when you were told you were stupid and not good enough. Everything changed for you. It is natural for your emotional brain to take you to this previous place of old hurts. But God wants us to go to a new place that is spacious and full of peace and hope, not an old place full of old experiences, fearful thoughts, and false beliefs. Intentionally reexamine this place. Determine where you allow your mind to run to. Actively dispute your negative beliefs. Say, "No, I choose to go to the open, spacious, true, and peaceful place instead."

This sends you on a different track, and the negative belief no longer has any power over you. Dr. Seligman, one of the primary founders of positive psychology, has discovered that the key to disputing automatic negative thinking is first to recognize it. Then view these thoughts as if they were outside of your being, said by someone else who has the intention of stealing your peace and making you miserable. Argue against these negative thoughts, setting them straight with the truth.[5]

CONSIDER THESE QUESTIONS

Look for evidence. What evidence is there for the negative belief? Is it an overreaction, catastrophizing the situation? Is there a kernel of truth that has been blown out of proportion?

What are the alternatives? Is there a better way to think about this that is more objective and not so destructive? What is God's truth regarding this? Am I latching on to the worst possible scenario? Make a list of all the possible contributing causes of the negative belief. Then write out the negative thought on the left and the realistic disputed truth on the right. *I am always just going to be a worrywart. / I can intentionally change my thoughts.*

What are the implications? Look at the evidence. Maybe the negative belief is true. Even so, is it really as bad as you're making it out to be? What is God's perspective? What is the worst-case scenario, and how could you handle it? This is called *de-catastrophizing*.

How useful is this belief? If the belief is destructive, don't focus on it. If it is true, ask God to help you find a constructive way to spend your energy on resolving or unlearning thought patterns that developed as a consequence of those experiences.

ABCDE. Learned Optimism. Learned Faith.

Dr. Albert Ellis developed Rational Emotive Behavioral Therapy and the ABC model, which uses rational understanding of emotions to help change behavior.[6] Dr. Seligman added to this by creating the ABCDE model, suggesting a pathway from negative thinking to positive thinking, decreasing worry and resulting in tranquility.[7]

A—Adversity We interpret activating events, our experiences, and adversity through automatic habitual ways of thinking—either hopeful and optimistic or fearful and pessimistic. *Write down an event or situation that is causing you stress.* Let's say you get a speeding ticket while rushing because you are late.

B—Beliefs Adverse events can trigger distorted, self-deprecating beliefs that support our interpretation of the situation. Because they are automatic from past experiences, the influence of parents and teachers, and bad thought habits, we accept them as reality without being objective or scrutinizing. *Write down the thoughts that go through your head about this event.* What core beliefs are influencing your interpretation of the event? *Something always goes wrong when I am in a hurry. Why did the police have to pick on me? / Oh well. I should have left earlier so I wasn't so rushed.*

C—Consequences Thoughts and beliefs have a direct connection to your mind-set, emotions, and resulting actions. *Write down the feelings you are experiencing as a result of the stressful event.* Ask yourself how you feel. What are you thinking? (Anxiety, frustration, worry, anger, sadness, embarrassment, shame.) *This has just put me over the edge. Now I'm all stressed out. / It's just a ticket. I'm not going to let it ruin my day or the next event.*

D—Disputation Here is where you can change your negative thought patterns and feelings. If the belief isn't accurate, you worry and suffer for no reason. If there is some truth, you can come up with a plan to resolve the concern. Stand back and objectively be aware of your thoughts and beliefs. Dispute your beliefs with the evidence, alternatives, implications, God's truth, and usefulness of the belief. *I haven't had a ticket like this before, so I will just do traffic school. He wasn't picking on me. I wasn't watching my speed. Things like this happen, and they aren't worth stealing my joy. Now I know not to speed down that hill and to be more aware of my time and leave a little earlier.*

E—Energization When you let go of negative thinking, it frees you from worry and other negative emotional states. Your brain is able to problem-solve and think more clearly and more creatively. You realign your system with God's Spirit and truth for peace, serenity, and tranquility. *This definitely was a frustrating event in my day, but I'm not going to let it steal my peace and joy. It will all work out, so I will let it go.*

Extinguish Worry

Worry is like a cow chewing its cud . . . chewing and chewing and chewing. You go over and over things in your mind, ruminating until they create more stress. There is no end to it. And worry is like a rocking chair. It gives you something to do, but it doesn't get you anywhere. Worry is not solution-oriented. In fact, it is destructive.

Have you heard of polar bear theology? Russian writer Leo Tolstoy tells of how when he was a boy, he and a few friends started the White Polar Bear Club. The initiation requirement was to sit on a stool in the corner and not think about a white polar bear for thirty minutes.

When you try not to think about something by saying, "I must not think about the polar bear. I must not think about what's worrying me," you actually feed your preoccupation with it. But there are some effective ways to deal with worry.

DISTRACT YOURSELF

Here is a little exercise you can try. For the next ten minutes, try not to think about what you are struggling with. (Don't think about the polar bear.) Is it worry, anger, disappointment, a negative self-image? Let's take worry, for instance. Say ten times, "Don't worry, don't worry, don't worry . . ." Does that help? No, it doesn't. It is still there.

Instead, distract yourself so your mind has something else to focus on. Get completely engrossed in an activity for at least ten minutes. Watch a TV show, read something inspiring, bake or clean, go to the store, or get out and focus on your surroundings. Those who have studied ruminating and worry say that if we distract ourselves by concentrating on something else for at least ten minutes, it breaks the worry cycle.

EXTINGUISH WORRY BY WORRYING

Another way is to worry about something for fifteen minutes, and it will extinguish. What incubates worry and feeds it is to worry for between three and fifteen minutes. You either have to cut it off short or keep worrying past the fifteen minutes. Set a timer for fifteen minutes, and let yourself worry away. Really have a go at it. Catastrophize and ruminate all you want. Then, when the time is over, stop worrying.

SEE WORRY FOR WHAT IT IS

Jeffrey Schwartz has done studies on people with obsessive-compulsive disorders who had MRIs showing their brain lesions.

He taught them to look at their brain and say, "This is just brain activity. It's just electricity. I'm okay." And the lesions actually changed. They literally went away. It didn't take long, only fifteen minutes of this exercise a day. You too can have this kind of change in your brain through the way you think about yourself, people, and situations. "It's just hormones," "They're just teenagers," "This too will pass." What are you worrying about? Speak thoughts like that to your brain right now, and improve your perspective, emotions, and overall well-being.[8]

WHAT IS THE WORST AND BEST
THAT COULD HAPPEN?

Having worried and ruminated about all possible scenarios, visualize yourself handling the most extreme outcome. What would you do in the worst-case scenario? How would you handle it? Come up with some realistic solutions. Then imagine the best possible outcome. When you start being more positive, your brain functioning will be more expansive and you will have a better frame of mind to be creative and assess the situation more realistically.

MOVE FROM WORRY TO CONCERN

Turn your worry into a prayer concern. Write down what it is that is worrying you. Externalize it. Journal it. That helps your brain see it and sort out what is real and what is imagined. Then you can take this worry and dispute it with reality. Do your fifteen minutes of worry. When you have worried enough and done all you can do, then shift your worries to concerns and pray. Now write a prayer list. "Instead of worrying, pray. Let petitions and praises shape your worries into prayers, letting God know your concerns" (Philippians 4:7 THE MESSAGE).

DON'T WORRY. TAKE ACTION. DO SOMETHING.

Ruminating and worrying will take you on a downward spiral of constrictive thinking, leaving you feeling stressed, helpless, and hopeless. This leads to anxiety and depression. After you have made your stress and worry list and worried enough, make a prayer list and begin to pray over your concerns. Then respond to these concerns with positive action. Make an action list. What is your part, your assignment from the Lord to partner with Him? Do what you have to do, then just let go and trust. This restores a sense of control and directs your brain in an upward spiral, and it keeps the biological anxiety at bay. Avoid the hopelessness of, "I tried it once and it didn't work, so I won't try again." It might not have worked that way, but try again in a different way. Learned helplessness is very destructive. We flourish when we overcome the belief of "I can do nothing," which stops you from trying. What you can do is pray, take action, let go, and practice your faith.

Create Serenity Through Virtual Reality

Close your eyes and imagine a scene, somewhere you have been that has been a safe, peaceful place, or a situation that has been life changing for you. It could be when you were a child, or more recent. It may be a place or situation you would like. Remember or imagine every detail of the countryside or the sea, the warm sunlight, or the people with you. Imagine the pleasant sights, sounds, and sensations. Imagine feeling inner peace, serenity, and tranquility in all areas of your life—body, mind, emotions. Take a few deep breaths and think, *Relax. Peace.* Train your brain what to feel.

The Antidote to Worry Is a Flourishing Faith

The antidote to worry lies in a vibrant, flourishing faith. Our brains are hardwired for God and sacred practices. Modern living doesn't naturally take us down the path of tranquility and peace, and neither do most of our faith practices. That is where contemplative spirituality is essential for us to learn the fine art of living in peace and tranquility.

PRAYER: THE ULTIMATE PEACE PRESCRIPTION

Prayer and meditation can change the state of your mind and your brain. Scientists are becoming more convinced of the benefits of religion and spirituality. I hope you are, too. Christianity has such rich treasures of faith practices in our heritage that we would do well to begin embracing them and gaining the tremendous benefits in our daily life.

The most profound, proven peace prescription is found in Philippians 4:6–7. *The Message* says it beautifully: "Don't fret or worry. Instead of worrying, pray. Let petitions and praises shape your worries into prayers, letting God know your concerns. Before you know it, a sense of God's wholeness, everything coming together for good, will come and settle you down."

Framed as a prayer of the heart, you could say, "Help, Lord, with [whatever you're concerned about]. Thank you. I receive your peace." This is the key to guarding your heart and mind from peace pilferers and opening yourself to receive God's peace.

If we prayed and meditated more consistently like this instead of worrying, we would have a lot less to worry about. There are many forms of prayer and meditation in the Christian faith tradition that are helpful for the ruminating or obsessive soul.

- *Listening prayer.* Hearing and discerning God's voice through prayer and Scripture, and then obeying the Lord's direction.

- *Centering prayer.* Connecting with God in a silent, personal way, being aware of God's presence very closely within.

- *Scripture prayer.* Personalizing Scriptures and prayers in the Bible.

- *Breath prayer.* Present short words, phrases, or simple heartfelt desires to God.

- *Praying in the Spirit.* Prayer led by the Spirit, in the power of the Spirit, often from deep within, that words can hardly express.

- *Contemplative prayer.* Opening your heart, mind, and whole being authentically to be aware of God in a process of interior purification and transformation.

- *Prayer walking.* Being open to the Spirit of God, presenting prayers, intercessions, and gratitude while walking.

- *Examen.* Daily reflecting on how you feel closest to God, what you are most grateful for (consolations), what depletes a sense of God's presence, leaving you feeling out of touch or uncentered, what you are least grateful for (desolations).

- *The Jesus prayer.* Repeat this phrase in heartfelt prayer: "Lord Jesus Christ, Son of God, have mercy on me, a sinner."

- *Practicing the presence of God.* Develop a continual openness and awareness of God's presence in your life, Christ living in you, and the Holy Spirit flowing through you.

- *Lectio divina.* This sacred reading of Scripture and praying has four stages: *lectio* (reading); *meditatio* (meditation); *oratio* (prayer); and *contemplatio* (contemplation).[9]

- *Visio divina.* Along with lectio divina, use images from nature and visual art to reflect on and experience the presence and living Word of God in our life.

- *Constant prayer of the heart.* It is like breathing, like the heart beating. Our blood flows and our breath continues without ceasing. We are not even conscious of it, but it never stops. Prayer like this is not an exercise; it is a way of living, it is life.[10]

Daily prayer and meditation provide a deep sense of well-being, peace, and joy, and this feeling follows through the daily routine. You build up your psychological immunity, which benefits you beyond the time of prayer. The time of quieting the mind from typical worries and "letting go and letting God" in prayer and meditation provides a way to slow down the automatic stress response and reactions to anger or frustration. We are better able to access the thinking brain (prefrontal cortex) and get control of and talk to the emotional brain (amygdala, basal ganglia, fearful brain centers). God promises that prayer changes everything. It certainly changes us—our brains and body chemistry.

Neuroscientists have shown that regular contemplative prayer and meditation contribute to changes in brain chemistry, allowing the brain to be more peaceful.[11] Biology and spirituality work powerfully together. In chapter 6, I mentioned the study done with nuns during times of meditation and prayer and the ongoing effect it had afterwards when they went about their normal daily routines. The front left side of the brain (clarity and happiness) lit up; the back part of the brain (emotional, fear, reptilian brain) was subdued. Many studies like this show that while in prayer and deep meditation, your brain is able to let go of negative thinking and the need to control, clearing your mind to simply relax and go with the flow.[12] When your heartfelt prayers are voiced to God and shaped with gratitude, worries are unburdened and anxiety is released. Divine calm then fills you with peace like a river, enough to whisper, "It is well with my soul."

Christian Meditation

Most people would agree that physical exercise is good for our health and well-being. In the same way, we are now discovering that our mental fitness is just as important. If we exercise our inner life, training our brain to transform our emotions, we flourish in well-being and are much calmer. Meditation is the primary natural treatment for reducing fear, worry, and anxiety.[13]

The lost art of Christian meditation is not dangerous; rather it "has been an important contribution to Christian living since the first days of the Church."[14] The slow, thoughtful, quiet reading of Scripture known as lectio divina, or "divine reading" (described in the previous section), was used in the daily life of a Benedictine monastery, and is still practiced in meaningful ways today. The spiritual exercises of St. Ignatius of Loyola, the founder of the Jesuits, are still used today as an experience of Christian meditation.[15] These and other forms of Christian meditation are based on very solid biblical teaching that doesn't focus on particular methods, positions, or chants. Instead, by concentrating and using your imagination, you can learn to turn your heart and mind in a devotional way toward God as a form of spiritual resting in prayer or reflection.[16]

In Hebrew, the word for meditate is *hagah,* which means "to reflect, ponder, or contemplate" something as one repeats the words. It is not like the English word *meditate,* which implies a mental exercise only. One Hebrew way of meditating was to repeat Scriptures softly and quietly while abandoning outside distractions and getting lost in communion with God. If you know how to worry, you can learn how to meditate. (For more information on relaxation and Christian meditation, and to download a free meditation exercise, visit *www.howtoflourish.com.*)

There are many references in the Bible to meditating so we can calm our souls and get to know God better. Other terms used to describe *meditation* are remember, think on these things, ponder, consider, let the mind of Christ be in you, and set your mind on things above.[17] Jesus himself had a daily practice of being in a quiet place, spending time just abiding with God in His presence. This doesn't need to be overwhelming and intimidating. You are the result of what you think about all day. So be intentional about including this practice in your everyday rhythms. Simply surrender your will to God. Reflect on Scripture and who God is. Be aware of God's presence in the ordinary moments of the day. Use the time while driving in the car, taking a shower, gardening, lying in bed in the morning and evening, waiting for appointments, or before a church service. At any time you can begin altering your life by altering the attitude of your mind. When you are able, take more focused time to learn the lost art of meditation and be blessed with the benefits of more peace and tranquility, insight, a positive outlook on life, growth, clearer focus, and a heart of love and worship toward God.

In *Biblical Meditation for Spiritual Breakthrough*, Elmer L. Towns identifies at least ten ways to meditate:[18]

The David Model: Considering God's creation and majesty

The Mary Model: Pondering the person of Jesus

The Saint John Model: Thinking about the cross

The Joshua Model: Focusing on biblical principles

The Saint Paul Model: Becoming like Christ

The Timothy Model: Meditating on your calling and gifts

The Haggai Model: Considering your failures

The Asaph Model: Meditating on God's intervention

The Malachi Model: Meditating on God's name

The Korah Model: Contemplating intimacy with God

LET GO OF ANXIETY

François de Fenelon, a revered archbishop in the 1600s, wisely said, "Let your anxiety flow away like a stream. When you are calm and collected, you will find the will of God more clearly. Simply bringing yourself quietly before God will do more than worrying or being too religious. Silence encourages God's presence, prevents harsh words and causes you to be less likely to say something you will regret. Out of the silence that you cultivate, you will find strength to meet your needs."[19]

Spending time with God in reflective silence and solitude, and meditating on His Word, will strengthen your relationship with Him; make you healthier; and provide more joy, peace, and contentment in your life. I have found Christian contemplative spirituality and meditation to be tremendously helpful in calming and focusing the scattered and worried mind.

Healthy Habits of the Mind

SOW GOOD THOUGHTS

Now we come to the biggest challenge in living out the gift of God's peace: calming our fearful, anxious, emotional brain and stress response system so the peace of the Spirit can flow in our lives. This requires times of quieting the mind, sorting out our negative thinking, and getting some silence from the busyness of life. Meditating on good things and positive promises that calm our worried minds assures us of God's love.

There is a fable about a woman who went shopping and was shocked when she realized that God was the one behind the counter. So she went over and asked, "What are you selling?" God replied, "What does your heart desire?" "Oh," she said, "I would love happiness, peace of mind, freedom from worry and fear—for me and the whole world." But God smiled kindly and responded, "I don't sell fruit here. I only offer seeds."[20]

If you feel weary of being unhappy, anxious, and fearful, or want more peace and tranquility, begin sowing good seeds of thoughts, actions, and responses. It is God's natural law that these seeds of the Spirit in our mind and heart will eventually give results. The seeds you sow today will determine what fruit you reap tomorrow. What we seed and allow to flourish in our thoughts will determine who we are and who we become. As you think in your heart, so you will be. (See Proverbs 23:7.)

This means guarding our hearts and minds and weeding out the negative. We will have challenges, but Paul warns us to be diligent to deal quickly with negativity, wrong perceptions, and offenses before they take root. (See Hebrews 12:15; 2 Corinthians 10:4–5.) Pull the weeds out while they are small. Practice mental hygiene, keeping your thinking clean and clear, lined up with God's truth and Word. Ephesians 4:23 says we are to let the Spirit change our way of thinking. Romans 12:2 says we are transformed by the renewing of our minds. That's where it starts. As we allow God to transform us—like a caterpillar changes into a butterfly—we are changed from the inside out. In Philippians 4:8–9 (THE MESSAGE) Paul says, "I'd say you'll do best by filling your minds and meditating on things true, noble, reputable, authentic, compelling, gracious—the best, not the worst; the beautiful, not the ugly; things to praise, not things to curse." In the Amplified version, the passage ends this way: "Practice what you have learned and received and heard and seen in me, and model your way of living on it, and the God of peace (of untroubled, undisturbed well-being) will be with you."

Our thoughts become our words. Our words become actions. Our actions become our habits. Our habits become our character. Character is everything, becoming our destiny, giving us a good life, a life well lived. It all starts with "good seed."

LIVE OUT AFFIRMATIONS OF WHAT YOU BELIEVE

Our actions can reflect our false distorted beliefs—what we fear, not what we truly believe. What do you truly believe? Write down what you believe on all levels of your life: spiritual, emotional, relational, and physical. How much of what you truly believe are you able to really live out in your daily life? When you doubt what you believe, tell your brain how to think and feel according to what is true. Write out affirmations and the truth of how it really is and who you want to be. Read over these, and speak these to yourself so your mind and brain can be convinced of what you believe. Align your lifestyle and choices according to what you believe. Now intentionally live this out.

LIVE IN THE MOMENT

Yesterday is gone, so make peace with your past. Tomorrow might never come, so don't worry about what you have no control over. Most of our stress and worry is extra weight about the future or the past that we can't change. The present is the only current gift you have, so live in the moment. Even if the moment is stressful or painful, we do better by just being fully human and fully alive to the moment.

When our minds get stuck in brooding and worrying on the past or the future, we miss the present. Focus on where you are now. Feel the vibrant life you have through all your senses. Feel the air on your skin, the taste and texture of your food, the sights and sounds around you. Be aware that God is always with you. How is God present for you in the moment, in your situation now?

Surrender and Open Up

RESISTANCE

Be aware of the resistance in your life. You may want to change, be transformed, and become your best, most authentic self. But by default, as humans we have a tendency to resist change and overreact to fear. Even if it is for the good, it's sometimes hard to let go and trust. This resistance can also happen to caterpillars during metamorphosis. When it's time to spin a chrysalis, some of them actually resist and cling to their larval life. They put off spinning a cocoon until the following spring. This state of clinging is called *diapause*. Out of fear, we hold on to what is familiar and comforting or we bolt. What worries, fears, doubts, hurts, or discouragements are holding you back?

SURRENDER AND TRUST, DON'T BOLT

In his book *Life Lessons From a Horse Whisperer,* Lew Sterrett tells the story of taking a shortcut through some woods on his horse Spotlight, when all of sudden the horse came to a stop. Spotlight was a good horse, always eager to please, so when he didn't respond when being told to move, Lew decided to listen to him first. When he looked down, his heart nearly stopped. They had run into a fallen-down barbed-wire fence, and across Spotlight's forearm as well as both his rear legs were strands of barbed wire all tangled up. He was trapped.

Horses don't think in situations like this. They react. When they are trapped, they panic, bolt, and run as fast as they can. It's a survival instinct to stay alive in the wild. Our stress response system can make us do the same in a crisis when we are afraid. We tend to want to fight, flee (bolt), or freeze. How often have you felt like just running away when afraid or stressed?

With Spotlight trapped, any more movement or struggle would have tightened the barbed wire and caused the horse to panic even more. Bolting would make it worse, even fatal for the horse and the rider. For the first time in years, Lew says he was terrified. He had no way to cut the wire, no cell phone to call for help. "I've seen horses panic and beat themselves to death against the side of a trailer, or kill themselves by getting tangled up in a fence. I saw a horse panic and throw herself to the ground so hard that it killed her."

Bolting, when we over-react and lash out, often makes things worse. I've seen people cause damage to themselves and others as well (and I've done a little myself along the way). We say mean things that hurt. We slap and hit, or scream and shout. We try to run away, only to tighten the cords that are strangling the situation.

Seeing no solution with Spotlight, Lew cried out, "Oh God, help me." We often pray our most desperate prayers in situations like this when we feel most helpless and trapped in sudden stressful crisis, don't we? And the Lord hears us, and comes to us to lead us in His way out.

While Lew was praying, a thought came to his mind about a technique he had learned for getting a horse to raise its feet. He reached back and squeezed Spotlight's hock, and rather than fight and kick or bolt, Spotlight did what he had been taught in previous training. He lifted his rear feet gently one at a time until they were out of the barbed wire. He had also learned when a rope was tied around his feet not to react, but instead, when the rope was pulled, to yield and follow. In this dangerous situation, rather than resist, Spotlight overcame his fear, putting his trust and faith in Lew, allowing him to gently pull his front feet out of danger as well.[21]

Surrender, let go of what you are tightly holding on to. Allow the peace of God to soften your heart, open you up, and slowly release you from your fears and worries. As you allow God to lead you to still, calm waters, be refreshed and soak in His presence, softening the hardened, tight, painful, difficult, and longing areas in your life.

As you sit quietly, pray, "I open my heart to you," or "I place my trust in you." Continue this prayer until you come to a sense of peace.

Flowering Tea Soaking Reflection

You may want to reflect on this section while listening to inspirational music and soaking a flowering tea pod. When ready, place the flowering tea pod into hot water in a clear pot or mug. Watch the pod open up and blossom into a flower. You could also imagine this exercise or take a soaking bath. Meditate on how you too can soak in the streaming flow of the Spirit, softening your heart, calming your worries, and opening your heart up to flourish. As your flowering tea softens in the presence of the warm water, likewise, let your heart, soul, and spirit soften and open up as you soak in the presence of the Lord and worship Him. As you take a soaking bath for your soul, imagine your heart soaking, softening, and opening up to God, a person, or a situation. Now choose positive environments and people that can seep goodness into you.

Here is some timeless wisdom on serenity and tranquility from *As a Woman Thinketh*. Embrace this for yourself. Calmness of mind "is the result of long and patient effort in self-control . . . Who does not love a tranquil heart, a sweet-tempered, balanced life? . . . That exquisite poise of character which we call serenity . . . is the flowering of life, the fruitage of the soul. . . . Humanity . . . is blown about by anxiety and doubt. . . . Self-control is strength;

Right thought is mastery; Calmness is power. Say to your heart, 'Peace, be still!' "[22]

Prayer

Lord, may you keep me in perfect peace as I trust in you, and as my thoughts are fixed on you!

Adapted from Isaiah 26:3 NLT

Reflective Questions and Flourish Practices

1. Where are you on your journey? What are you stressed, worried, fearful, or anxious about right now?

Are you struggling with transitions or change (midlife, healing process, a new calling)?

Are you in crisis due to intrusive events (major loss, relationship conflict, illness, problems with children)?

Are you experiencing internal uprisings (burnout, depletion, overstimulation, a wilderness, disappointment, inner conflict, emotional wound)?

2. Jesus said, "My sheep recognize my voice. I know them, and they follow me" (John 10:27 THE MESSAGE).

Take a moment and consider all the different thoughts, voices, and events that are clamoring for your attention. What event or voice stands out the most?

Now picture Christ ahead of you, waiting for you, being present with you and speaking to you. What does He have to say to you?

What do you want to say to Him? Say it now.

Make these simple words your prayer today:

May I know your presence, Christ, in my life, your closeness to me in every moment of this day. I welcome your presence with an open heart.

3. Write down the things that worry you the most and then ask yourself, "How can I turn each worry into a concern?" Remember your mind and body gets a totally different message when you worry uselessly than when you acknowledge a concern.

4. Do a surrender stone exercise to deal with your worries. Pick up a stone representing a worry or whatever you want to surrender. Using Philippians 4:6–7, surrender your concerns, give thanks, and then think on God's goodness. You may want to write a word representing your worry on the stone. When you are ready, throw the stone as far as you can as a symbol of releasing it to the Lord. Then go in peace.

5. Keep a journal with you this week and write down the automatic negative thoughts (ANTs) that keep coming to your mind. Then dispute each one with truthful, positive affirmations and promises of God.

6. Write out, memorize, and meditate on a few Scriptures that remind your brain and mind to be serene, peaceful, tranquil, and hopeful. (See Isaiah 26:3.)

7. Go to *www.howtoflourish.com* and do the relaxation exercise. Discover how Christian meditation and relaxation can work for you.

PART 6

ENCOURAGING HOPE
FOR YOUR JOURNEY:
HOPE AND RESILIENCE SYSTEM

You flourish in
hope, meaning, and purpose
when trusting in God's faithfulness

chapter 10

Flourishing Hope
in Adversity

We continue to shout our praise even when we're hemmed
in with troubles, because we know how troubles can develop
passionate patience in us, and how that patience in turn forges
the tempered steel of virtue, keeping us alert for whatever God
will do next. In alert expectancy . . .

Romans 5:5 THE MESSAGE

On your journey to flourishing, you grow and mature in divine
harmony and well-being with yourself, God, others, and all creation. And one of the main ways this happens is through life
challenges.

In this chapter you will discover faith-based flourishing in
adversity. It's not enough to know how to thrive during life's high
points. We also have to learn how to thrive in adversity—cultivating
bounce-back-adaptability.

Psychologists have been researching for decades the ways people cope with adversity, naming this adaptability "resilience." In the past fifteen years research has gone further to consider how people can actually gain benefits and grow through adversity, referring to this as "post-traumatic growth."[1]

Challenges Release Growth Hormones

"We must accept finite disappointment, but we must never lose infinite hope."

—Martin Luther King Jr.

Although the concept of flourishing denotes a strong, positive image, it does not imply a life with ideal circumstances and everything lined up perfectly. We must respect the entire growth process and cycle of the seasons of life. There must inevitably be a winter following a summer. There is a season for everything, and it is all part of flourishing and abundant living. So we have to surrender to the seasons. There will be trials and struggles, seasons of drought. Yes, they are our falls and winters. Some of our greatest growth happens during these seasons.

In nature we see examples of flourishing in adversity all the time. A palm, a cedar tree, a blooming rose in the desert, or a lily among thorns—much of nature is designed to flourish even in adversity. Botanists have discovered, for instance, that when a tree is injured or experiences a challenge, it produces more growth hormones. This results in the roots growing deeper, ensuring stability and ultimately producing more fruit.

Bounce-Back-Adaptability

Our ability to bounce back and even grow from adversity is admirable but not unusual. Although we may be sad, miserable, and even devastated for a while, studies show that people are able to overcome all sorts of hard times. Our capacity for resilience is a very generous God-given gift. We are designed to heal when injured, grow when handicapped, and flourish in body, mind, relationships, and spirit in the face of challenging times. We have innate systems that adapt and become stronger and more effective to protect us the next time trouble raises its head, build better character, and help us return to happiness in surprising and simple ways. In fact, we often need adversity to discover our best strengths and fully flourish.

Hardship and catastrophe, while not pleasant, can provide an enormous impetus for growth. God uses affliction in our lives to stimulate growth and to prepare us for fruitfulness. Although we would like to totally avoid struggle, sometimes, like Paul with his thorn in the flesh, God's grace enables us to accept it and turn it into genuine growth.[2]

Paul reminds us that when we go through struggles, there is a divine purpose. It builds our faith and our character because it drives us back to God. It helps us discover our strengths and become a source of blessing to others. The painful and unwanted conditions of life, through the redemptive power of God's Spirit, can also become the "soil of sainthood," or at least the catalyst for building character and being helpful to others. The difficult situation you are in now may be God's invitation to your growth in holiness, grace, and blessing. Turning your suffering into seeing God's possibility for redemptive living may be the beginning of the greatest miracle of your healing.

If you keep persevering, the Spirit of God will give you a flourishing finish.

Growing in Adversity

We all develop ways of dealing with difficulties and tragedies in our lives. The palm's trunk has been created to bend but not break in strong winds. The cedar, needing nutrients and support for its height, adapts by connecting its root system to a broader network to stay strong.

All of us, like the palm and cedar, need to discover and hold on to our own unique ways of being resilient in adversity. I remember when my sister Sharon lost her husband in a tragic car accident on March 21, 1995. In the hospital she stood over her dying husband and felt the Lord say, "Nothing enters your life that hasn't first been sifted through my hands. I saw this coming and I have prepared your way through it." In the midst of her grief, she could not read the Bible. Praying was very difficult. But reviewing meaningful verses she had memorized earlier in her life comforted her. It was as if God knew she couldn't sit and read anything, so He consoled her by prompting scriptural reassurance from deep within her memory.

"Friends, when life gets really difficult, don't jump to the conclusion that God isn't on the job. Instead, be glad that you are in the very thick of what Christ experienced. This is a spiritual refining process, with glory just around the corner."

—1 Peter 4:12–13 THE MESSAGE

Obviously, we all differ in how we respond. How can people go through the same terrible situation yet respond so differently? Why do some people seem to cope remarkably well and grow while others are vulnerable, wilt, and languish? It's because we bring differing life experiences. Some of us have been better learners than others, so we have the tools of survival ready at hand. Some have had good models and mentors, so they do better in challenging situations. No doubt our differing personalities and temperaments, childhood, and previous history of struggles are a factor. But no matter our scars and wounds, it is always possible for us to learn how to adapt and grow. We are not victims of circumstances over which we have no control. There is always a way back to the flourishing road.

How Can God Help You Flourish Through Adversity Now?

God's plan is that we be like the palm in the desert. We may sway, but we must hold strong in hope against the wind of adversity. Perhaps we need to be like the cedar and dig deeper as we reach out for help from others.

The poem "Invictus" by William Henley, the inspiration for the recent movie title, ends with these self-encouraging words:

> It matters not how strait the gate,
> How charged with punishments the scroll,
> I am the master of my fate;
> I am the captain of my soul.

Nelson Mandela embraced these words while he spent all those years in jail. They helped remind him that no matter what happens, he can choose who and what he wants to be.

To help you embrace God's plan for you to flourish in hope during times of adversity, I have compiled a few focus points from scientific research, my own journey, stories I've heard friends tell at the Strength for the Journey retreats, and some important biblical truths.

You may want to make a list from your own experiences and observations of others. What matters most is that you continue to build *your* hope, so you can be strengthened on your flourishing journey.

1. BE PREPARED TO BE SURPRISED BY THE EXPECTED

Most of life's challenges come unexpectedly. However, expect them and remember that nothing comes into your life that isn't sifted through God's hands. Life in Christ isn't a smooth pathway or a bed of roses. And even though there are some roses, they also have thorns. None of us are strangers to trials. If you reflect over your life, I'm sure there are situations and circumstances that you didn't imagine happening. Life just doesn't always go the way we plan. Our kids won't turn out exactly the way we expect. The economy won't be stable. We will have health problems and relationship issues. Our default nature will lead us astray.

So, be kind and compassionate to yourself and others around you, because we are all either heading into, recovering from, or going through something. We are surrounded by events and challenges from within and without. We battle against the default settings within us and the vandalizing of shalom all around us. It's a battle for some to keep their weight down, and a battle for others to not be driven by their insecurities or past wounds. We are all battling something—in order to live life in the Spirit and to live out our most authentic calling on earth.

Most of us unconsciously wish we could live a spa life. I get pooped out and tired of pain, don't you? I think we tend to shut the pain down because it's too stressful. It triggers fear, worry, and anxiety. Instead, we go around in our robes, walking in flip-flops waiting for a massage. We deeply long for what we are ultimately created for—continual love, peace, and joy—heaven. We long for paradise, the "wonderful" life. And in time, in heaven we will finally be fulfilled.

But for now we don't live in a controlled environment. We can't control the people and circumstances around us. We can only choose the path we take each moment. Although doing the spa occasionally is good for you, don't stay in your robe and flip-flops all the time. Get dressed and ready for reality. Intentionally choose the pathways that will prepare you for resilient well-being and flourishing. Expect to be surprised by difficulties that you actually can expect in life—with the purpose of building your character and making you stronger and more fruitful.

Exercise prepares your body for the sudden challenges in life. The cumulative benefits of consistent exercise continue throughout the day and long after. Exercising your body builds up strength, endurance, flexibility, and overall well-being. By exercising, you will be more prepared to run through the airport to catch an unexpectedly close connecting flight. (My dad taught me to always go two hours early to the airport. Be prepared to expect surprising changes in air travel.) Exercise prepares you to have a stronger immune system to fight off the germs that you can always expect to be going around. Exercise prepares you to recover better from expected stress that will still come as a surprise.

Likewise, when you exercise and prepare your inner life—your mind, heart, soul, and spirit—for the inevitable surprises in life, you will be more prepared to handle them. Prayer and meditation in the morning, journaling, and memorizing Scripture might not seem very dramatic at the time—after all, it's just an ordinary part of your life. But you will be better prepared in your heart to face whatever challenges come into your day. Listening to uplifting music will put a song in your heart that will see you through a sudden stressful challenge. God might have given you a word or Scripture that morning that is just what you need to know when a situation suddenly arises. Ongoing connection with friends, family, and small groups might be just a regular rhythm of your life. But when you are surprised by a crisis, it will be so important to have those close to you who love and care about you and will be there for you.

2. EXPECT TO FLOURISH

You can expect to have challenges in this vandalized world. But you can also expect that God's restoring plan for you is to flourish. We all have the promise like David did. Like Psalm 92:4, 14 promises: "I will triumph in your hands. . . . [I will be] fresh and flourishing" (THE MESSAGE). God provides a fresh anointing for us to flourish through the adversity we face today. In Psalm 23, this anointing reflects the loving Shepherd caring for us by providing protection, healing, and joy. The anointing represents the flow of the life of the Holy Spirit, who is constantly renewing, refreshing, and sustaining us, especially in times when our flourishing is hindered.

Expect miracles in your everyday life. God will touch and protect you, heal you, and speak into your life in powerful ways. Expect the great things of God working through His Son in you.

Expect to be surprised by spiritual refreshing and a fresh anointing. Expect strength for your journey and a new light for your path. Expect redeeming restoration. Expect to be surprised at your character strengths and how you are able to cope—even flourish. Expect that God will see you through to a flourishing finish, and He will be glorified by the fruit of your life.

During a memorable performance at a concert during the early 1800s by famed violinist Niccolo Paganini, a string of his violin snapped at a very intricate passage. The audience gasped in dismay. How disappointed they must have been, as it cost about three times more to see this famed musician than anyone else.

But when Paganini continued playing impeccably on only three strings, the crowd exploded with wonder and awe. He instantly became a revered star. From then on, Paganini would often use this device on purpose, using thin, worn-out strings that would snap to further enthrall his audience. He would complete his performance on three or even two strings, and eventually wrote an entire piece for a single string.[3]

At some time along our journey, we all feel as if we are playing with fewer strings. Parts of our lives get broken. We lose our health, relationships, dreams, or money. However, each of us can become more determined to play well with the strings we have left, in ways that bring cheers and glory to God rather than dismay from onlookers.

How many strings are you playing with right now? All of them? Then rejoice and be grateful. Are you playing with just three or two, or are you down to one? Then play them well. I know I want to play with what strings I have as well as I can, with hope.

Whatever your instrument or the melody of your song, join the orchestra of the kingdom of God, crying or laughing, sharing the melody of your life music. What melody are you learning to play? Who are you playing for? Like Orpheus, the New York orchestra without a conductor—listen for the hope, the song, and the part God wants you to play. And listen to the stories and the melody being played on the strings of those around you. Become a hope-giver, cheering them on.

Whatever your challenge, don't go through life alone.

Ways we flourish in adversity

The large body of research on resilience shows that through adversity, we can expect to grow, become stronger and closer to others, and discover joy in the following ways:

- When we have to rise to a challenge, it reveals our strengths and helps us grow in character and confidence to cope. (See Romans 5:3–4.) We become stronger.

- Going through hard times changes our relationships. Suffering is a great leveler. We find out who our friends really are. It opens up our hearts to one another and strengthens our relationships. We feel much deeper love and appreciation for those we care about, and compassion for others going through hard times.

- Besides changing our approach toward others, struggles change our priorities. We learn not to sweat the small stuff, living each day to the fullest, carefully and intentionally making the most of each opportunity and the time with loved ones. When we allow each struggle to refine our character, we become more focused on the goal of reflecting Jesus and living each day being fully alive.[4]

3. BUILD YOUR PSYCHOLOGICAL AND SPIRITUAL IMMUNE SYSTEMS

Just as we can prepare our body's immune system to fight off disease, so we can enhance our psychological and spiritual immune systems to ward off emotional and spiritual languishing. There is no way you can be totally immune to all trials and challenges that come your way, but you can take certain steps and build buffers that will strengthen you to cope and have a healthy crisis.

I live in California, the earthquake and fire center of the country. There are some things we are told we can do to brace for the shake-ups and fires that come our way. Certain actions and attitudes can increase your odds of survival in challenging situations.

"Things turn out best for the people who make the best out of the way things turn out."

—Art Linkletter

Here are some critical factors that can boost your spiritual, mental, and emotional immune system. Many have been proven to help us grow and flourish through adversity. What is most helpful to you?

- Stay closely connected to God, growing strong in your faith and hope.
- Daily practice prayer, Christian meditation, and other spiritual practices for inner tranquility of mind and body that equip you when facing stressors.
- Discover which stress management and coping strategies work the best for you.
- Build on your strengths and what helps you cope the best.
- Stay mentally healthy.
- Be optimistic and cultivate hope.
- Pursue laughter and humor.
- Meditate on and memorize Scripture.
- Take God's promises into your heart and mind.
- Appreciate the positive and be grateful.
- Nurture and strengthen healthy relationship connections.
- Exercise your body to keep physically fit.
- Stay well nourished and rested.

4. CULTIVATE HOPE IN HARD TIMES

Hope can be a personality disposition (trait) or a frame of mind (state). The person of hope lives in the moment with the knowledge and trust that all of life is in God's good hands. All the great spiritual leaders in history were people of hope. They all lived with a promise in their hearts that guided them toward the future without the need to know exactly what it would look like. Choose to live with hope.

A robust faith produces robust hope.[5] Hope is essential to recovery from hardship, stress, and depression. When I attended the first World Congress on Positive Psychology, presenters from all over the world made it clear: Alleviating suffering works best alongside the building of hope and happiness. One of the best ways you can help suffering people is to build a positive and hopeful view of the future.

A despairing or anxious world needs more than just the relief of suffering. People want to know that there is hope for the future, and they are also desperate to know how to live with some meaning and purpose. They want to make sense of their lives and keep growing and moving forward in some significant way. And this is what a godly hope gives us. Experiences that enhance positive spiritual emotion can cause negative emotion to dissipate rapidly. More love, more joy, more peace, more gratitude, and more hope buffer against languishing and psychological disorders, providing pathways to resilience in times of trouble.

That is God's message of redemption and restoration, a hope and a future—here on earth and in eternity ahead of us. We all have to cultivate this hopeful sense of purpose, a vision and mission for life. The Bible says that without a vision, we "perish"—we fail to flourish—we just aren't living life to its fullest. (See Proverbs 29:18 KJV.)

Be a hope giver

Earlier in the book I encouraged you to be a shalom bringer, then a joy spreader, and a peacemaker. Now I'm suggesting that you also become a hope giver. This is someone who can speak good, hopeful words to themselves and others. People with hope and confidence in their abilities to succeed engage in more self-supportive statements such as "I know I can do this" and "God can do all things."

Hope has been aspired to since the beginning of time and just recently more vigorously researched. Hope is important to all aspects of our lives, well-being, and relationships. If we want to be successful in our relationships and family, we must instill hope—be a hope giver—that others can grow and accomplish their goals.[6] For parents it is essential to reflect hope to your children.

Seed hope and positive thinking into your own mind and heart and into others. Bolster hope with positive emotions and thinking.

Humorous films, laughing out loud, constructive visualizations, and other positive feelings increase hope. Even building confidence in our abilities to work together builds hope and replaces despair.

Good and pleasant words are sweetness to the soul and healing to the bones. (See Proverbs 16:24.) Hopeful, encouraging words are like medicine to our entire being. (See Proverbs 15:30.) We flourish and grow through adversity when we daily water and fertilize our lives with good words that cultivate faith and hope—being hope givers.

> *"A pessimist sees the difficulty in every opportunity; an optimist sees the opportunity in every difficulty."*
>
> —Winston Churchill

When a Door Closes, a Window Opens

Put problems in perspective. When you encounter a loss or a door closes, look for God to open another door, or perhaps a window, of opportunity. Is there a door in your life that has closed recently? Are you hoping for something new to open up? Think of times when something important went wrong, when a big plan collapsed, when you failed to get a job you wanted, when things didn't turn out as you expected. When one door closed, did another door or window of opportunity open? Reflect on these past experiences, because just reminding yourself of them can help to build hope. What doors closed? What opened up next? Did the new door open immediately, or did it take a while? Did your disappointment, sadness, or bitterness (or other negative feelings) influence your ability to find the open door?[7]

5. NOURISH YOUR SPIRIT

How do you respond when you are stuck, when it seems there is nothing you can do? When our emotional and spiritual reserves are drained by the challenges of life or our own weaknesses, we can wilt and languish. We need nourishment for our souls to strengthen us. Without spiritual food, we don't have the energy for living deeply in the spiritual life. We starve our souls in ways we never would do to our bodies. Or we offer shallow, spiritual junk food.

Learn to be self-soul-nourishing so your inner life will be strengthened to live authentically and purposefully. Return to what replenishes and energizes you, makes you feel most alive. Feed your soul for vibrant, life-giving transformation. Allow yourself, as I often do, to be nurtured and shepherded as Psalm 23 offers: lying down in green pastures and being led by still waters. You can also:

- Cultivate personally meaningful spiritual practices.
- Read the Bible every day, memorize Scripture, sing songs of praise and worship.
- Spend time appreciating nature and beauty.
- Reflect, journal, and ignite creativity through your senses and with images and symbols.
- Take time for quiet, solitude, retreats, and Sabbaths.
- Get together with someone you feel close to and share your heartfelt stories to encourage each other along the way.
- Connect with regular support and worship in your local church community.

235

- Live fully present and fully alive, aware of the divine presence of God in everything you do.

Memorize Scripture—it will sustain you

I heard an interview recently with a woman who was trapped in the Haiti earthquake. Mireille Dittmer said the earthquake happened so quickly that in a split second she was cocooned, kneeling down to protect herself, and then remained trapped in that position for five days. It was excruciatingly painful. Her leg was very bruised and had sores all around it.

When asked, "How did you not go crazy?" she smiled and said, "My faith in Jesus Christ. I have a very strong faith. I read my Bible every day. Whenever I started feeling weak, I started reciting psalms, and that gave me strength again." She didn't eat, sleep, or drink, and lost track of time in the total darkness and silence. Eventually she heard the voices of a man and a little girl—total strangers with whom she instantly bonded. They prayed and talked and gave each other strength. They kept tapping so they could be heard. She never doubted she would be rescued, although the others felt weak, dehydrated, and scared. They kept talking and saying, "We should not lose faith. Our faith will save us. Don't give up. That's the only thing we have to hold on to, because there is nothing else you can do." They were finally all rescued after five days and are expected to fully recover. She ended the interview with the words we need to remind ourselves: "Nothing is impossible with God."[8]

Is this not similar to what Paul did when he was stuck in prison? He prayed and sang. What did my friend Gary Oliver do during his battles with cancer, when his son died, when his wife died, when his sister died? He tells me that he drew strength from his faith and faith practices, staying close to the Lord, continuing in joy and gratitude, surrounded by close friends.

What did I do during challenging times along my renewal journey that I related earlier in the book? What did my friend Beth do when her cancer fight was overwhelming? What did my sister

Sylvia do when her husband was seriously ill in the hospital? What did my sister Sharon do when her husband died in a car accident? We all reflected on Scriptures so we could tell our brains what our heart and soul could believe and feel.

These and many other stories show us what we can do when we feel stuck. Develop antidotes, buffers, coping strategies, and resources to strengthen you through times of stress, worry, and fear. Nourish your soul to be a life-giving resource of hope.

6. NURTURE, STRENGTHEN, AND APPRECIATE RELATIONSHIP SUPPORT

Trials and disappointments can become so overwhelming that we can lose our hope to believe in joy. When in pain, it is a natural tendency for our world to become small and for us to withdraw. The people we value the most become even more cherished. Our closest friends and family lighten the load by sharing in our grief. They hold out reminders of truth and hope, like the fact that God is always with us and wastes nothing, and that smashed grapes can produce tasty wine.

The Strength for the Journey retreats I am a part of leading were developed out of the fruit of my friend Beth's painful and continuing cancer journey. A whole new community of women developed as a result of supporting her through this illness, and we now gather together regularly to be encouraged and strengthened with God and one another amid whatever we are dealing with on our journeys. We have come to deeply appreciate that behind every person on the battlefield, there are others in the supply lines offering support.

Dr. Dennis Charney, professor of psychiatry at the Mount Sinai School of Medicine, has been studying people who have shown exceptional resilience after trauma. I am amazed by one of his research interests, former navy pilot Bob Shumaker. His story shows the power and importance of supportive relationships to strengthen us through adversity. Bob was ejected from a plane during combat in Vietnam. He broke his back and was caught and held in a North Vietnamese prison, where he was brutally tortured. He was in solitary confinement for three years.

Although he was in isolation, there were others imprisoned around him. They developed a tap code of the alphabet, arranged in five rows and five columns, and were able to communicate with each other through taps. The tap code kept their spirits, hopes, and dreams alive. It became quite sophisticated as they transmitted things like French lessons, music lessons, biology lessons, and how to fix a television set. They spent a lot of time tapping on the wall. This connection and their tapping conversations were crucial to their survival.[9] We all need to develop a way of communicating with others in order to get through rough times.

Reach out and connect

This and many other stories affirm the idea that social support, no matter how rudimentary, is a key factor in our ability to have hope and flourish in adversity. We can't do it alone. We need others around us, even if they are only taps on a wall. Just knowing that there is someone else on the other side of the tap can work miracles. We need our family and friends, our church community, and small groups. We need the sisterhood of other female companions along the way. For some, nothing surpasses the fellowship of regular participation in a twelve-step group. AA creates an opportunity to be supported and helpful to others. Everyone needs a "tap code," a fellowship, a way of communicating with other people to establish friendships that are supportive, where we too can be shalom bringers through tough times.

Who is in your supply line? Who is listening to your tapping conversations? Who is in your circle of fellowship? And who can you be there for as well?

Research is clear that when we give our time, talents, and presence to something greater than ourselves, we benefit with a sense of meaning and purpose that brings increased fulfillment and happiness. When we serve others who are in greater need than we are, even in the midst of our own struggles, it serves as a healing, renewing antidote to our own stress. Make a pot of soup. Write an encouraging note. Do an act of loving-kindness for someone else in need. You will feel purpose and connection, and be strengthened and encouraged.

7. KEEP LOOKING TO THE FUTURE

We have this assurance in Jeremiah 29:11: " 'For I know the plans I have for you,' declares the Lord, 'plans to prosper you and not to harm you, plans to give you hope and a future.' " Throughout this book, we have considered God's plan for you to flourish, and how to discover your personal plan to flourish—even in adversity. God uses all our life experiences to help us to flourish and be fruitful. Nothing is wasted, so don't give up. Nothing is impossible, so keep hanging on.

Whatever difficult situation you are facing right now, hold on to Jeremiah's promise for your future. Set goals and make plans toward ways you can flourish in adversity. Don't give up. Keep purpose and meaning in your life experience and believe that God can use your adversity to mature you to be a fruitful blessing to others. Studies show that those who made it through very serious times of being imprisoned or trapped in earthquake rubble, or times of serious illness, had small goals every day and kept hope for the future.[10]

Pass on what you have received, and let the fruit of your life nourish others. Discover the passions and desires of your heart, and follow them. In appendix A you will have the opportunity to create your own plan. You may also consider reflecting on your goals, life purpose, calling, vision, and mission. Dream about and visualize your future. In the sidebar I suggest some ways you can set goals. Write these out and review them frequently. See God fulfilling His redemptive plan for you to flourish in your best self, using your unique gifts and strengths to make a difference.

239

Write Your Goals and Visualize Your Future

James Pennebaker has researched and shown the benefits of expressive writing for healing and the positive approach to the future. He discovered that those who wrote about their future, realizing their dreams, and achieving their goals for twenty minutes a day for four days showed increased happiness.[11] You may try that exercise for four days, or this variation on envisioning your life and a flourishing future: [12]

1. Imagine the full picture of your life journey overall. What things have happened to you? What have you accomplished? What kind of person are you? Imagine that everything has gone as well as it could. You have flourished, living fully alive in the Spirit of God and overcoming challenges. Describe this life.
2. Now imagine your best possible flourishing self, living the abundant, vibrant life that God created you for. Consider your life flowing with positive spiritual emotions and character virtues, connecting with God and meaningful relationships. Describe yourself.

- **Write a List of Your Goals**

On a three-by-five card, write goals that you have in mind. On the back of the card write, "I will become what I think about." Think about these goals cheerfully and hopefully in a positive way every morning.

Find tangible ways of staying motivated to remain on your path. Have a visual idea of what your goals are. Find a picture or a collage to represent your goals. You need motivation. Create a mental picture of the pathway that will take you on the journey to flourish.

What character qualities do you want to have? What thoughts do you want to seed and nourish? What new habits can set you on a new pathway? What visuals, symbols, habits, or exercises will help you stay on this road to flourishing?

- **Write summary affirmation statements about the following:**

Your Life Purpose—What God desires for your life; the kind of person you want to become; your primary reason for living. Your Life Calling—What you give yourself to that energizes you; what you are able to do because of your passions, interests, and abilities. Your Life Vision—A mental picture of what you want to accomplish; your dreams; how you want to be most useful. Your Life Mission—Your plan for what you will do and the steps for how you will get there.

Prayer

Lord, I will put my hope in you and your unfailing love (Psalm 130:7). I will be joyful in hope, patient during struggles, and faithful in prayer (Romans 12:12). Thank you that I can be confident in the plans you have for me (Jeremiah 29:11). I have hope that everything will work together for your good, because I love you and I am called for your purpose (Romans 8:28). I will wait on you, Lord, for renewed strength and hope when I am tired and depleted. I will try to see my stresses and challenges as gifts to show my true colors and as opportunities to strengthen my faith and become mature and build character (James 1:2–4). Thank you, Lord, for bringing out the best in me, continuing your great work in me, and preparing me for a flourishing finish. Amen.

Reflective Questions and Flourish Practices

1. Think about a struggle you've gone through. What have you learned from this situation? What wisdom are you now more aware of? About yourself, about others, about life, about God?

2. What vulnerabilities and weaknesses have you become more aware of in yourself? How did this bring out the worst in you?

3. How do you see God present in your life right now? How is this building character and making you a better person?

4. How has this crisis strengthened positive character traits in you? In your relationships, marriage, work, and other areas of life?

5. Who do you now want to be? List the character traits and lifestyle that you aspire to. Where do you go from here?

6. How do you now choose to live? Write some affirmations of who you aspire to be and the life you intentionally choose.

7. What is your healing journey plan to flourish in daily joy and abundant, vibrant living? This is your intentional lifestyle renewal plan to flourish. Include your overall goals and aspirations, daily, weekly, monthly, annually. (Refer to appendix C.)

chapter 11

A Flourishing
Finish

There has never been the slightest doubt in my mind that
the God who started this great work in you would keep at
it and bring it to a flourishing finish on the very day Christ
Jesus appears.

Philippians 1:6 THE MESSAGE

Most of us don't get to choose our beginning, our family of origin,
or life's difficulties. But we do get to choose what we do with them,
how we run the race, and most important, how we finish. In our
youth, because of our immaturity or our default human nature,
we make decisions that may lead us to languish. But no matter
what season of life we are in, what developmental stage we are
passing through, or what struggle we are facing, we can pause and
intentionally choose who we want to be. We have an incredible
opportunity to choose the pathway toward a flourishing finish.
Each season of life brings both blessings and struggles. This is why

flourishing, especially faith-based flourishing as I have presented it here—is so important. When flourishing is infused with our faith, the emotion virtues of love, joy, gratitude, peace, and hope all become available. And they, in turn, provide the foundation for a maturity and inner fortitude to stay the course and finish well. God is love. God is good. God is in everything and wastes nothing.

It is the Saturday before Easter as I write, so I cannot help reflecting on themes and images of the Easter story. I am reminded that it was with the death of Christ on an Easter Friday two millennia ago that our redemption began. I wonder what being a disciple then must have been like. For certain, it must have been a very painful time. It seemed that all they had hoped for had perished. The disciples did not celebrate the death of Jesus. They were shocked and disappointed. They feared for their own deaths. They believed that all was lost.

Then Easter Saturday came. This was their day of waiting, worrying, and wondering, "What's next?" Finally, Sunday came. They had no idea at first what that Easter Sunday promised. The first mourners to arrive found the stone rolled away. Jesus had risen and now promised a new life. It must have been an overwhelmingly bewildering time. Soon it became a time for celebration. The long-awaited fulfillment of the promises Jesus had made ushered in a new era of adventure and challenge. Friday's loss, then Saturday's waiting, and finally the Sunday celebration of a risen, living Christ who brought new life to the whole world.[1] And with it came the power and promise of flourishing, so we can thrive in a world full of loss and disappointment. That's the redemption story!

The Fridays of Life

In each season of life there is a Friday, a Saturday, and a Sunday. At some time we will all face a dark, despairing Friday. Suffering is a great equalizer. No matter our social status, age, gender, accomplishments, or failures, adversity levels us all. In a sense, it also unites us on our journeys. Things haven't turned out the way they were supposed to or the way we would have liked them to be. In 1 Samuel 4–6, the Philistines, in a shocking and disastrous battle, defeated the Israelites. The Ark of the Covenant was captured, and for the Israelites this meant that God was also taken captive. Without the ark, how could they possibly commune with God? Like the disciples at Easter, they were devastated. All their hopes were dashed. For centuries many have asked similar questions: *How could we, the chosen people of God, have been defeated? How could Jesus the Messiah have been crucified on a dark, despairing Friday? Why has my husband, who has so faithfully served his company, been let go? Why is my teenager being a prodigal or my friend struggling with cancer?*

For many, despairing Fridays can be plentiful—and painful, because it just wasn't supposed to be this way. In the psalms, King David so articulately expresses these sentiments. After he had been chosen by God to be the king, instead of newfound glory, he found himself surrounded by troubles and tribulations. He eventually ends up in a desolate cave—and spends about ten years in isolation.

We also sometimes end up in a cave of disappointment, sometimes of our own making. We suffer loss, defeat, failure, fear, illness, regret, relationship conflict, parenting challenges, health problems, financial distress, and lost dreams. It's inevitable because we live in a vandalized world.

To add to our misery, most, if not all, don't like these "trapped in a cave" experiences. Caves are dark and too quiet. We want action and resolution. We are also pretty good at trying to avoid caves or prematurely escape. We try to compensate with defensive strategies, such as being controlling, grasping for more success, becoming overly religious, or using our smarts to outsmart hard and painful times. But at some point, despite our attempts to escape, we still end up in a desert place, a desolate cave, or a cocoon, desperate for God. These are the Fridays of life. Take a moment and reflect on the Fridays in your life right now.

Hope–Based Waiting

Then come our Saturdays, when we must wait. And wait. And wait! And question. *What is really going on here? Why the delay in getting resolution? Where is God in all of this? Will He ever show up? Will this dark cloud ever lift? Is this all I will ever know? What will be the next chapter of my life's story?* So we just sit and wait, like the disciples did on that Easter Saturday. What are we waiting for? Some breakthrough? Perhaps a victory? Certainly, for the rest of our life's story.

We wait for a relationship to be reconciled, our wounded hearts or bodies to heal, wisdom to raise our children, and victory in battling for their souls. We wait and trust for the right spouse to come along, financial breakthrough, a job, freedom from what hinders us from living full of the Spirit of God, authentically becoming our best possible self. In the light of your Fridays, also take a moment to reflect on your Saturday—what is it you are waiting for? Journal whatever comes to mind. It will help you to clarify your hopes and dreams for whatever comes next in your life.

Often, it's only at a later time, in retrospect, when we look back on our lives, that we can see how things come together, when we see the beautiful harvest, how we and others have changed. We are told so many times in the Bible to wait. And that is what our Saturdays are all about. Waiting is not a bad thing. Some of us do this better than others. It doesn't mean just sitting around, biding our time or stressing out. Instead, we are to wait hopefully with expectancy. I call this "hope-based waiting." It is easier to be patient when we are trusting in God and anticipating what He will do. During difficult times especially, we are encouraged to wait like Jeremiah did in Lamentations 3. Like Noah and David did (Genesis 7; 8:1–15; Psalm 31:24; 33:18; 130:5, 7; 147:11). Even during all the overwhelming hard times they went through, they had hope in God's deliverance and were willing to wait for it. The Lord is good to us when we wait for Him, when our soul seeks Him. It is good that we should hope and wait quietly for the Lord. (See Lamentations 3:25–26.)

So take a few minutes to reflect and journal what you perceive to be your crucibles of hope-based waiting. What are the longings of your heart—the things you are waiting to see flourish in your life?

Waiting for the Resurrection—Your Breakthrough

And now we come to Sundays—days of resurrection and resolution.

Julian of Norwich, a Benedictine nun who lived in the 1300s, noted that our *wounds* become like a *womb*. This transformation happens when we are able to turn our pain (the tomb) into a fertile place where life is birthed (the womb).

The darkness of the cave, the silent tomb on Holy Saturday, now becomes a life-giving womb on Sunday, preparing us for the promise of a new, radiant, and abundant life. It is in the cave, in the cocoon, where God can do some of His best, most profound redemptive work in us and our life situations. May your cave become a *womb* for God's life-giving resurrection power in you. Transformation. New life is forming. Miracles are being prepared. All is being made right with God. Life is being restored and renewed.

We like exuberant beginnings and victorious endings. But most of life is lived in the "in-between"; the daily routine of mundane challenges. In some ways, we all live mainly in a Holy Saturday, waiting for our full redemption and restoration in Christ.

God Does His Greatest Work in "Saturday Caves"

This brings us to a very important, but often overlooked, flourishing principle. There are times when you may feel like nothing worthwhile is happening in your life. These are the winter seasons, the never-ending Saturdays. For a butterfly it is the time of metamorphosis in the cocoon. The days can be long and dreary. You hear of great things happening to others around you, but you feel like the

"I believe in the sun, even when it is not shining; I believe in love, even when I do not feel it; I believe in God, even when He is silent."

—Author unknown

blind man on the side of the street crying out, "God, why don't you help me?" Vaclav Havel, former president of the Czech Republic and one of the great leaders of a genuine revolution, once said, "The feeling that 'if nothing is happening, nothing is happening' is the prejudice of a superficial, dependent, and hollow spirit." In other words, when nothing is happening, a great deal may be happening![2] We need to write these words on our heart and carry them everywhere. It is particularly true when it comes to God's work in our heart. When nothing is happening, God could very well be doing His finest work in you.

So we may need to adjust our feelings when we feel disappointed and depressed, even like a failure. When it seems like the Lord is doing nothing big in your life, He may be doing some small but miraculous transformation that you can't even see. God doesn't shake us up with dramatic catastrophes so much as He blows like a gentle wind, trying to change our direction in life. Everyone else may seem to be getting better opportunities or more rapid healing; they may find a new job quickly; their kids may thrive better than yours; or others may seem to have a happier marriage. Don't judge your own circumstances by what others seem to be experiencing. Try to stay away from thoughts like *Lord, why aren't you doing anything for me? Where are you? I need some action here from you!* Sentiments like this feed depression and despair. Yes, we can feel desperately alone in our caves. But remember: When nothing seems to be happening, a lot may be happening. As Yogi Berra would say: "The game isn't over till it's over!"

The enemy of your soul likes to hover around, keeping you aware of your failures and shortcomings and luring you into looking for alternative ways to find your life source and strength. In the midst of all this turmoil and hardship on your soul, threatening to wilt you, the Lord wants to lead you to a safe place, to green pastures and quiet places. In times like this, you need to find a place of peace and security. You need to have a quiet faith in the midst of calamity. In Isaiah 30:15 the Lord says that "in returning and rest you shall be saved; in quietness and confidence shall be your strength" (NKJV). Even though nothing may seem to be happening, something is happening, and God is with you. So be assured; you are loved by a God whose love transcends all others. You are not forgotten in the cave. Embracing this truth can help you see your life from His perspective and keep you faithful to His plan for your life's journey.

Welcoming God Into Your Saturday Cave

In really bad times, you may be tempted to look for some big miraculous sign or dramatic action on God's part. You want God to come down in fire or part the ocean of your despair. But chances are that God will not make some dramatic rescue. More than likely, He will call you gently and invite you to have a quiet faith in Him. And if disaster ensues, He wants you to stay close so He can comfort you. The Lord is good, and in quiet confidence He will provide exactly what you need.

When God was instructing Solomon to build the temple, large limestones were quarried from the other side of the mountain and carved to precision in underground caves outside the temple. Today, these sites in Israel are known as King Solomon's Quarries or the Cave of Zedekiah.[3] According to the first book of Kings it was forbidden to use iron tools on the site of the temple. There was no banging and clanging permitted to reach the temple site. It was a sacred place. When the stones were ready, they were brought to the temple and slid into place without metallic tools or loud sounds.

This picture of the temple is a metaphor for our souls. Each one of us is now considered the temple of God, where His Holy Spirit lives. Just because there isn't noise and action going on doesn't mean that nothing is happening in your life. The Lord works by His Spirit and His Word. He is doing a deep work when we are by still streams, when our roots are going down deep, drawing from and soaking in His presence. What happens in our cave seasons is not lost. What lasts and carries over from our cave seasons is who we have become: how we face aging parents, deal with difficult two-year-olds, manage the junior high years, survive financial difficulties, and cope with the loneliness of waiting. What you learn and how you are shaped by the Saturday season is what matures you and strengthens you for the rest of your journey. The grace and mercy you receive and treasures you discover in these dark places are what you pass on to others.

That's when He is creating what we need—a new heart, mind, and spirit—and slipping it right into place without a big commotion. You don't need to see a lot of action and hear a lot of noise to know God is doing a great transformation and restoration in the deep, inner sacred places of your life. God is building a great temple and cathedral in you, and the work is being done skillfully, in quietness and confidence.

You don't have to strive and struggle to make this grand transformation happen. It is God who does the work in you. It is the Holy Spirit that transforms and flows through us. You don't have to strive for good character and fruitfulness in your life. That is ultimately God's part. It is His life-giving power that does great work in caves, in our inner beings.

We must open our hearts to God in relationship and partnership, desiring to surrender and submit to His transformation. And we must not go alone. Invite others to sit with you, to listen and help you in the struggle for freedom. You can't just sit on the couch in your cave life, indulging in disappointment, resentment, and bitterness with no intentional plan or commitment to growth and transformation. Be careful not to get too comfortable with the familiar and lose your strength to break free and finish well.

By God's grace in you, He will rebuild your life so that His glory will be seen. You can decide that in the temple of your heart, soul, and mind, you will glorify God. That out of the good tree of your life, you will bear good fruit.

Discovering What Matters Most

Are you stronger now and a better person for having gone through the cave experience? God wastes nothing. When people are asked if they would eliminate difficult experiences or challenging times, most people say no. Haven't you learned about yourself and become stronger in ways that equip you for the rest of your life? You then pass this on by becoming a shalom bringer, joy spreader, and hope giver to others on their journey. The flourishing redemption in your life becomes nourishing bread for others.

Flourishing in adversity helps you focus on what really matters most. When you are battling for your life, for a marriage, for the future of your children, for a roof over your head, for breakthrough in your soul, you discover that there are a lot of things that just don't matter—that you can do without.

What really makes life worth living and brings happiness are the most simple and cherished things in life. People matter. I have learned so much about living life to the fullest from struggles along my journey and walking closely with others on their journeys. My friend Beth lives each day to the fullest, totally dependent on God, not knowing the direction of her years of battling with metastasized breast cancer. She embraces each moment of abundant, vibrant life. This is when you realize what really matters most. Let us live each day carefully, fully human and fully alive, open to the Spirit of God flowing through us to flourish in mature Christian character.

When David was running from all the men trying to kill him, he ended up alone in a cave. When he was stripped of everything, God was all he had. He found strength in the Lord. God was more than enough.

God Is All You Need When God Is All You Have

In Isaiah 40:29–31, God says He gives power to the weak, and to those who have no might He increases strength. Those who wait on the Lord will renew their strength. In Isaiah 41:10, He says don't be afraid, I am with you, I will strengthen you. In Jeremiah 16:19, we are to look to God for our strength and help: "O Lord, my strength and my fortress, my refuge in the day of affliction." Isaiah 35:2–4 describes a picture of us flourishing in the kingdom of God. How are we to strengthen those who are weak, in the cave experience, stuck in desert places, anxious and fearful? Tell them to be strong and not to be afraid. The Lord will come and save them.

Inner strength comes from communing with God. It's during these quiet moments alone with God that He restores our souls. Let Him teach you how to be still, to rest awhile and gather inner strength, and resolve to compensate for your weakness when spiritual warfare begins. The quiet times you spend with God in solitude and prayer will strengthen and restore your soul and help you be aware of His love and care for you.

In times of need, God strengthens us. He gives us a fresh anointing of His Spirit to refresh us. In Psalm 92:10 the writer declares, "I have been anointed with fresh oil" (NKJV), and in Psalm 23 David declares that the Good Shepherd anoints his head with oil. Many passages refer to metaphors of the Holy Spirit of God being poured into our lives as oil and water, healing us, protecting us, refreshing and nourishing us, providing us with what we need.

When you are at your end, facing your Friday losses and your Saturday waiting, when you feel all is stripped away and God is all you have, maybe the Spirit of God is all you need. He is more than enough. It is during these times that you pray your most heartfelt prayers that draw you closer to God so He can do some of His best, most life transforming, beautiful work in you.

A Flourishing Finish

As I finish writing this chapter, it is Easter—resurrection Sunday. This is the most glorious day in Christian history because it is the climax of God's plan for salvation. It is the ultimate Sunday, the day when Jesus broke out of the tomb of death and now promises all of us an abundant life. The same life-giving power that got Jesus through the grave to the victorious Sunday is now available to you and me. During the Fridays and Saturdays along our journey, we basically just try to hold on and let God and others hold on to us.[4]

Now we have to be patient again and wait for God to work His deep, life-transforming changes in us. All we have to do is surrender to the experience and submit ourselves to the life-giving process. Then, when our Sunday comes, we burst out of our cave and celebrate our victory. We can join with the sentiments expressed in Psalm 30:11 in *The Message*: "You did it: you changed wild lament into whirling dance; you ripped off my black mourning band and decked me with wildflowers."

This morning I made a cross of fresh flowers from my garden. A flowering cross is a perfect symbol of the flourishing that His redemptive suffering offers. The same power that raised Jesus from the dead in His cave is available to you in your cave. God wants you to have a flourishing finish.

We were just finishing our Easter lunch as a family today when we experienced an earthquake here in Los Angeles. The shaking reminded me of how often God has to shake me up a little just to get my attention. A shaking up certainly brought new life that Easter Sunday two thousand years ago. The stone blocking the cave was rolled away and new life came bursting out. Sundays are the days when we thankfully celebrate seeing these glimpses of hope, new opportunity, and answers to prayers. The bad habits are finally changed. There is a turnaround, healing, breakthrough, and renewed joy as new life streams through the once stagnant, wilting, and languishing places.

Take a moment to reflect on these questions:

What are the Sundays you are waiting for?
What are the breakthroughs to be celebrated?
How has God surprisingly brought you new hope and
new life?

All Shall Be Well

I received an Easter card from my friend Debbie, with a photo
she took of the Garden Tomb of Jesus in Jerusalem. There is a sign
on the tomb that says, "He is not here—for He is risen." As Julian
of Norwich said, "The worst has happened and been repaired,"
so all will be well. The worst happened on that Friday and endured
through Saturday. But then came Sunday. He is no longer in the
cave. He is now living again and has the keys to free you from
what you feel is the end.

The same life-giving, cave-busting spiritual power that freed
Jesus is available to breathe new life into you in whatever situation you are in. The Lord knows where you are. He sees you
and knows exactly what your hopes and aspirations are. He does
some of His greatest work in caves, breaking us out with life-
transforming power.

New resurrection, abundant life is available to you, and it
is always on its way with God. God created and designed the
beginning of your life, and He will finish what He has started.
Our choice is to be in a relationship with Him or be apart. His
invitation is to walk with Him, live with Him, and let His Spirit
give us transforming life.

Yes, it is a lifelong journey. But you can know for sure that
you are created to flourish as your best possible self in all your life
systems, and God desires to give you a flourishing finish. Nothing
can write the ending except Him. Not fate, fear, failure, or the
limitations of our flesh.[5]

God's purposeful plan for your life is redemption. Restoration.

Abundant, vibrant life, being fully alive in God is the gift for you. It may not be the way you expect, but expect that it will be His perfect will in His best timing. Jesus came to give us abundant life so that we won't perish or languish. "Because Jesus was raised from the dead, we've been given a brand-new life, and have everything to live for, including a future in heaven" (1 Peter 1:3–4 THE MESSAGE). That is a promise of the high purpose of eternal life. The ultimate flourishing finish is when we are in heaven with no more tears.

There will be some things in life that you will always struggle through and only get resolved on the final Sunday, in heaven. Faith-based flourishing is God's call for us to live well and stay the course to the end. God makes all things beautiful, in His way and in His time. God's desire is for you to flourish. He wants to see His shalom fulfilled in your life and mine, delighting in our maturity and fruitfulness.

Open your heart to discover and embrace the fullness of this new life in God's loving, transforming Spirit. Cultivate this life in every aspect of your being, in all your life systems, so you can have the life-giving fruitfulness of spiritual emotions and character maturity streaming through you, making a difference to those around you—being a flourisher.

May you go in the fullness of God's Spirit—growing in love, joy, gratitude, peace, and hope—and flourish!

Prayer of St. Teresa

Let nothing disturb you
Let nothing distress you
While all things fade away
God is unchanging
Be patient, for with God in your heart
Nothing is lacking, God is enough.

Reflective Questions and Flourish Practices

Meditate prayerfully on this passage about flourishing and how it applies to your life.

> The person who trusts and hopes in the Lord will be blessed. They will be strong, a tree planted near water that sends its roots by a stream. It is not afraid when the days are hot; its leaves are always green. It does not worry in the year when no rain comes; it always produces fruit.

Adapted from Jeremiah 17:7–8 NCV

BE LIKE A TREE PLANTED NEAR WATER

The environment where you are planted will determine how you flourish and bear fruit. Being planted near the waters of the Spirit provides continual renewal, refreshing, and nourishment. When you are planted in relationships, a church, or a small group you have the opportunity to grow in your gifts and strengths; be encouraged and contribute by serving others. *What environments in your life right now are most nourishing to you?*

SPREAD YOUR ROOTS OUT DEEP BY THE STREAM

When roots go deep and are spread out to reach to the streams of water, they are continually nourished by the Spirit and the Word and not easily uprooted. Be rooted in the love of God and Christ. People with deep roots love others. They participate and contribute. They build deep, solid friendships and relationships. They benefit from spiritual and relational nourishment, flourishing the way God intended. *How can you go deeper in your love of God and in relationships?*

DON'T BE AFRAID OF HEAT

When the heat of trials and challenges comes, a flourishing life can stand firm and not be thrown off. If you are planted by refreshing, nourishing streams, no matter what you go through, you can stay strong and be victorious. *What is the "heat" in your life right now? What can help keep you watered and refreshed?*

ALWAYS HAVE GREEN LEAVES

Green foliage is a sign of growth and health from a deep resource within. To stay green requires continual spiritual nourishment. Daily lifestyle habits and positive practices cultivate well-being and spiritual vitality. If we neglect to feed our spirit and souls daily, thinking we already know it all, we will lose vibrant vitality, wither, and become weak. *What is most nourishing to you for continued growth and renewal? Use the appendix to create a lifestyle rhythm for well-being and vitality.*

DON'T WORRY IN DRY TIMES

There will be dry wilderness seasons and fiery times. The economy may crash or illness might strike. There may be relationship conflict or difficult decisions to face. Your heart may experience sorrow watching your children suffer. But you can't be controlled and depleted by these dry seasons. When you trust in God and are planted in the house of the Lord around strong believers, you can have strength and faith. *Tell the Lord about your worries so He can turn them into concerns and help you trust in Him. Turn your mind toward what you are grateful for and what is good. Then embrace God's peace and joy.*

ALWAYS BLOSSOM WITH FRUIT

This blossoming and fruitfulness is evidence of ongoing, vibrant life being passed on as a blessing to others. Living in love, generosity, and gratitude is a lifestyle that reproduces good fruit. When you flourish, the fruit of your life is a source of nourishment for others, no matter what season you are in. In Psalm 92 we are promised that like the palm tree, we can just keep being fruitful as we age. *Reflect on the desire of your heart to flourish, be fruitful, and nourish others. Take this before the Lord in prayer.*

Listen. What do you sense the Spirit of God saying to you about His continuing great work in you, toward a flourishing finish? Now it's up to you to respond.

appendix A

Creating My Intentional
Life Plan to Flourish

Although this is the end of the book, it is the beginning of creating and committing to renewal on your journey to flourish. What is your plan to flourish?

1. My definition of what it means to flourish is . . .

2. The flourishing botanical metaphors I identify with in this season of my life are . . .

BOTANICAL SOUL METAPHORS

- Flourish like a palm tree (Psalm 92:12)

    A palm tree thrives in dry places. It is resilient when tossed to and fro in winds and storms. It may bend and sway, but it won't break. The palm produces more fruit as it gets older.

- Flourish like a cedar of Lebanon (Psalm 92:12)

  The cedar of Lebanon grows tall and strong by sending out deep horizontal roots linking with other cedars for stability. We can link arms and souls throughout life.

- Flourish like an acacia tree (Isaiah 41:19)

  The acacia tree is able to survive in very barren surroundings by retaining moisture needed for dry times.

- Flourish like a tree planted by streams of water (Psalm 1:3)

  When a tree is planted by water and sends its roots down deep for nourishment, it will get through heat and drought and still stay green, showing evidence of life and vitality.

- Flourish like a crocus in the desert (Isaiah 35:1)

  Our life journey will take us through many desert experiences. Spiritually, this represents our full blossoming into spiritual maturity under the warmth of God's unconditional and very personal love during the challenges of life.

- Flourish like the lilies of the field (Matthew 6:28–39)

  The lilies of the field are wild flowers. They are not cultivated. God seeds them and takes care of them. He does the same for us.

- Flourish like a fruitful branch connected to the vine (John 15:1–17)

  We cannot be fruitful and truly flourish unless we are like branches connected to a vine so the emotion virtues can flow through us.

There may be another flower, plant, or tree that you identify with: apple, oak, olive, pineapple, daisy, weeping willow, jacaranda, sunflower, daffodil.

3. The name of the road that best describes the journey I am on at this time is . . . (Refer to chapter 1.)

4. Things I am afraid of as I begin the pathways to flourish are . . .

5. What are possible roadblocks that I will have to overcome on my path to flourish?

6. Flashing forward five years from now, after being on the flourishing journey, this is how I would describe my life. These are the images and metaphors that reflect my flourishing life in the future.

7. Cultivating my flourishing self: I will daily nurture and nourish my life with the vibrant Spirit of God and be aware of what drains, depletes, and causes me to languish.

LANGUISHING	FLOURISHING
What drains, depletes, wilts me	What energizes, fills, nourishes me

8. The spiritual pathways that reflect my unique temperament and help me best relate to God, draw near to Him, and feel most fully alive in Him are . . .

9. The streams of Christian faith traditions (contemplative, holiness, charismatic, social justice, evangelical, incarnational) that are most life-giving to me are . . . (Refer to chapter 2.)

10. The spiritual practices that energize me, nourish me, and make me feel the most fully alive to the Spirit of God that I would like to include in the rhythm of my life are . . . (Refer to chapter 3.)

- **Practices that nourish my inner life—spirit, emotions, mind, heart, and soul:**

    Personal Contemplation: prayer, Scripture reading, meditation, silence, solitude, fasting, retreat, simplicity, submission, worship and praise music, enjoying nature and beauty

    Learning: studying the Bible; inspirational reading; listening to teachings and songs; watching videos; attending retreats, seminars, and conferences

- **Practices that nurture my relationships:**

    Relational Interaction: spiritual direction, spiritual friendships, prayer partners, mentoring, small groups, time talking with friends, celebrating special occasions

- **Practices that enrich my life experience for impact:**

    Purposeful living beyond myself: using gifts and skills to serve others, volunteering, altruism, generosity, generativity, goodness, kindness

11. The new pathways, faith traditions, and spiritual practices that I would like to explore for renewal and a fresh flow of the Spirit are . . . (Refer to chapter 4.)

12. This is my plan to flourish during the challenges of a dry desert or cave experience:

For this next section, you may want to refer to the Flourish Practices for Well-Being assessment in appendix B.

13. Write a narrative description of what your flourishing life would look like. Be specific with goals and daily action steps. Start within twenty-four hours.

Discovering my invitation to flourish (chapters 1 and 2)
Arranging my days for intentional rhythms of life (chapter 3)
Love and my God attachment system (chapter 4)
Love and my relationship attachment system (chapter 5)
Joy and gratitude system (chapters 6 and 7)
Peace and tranquility system (chapters 8 and 9)
Hope and resilience system (chapters 10 and 11)

14. Consider creating a flourish scrapbook, journal, or collage of pictures, Scriptures, quotes, and images that express and inspire you on your journey to flourish. Take time when you are alone in quiet to look through these pages, focusing your thoughts on what is important to you, renewing your perspective on life. Keep adding to this as new inspiration comes to you.

15. **Practical ways to *Flourish*. Consider daily:**

What are my stresses, worries, and struggles?

What are my prayer concerns?

What am I grateful for?

What area of life am I motivated to *Flourish* in today? *(Body, mind, emotions, spirit, relationships, work, money, hobbies, etc.)*

What is the Spirit of God saying to me about how I could love, nurture, show kindness, compassion, joy, gratitude, encouragement, and hope to those around me?

(Smile. Say something affirming. Express gratitude. Call and see how someone is doing. Meet with a friend—listen. Remember birthdays. Send flowers. Give of my time, money, skills, and strengths. Celebrate with others on happy occasions. Support a cause for those less fortunate.)

Friends
Family
Community / Small group connections
School / Work
Church
Those in special need that I know about
People I encounter in everyday life

Flourish Practices for Well-Being as a Whole Person

Refer to chapter 2 to use this well-being outline as a guide, a resource of ideas, and affirmations to create your lifestyle practices for well-being as a whole person. What are your intentional plans, paces, rhythms, and ways of flourishing in each area of your life? Select a few in each area that you would like to begin focusing on, and then create your own intentional goals and affirmations to grow and flourish.

How to Flourish in Spirit

___ I embrace and surrender to God's love for me, learning to love Him in return.

___ I am becoming more aware of paying attention to the

sacred and God's presence with me in all things and at all times during the day.

__ I am open to being filled with the Holy Spirit flowing through me, choosing to live in the spiritual emotions and character traits of the Spirit—and allowing these traits to flow to others.

__ I am discovering my true self and the essence of who I am in God.

__ I am becoming aware of my false self, breaking free from unhealthy desires, patterns, and my "default setting" that drives me.

__ I have a daily quieting, reflective time when I slow down to listen, talk, and be with God.

__ I am learning a lifestyle rhythm of intentional healthy habits and transforming spiritual practices such as:

__ Silence and solitude

__ Bible reading—lectio divina (meditating on Scripture)

__ Prayer: listening and communing with God

__ Meditation

__ Reading, writing, journaling

__ Listening to good, uplifting music

__ Singing, praising, worshiping

__ Connecting with spiritual friends

__ Receiving spiritual direction

__ Keeping the Sabbath

__ I am becoming more intentional about creating a sanctuary in my soul and my surroundings.

__ I am aware of blessings in my life and becoming more thankful and grateful.

How to Flourish in Emotions

___ I am living more honestly and authentically out of the true, best self I am in God—diminishing the unconscious aspects that drive my false self.

___ I am discovering God's grace and mercy where I am wounded and vulnerable.

___ I am becoming more intentional about daily cultivating positive spiritual emotion.

___ I am developing awareness of my inner thoughts and feelings, expressing them in a healthy, constructive way.

___ I am learning to deal appropriately with difficult, negative emotions.

___ I am learning to grieve all my losses well.

___ I am discovering how to go through crisis in a healthy way.

___ I am becoming aware of and pursuing healing for emotional wounds and family of origin issues.

___ I pursue what nurtures and replenishes me.

___ I laugh more, keeping a sense of humor.

___ I am learning to be forgiven, to forgive, and to "let go."

How to Flourish in Mind

___ I am breaking free from unhealthy habits and patterns.

___ I practice healthy habits of the mind: hopeful, positive, encouraging thoughts.

___ I dispute negative self-talk that leads to negative emotions (fear, worry, anger).

___ I try to keep a positive (God) perspective, especially during difficult times.

___ I am growing in personal character strengths and talents. I have a to-be list.

___ I take a break from my regular routine for fun activities and creative hobbies.

___ I am learning healthy ways to reduce stress, anxiety, and worry.

___ I practice mental hygiene such as relaxation and Christian meditation.

___ I am aware of my body/mind connection, cultivating positive thinking, emotions, and actions.

___ I foster curiosity. I keep learning new skills and enjoying hobbies.

___ I pursue positive meaning and purpose in life.

___ I listen and talk with people to learn and enrich my life.

___ I keep learning—reading inspiring books, magazines, and journals, and listening to teaching that inspires me.

How to Flourish in Body

___ I care for my body, being in tune with my health.

___ I aim for a healthy brain that helps me make good choices, motivating me to flourish.

___ I eat balanced, nutritious meals.

___ I avoid unhealthy processed products.

___ I take vitamin and mineral supplements.

___ I drink eight to ten glasses of water daily.

___ I exercise regularly, at least thirty minutes at a time.

___ I get adequate sleep each night.

___ I rest, relax, and recuperate each day.

___ I keep the Sabbath—one day of recovery and enjoyment every week.

___ I practice healthy stress management and relaxation skills.

___ I remember to breathe deeply throughout the day.

___ I get regular medical checkups and attend to medical needs.

___ I express authentic, healthy sexuality.

___ I am growing in seeing self-care as a spiritual practice, making my well-being a priority.

___ I enjoy being out in nature.

How to Flourish in Relationships

___ I love others well out of embracing God's love for me.

___ I initiate and cultivate positive relationship attachments.

___ I am nurturing friendships and connecting with people I care about.

___ I am a friend for the journey.

___ I connect with family in as healthy a way as possible.

___ I practice showing love, kindness, compassion.

___ I practice forgiveness.

___ I show appreciation.

___ I am a shalom bringer, a flourisher, a loving safe place, a joy spreader, a peacemaker, and a hope giver.

___ I am learning to resolve conflict maturely.

How to Flourish in Life Experiences

___ I am intentional about my personal growth.

___ I am aware of and pursue my calling, passions, and purpose in life.

___ I set goals to live out my values and visions and dreams.

___ I focus on what matters most, which increases my life satisfaction.

___ I am honestly aware of my strengths, weaknesses, and limits.

___ I develop and use my strengths, gifts, and skills to serve others so they may flourish.

___ I serve, showing altruism and generosity.

___ I spend time enjoying nature and beauty.

___ During challenging times, I draw deeply on the Spirit of God to be strengthened.

___ During challenging times, I reach out to be strengthened and encouraged by others.

appendix C

Arranging My Life
to Flourish

Refer to chapter 3 and develop your own intentional renewal plan to flourish. From the resources provided and other ideas that come to you, write down what your heart desires most, what habits and practices you are most fully living for in this season of your life. Create your own intentional plan to begin with in each of the following areas. Be flexible, re-evaluating and updating often. What matters most is that you are always intentionally aware of how you arrange your life to cultivate growth to flourish.

Intentional Rhythms of My Life

Pray—*Connect with and love God*

Love and Relationships—*Love and connection with yourself and others*

Love yourself

Love others

Work—*Pursue meaningful service to God and others*

Play and recreation—*Delight in creativity and pure pleasure*

Rest—*Renewal. Restoration. Enjoyment.*

Arranging My Life to Flourish

Daily

Weekly

Monthly

Annually

appendix D

Flourish in Life and Relationships

Use this resource in a way that is most helpful for you to pay attention and become self-aware in how you are flourishing. The suggested rating scale is designed for you to use as a way of reflecting to see where you are doing well and where you may be languishing and need to grow. Each affirmation goal reflects criteria for flourishing in life and relationships. You may want to make a copy to read through regularly in your quiet time as a self-evaluation resource or as a reminder. It is not meant to be an overwhelming list you have to check off and live up to every day. Certain affirmations may stand out for you as areas you would like to grow in. Choose which affirmations you would like to embrace for yourself at this time, and be more intentional to live them out daily. Create your own affirmation goals drawing from this list or on your own.

1 = Not very true   3 = Mostly true
2 = Somewhat true   4 = Very true

Invitation to Flourish

___ I embrace the great abundance, sufficiency, and beauty that God intends for me.

___ To the best of my ability, I am living fully and freely in the light of God's generosity.

___ I embrace living an abundant, vibrant life to the fullest.

___ I am on the journey to continued personal and spiritual growth.

___ I aim for a "good life," well lived.

___ I view life as good, and I see God in everything.

Flourish Principles

___ I aim to be fully human and fully alive, bringing glory to God with the fruit of my life.

___ I am moving toward becoming my best, most authentic beautiful self, for God's delight and glory.

___ I am aware of what drives my life and how my false self hinders me from flourishing.

___ I am living as a whole person, pursuing well-being and harmony in all areas of my life.

___ I fully experience being my best self, reaching my potential and being a blessing to those whose lives I touch.

___ I am becoming self-aware, discerning my strengths and weaknesses where I have been careless, and hindrances that cause failure to flourish.

___ I find fulfillment in being creative and productive.

Intentional Living

___ I intentionally pursue positive habits, spiritual practices, and a daily lifestyle rhythm on a regular basis to keep me close to God, fill me with the Holy Spirit, and nourish my soul.

___ I consider the value and priority of each of the great realms and rhythm of life.

___ I am committed to growing in a vibrant personal life that includes emotional maturity, spiritual formation, and healthy relationship connections.

___ I commit to becoming authentically beautiful and finding a soul sanctuary that will require a daily discipline, not just a spa treatment or a consumer product.

___ I will be intentionally picky to order my heart and arrange my life around selecting the best and most nourishing things for the desires and longings of my soul.

___ I will explore the Christian faith traditions and spiritual formation practices to renew and enrich my journey to flourish.

___ My daily practices and lifestyle rhythm lead to greater well-being in life, family, work, community, and society.

Love and God Attachment

___ I am daily being filled with the Spirit of God, growing in love and being transformed into the best version of who God has designed me to be.

___ I am secure in my relationship attachment with God and the truth that I cannot make Him stop loving me.

___ God is my secure attachment base, and I pursue getting close to Him, finding encouragement, comfort, and help in my times of need.

___ I approach God with childlike faith, putting aside all my distorted images of Him and previous experiences, discovering Him for who He really is.

____ I practice solitude, silence, prayer, simple and sacrificial living, intense study and meditation upon God's Word and God's ways, and service to others.

Love and Relationship Attachment

____ I intentionally cultivate healthy, reciprocal, positive relationship attachments, being a safe place and a safe haven.

____ I am intentional to stay in touch with friends and family through letters, email, phone calls, or visits.

____ I am able to share my dreams and feelings, keeping a healthy balance of closeness and distance.

____ I feel lovable and that others are reliable. I see others as trustworthy and caring, confident that our conflict can be resolved.

____ I have an attitude of love and acceptance toward those around me, modeling the unconditional love of God.

____ When I receive what others offer, I recognize it reveals to them the gifts they have. I realize that it is in my receiving that others discover their gifts.

____ I acknowledge that forgiveness and letting go is the only way to healing myself and freeing and repairing my relationships.

____ I contribute to the well-being of others, paying attention to the decisions I make that affect a greater sense of well-being for myself and others.

____ I am aware that I can give to the point of depletion unless I also attend to self-care for myself and receive from others.

Joy and Gratitude

___ I intentionally cultivate positive emotions of joy and gratitude, which open up more awareness of my surroundings, creativity, and problem-solving.

___ I enjoy the simple pleasures that God provides now—in the present moment.

___ I realize that the joy God gives me is deeper than basic life happiness dependent on outward circumstances or other people. It is more like quiet contentment.

___ I know there is no true joy and happiness outside of the Spirit of God. I was created to find delight and pure pleasure in the presence of the Lord.

___ I aim to cultivate more positive emotion virtues in the face of the negative, being regularly cheerful and grateful.

___ I surround myself with people who uplift and nurture me to flourish.

___ I am a joy spreader, contributing to the lives of others out of a deep sense of gratitude for the gifts I have been given.

___ I spend money wisely on experiences that bring lasting happiness.

Peace and Tranquility

___ I am aware of what strains and drains me, and the symptoms of the effects.

___ I am listening to my life, my longings, my body, and my heart to be more aware of what stresses and energizes me.

___ I am eliminating busyness and hurry from my life, choosing the practices of slowing and simplicity.

___ I choose healthy ways to de-stress regularly.

___ I am taking good care of myself, managing stress, and recovering in active ways through exercise and passive ways through rest, Sabbath, and retreat.

___ I make solitude and silence a priority in the rhythms of my life.

___ When I experience negative patterns of thinking, doubts, fears, and feelings, I try to dispute them and replace them with healthier, positive thoughts that result in peace, hope, and faith.

___ I don't believe everything I think, and I am continually dealing with worries and fears so I am not contaminated or dominated by them.

___ Prayer and meditation are a regular rhythm of my daily life.

Cultivate Hope in Adversity

___ Even when going through challenges, I have the ability to be resilient, routinely experiencing hope and optimism.

___ Adversity in life develops my character and capacity for compassion and empathy.

___ I try to reflect on God's perspective, promises in Scripture, and His goodness around me both now and in the past.

___ I reflect on positive affirmations, encouraging words, and what is good in life that builds my faith and hope.

___ I am confident that God has a plan for my life with a hope for the future.

___ I look forward to the future with hope and anticipation.

Meaning and Purpose for the Future

___ As I look ahead, I have a sense of my passions, vision, calling, and purpose, and I live my life accordingly.

___ I am excited about learning new things and developing new skills and talents that can make a lasting contribution.

___ I am aware of the legacy I would like to leave and am actively developing it.

___ I want to look back at the footprints of my life satisfied that I have lived a good life and left a positive legacy.

___ I am making a positive impact and contribution to the lives of others using my gifts and skills through my vocation, work, and service.

Notes

CHAPTER 1

1. InterVarsity Christian Fellowship held a conference on the theme of human flourishing (*www.urbana.org/articles/human-flourishing*). The Yale Center for Faith and Culture has a "God and Human Flourishing" project, exploring how our faith in Christ enables us to flourish in the way we live and think as individuals and communities and why God matters for human flourishing (see *www.yale.edu/faith/ghf/ghf.htm*).

   I attended the first World Congress on Positive Psychology in 2009. It focused on new developments in the science of human flourishing and well-being from a psychological perspective, promoting the science and practice of positive emotions, character strengths and virtues, and healthy relationships and institutions (see *www.ippanetwork.org*; see also *www.authentichappiness.org*).

2. Siang-Yang Tan, PhD, "Applied Positive Psychology: Putting Positive Psychology into Practice," *Journal of Psychology and Christianity* 25, no. 1 (2006): 68–73.

3. The Templeton Fund in particular has provided a large amount

of funding for research for topics related to human flourishing (*www.templeton.org*).

4. Beth Fletcher Brokaw, PhD, "Applying Theory in Clinical Practice: Clinical Integration of Psychology and Theology," *Journal of Psychology and Theology* 25, no. 1 (1997): 81–85.

5. *www.renovare.org*

6. Linda M. Wagener and Richard Beaton, "Is Your Life in Balance? Flourishing 101," *Fuller Theology, News & Notes: Human Flourishing*, Spring 2010.

7. Rick Warren, "Are You Really Living the Good Life?" Purpose Driven Connection, *www.purposedriven.com/article .html?c=201707&l=1* (accessed August 5, 2009).

8. Nicholas Wolterstorff, Yale professor emeritus of philosophical and religious studies, refers to human flourishing as "shalom." Faith and Leadership, "Nicholas Wolterstorff: It's Tied Together by Shalom," *www.faithandleadership.com/qa/ nicholas-wolterstorff-its-tied-together-shalom* and Nicholas Wolterstorff, "God's Power and Human Flourishing," *www.yale .edu/faith/downloads/Nicholas%20Wolterstorff%20%20%20-%20 God's%20Power%20and%20Human%20Flourishing%20 2008.pdf.*

9. Sam Barkat, "Establishing and Restoring Shalom," *www.urbana .org/articles/establishing-and-restoring-ishalom-i.*

10. Flora Slosson Wuellner, *Forgiveness, the Passionate Journey: Nine Steps of Forgiving Through Jesus' Beatitudes* (Nashville, TN: The Upper Room, 2001), 115.

11. Gary Moon, *Falling for God* (Colorado Springs: Waterbrook Press, 2004), 7.

12. Henry David Thoreau, *Walden* (Nashville, TN: American Renaissance, 2009), 4.

13. Corey L. M. Keyes and Jonathan Haidt, eds., *Flourishing: Positive Psychology and the Life Well Lived* (Washington, DC: American Psychological Association, 2003), 294.

14. Corey L. M. Keyes, "The Mental Health Continuum: From Languishing to Flourishing in Life," *Journal of Health and Social Research* 43 (2002): 207–222.

15. Betsey Stevenson and Justin Wolfers, "The Paradox of Declining Female Happiness," *American Economic Journal: Economic Policy* 1, no. 2 (2009): 190–225.

16. Keyes and Haidt, eds., *Flourishing*, 296.

17. Catherine Hart Weber and Archibald Hart, *Is Your Teen Stressed or Depressed?* (Nashville, TN: Thomas Nelson, 2005), 5.

18. Some questions adapted from Linda M. Wagener and Richard Beaton, "Is Your Life in Balance? Flourishing 101."

19. Robert C. Roberts, *Spiritual Emotions: A Psychology of Christian Virtues* (Cambridge, UK: Eerdmans, 2007), 9.

CHAPTER 2

1. David G. Benner, *The Gift of Being Yourself: The Sacred Call of Self Discovery* (Downers Grove, IL: InterVarsity, 2004), 14.

2. David G. Benner, "The Gift of Being Yourself," *Conversations Journal: A Forum for Authentic Transformation* 1, no. 2 (2009): 24–25.

3. Margery Williams, *The Velveteen Rabbit* (New York: Avon Books, 1975), 17.

4. "The Happiness Project," *www.happiness.co.uk/about/about.php.*

5. John Ortberg, *The Me I Want To Be* (Grand Rapids, MI: Zondervan, 2009).

6. You can go to the following Web sites to discover more personalized help and online spiritual growth tools: *www.howtoflourish.com, www.monvee.com, www.strengthsfinder.com, www.authentichappiness.com, www.myersbriggs.org, www.keirsey.com.* Also: David Keirsey, *Please Understand Me II: Temperament, Character, Intelligence* (Del Mar, CA: Prometheus Nemesis, 1998).

7. Wagener and Beaton, "Flourishing 101: Is Your Life in Balance?" 5.

8. *Following Christ 2008*, Plenary Sessions, N.T. Wright (MP3 download one, two, and three), *www.intervarsity.org/gfm/resource/plenaries*.

9. Jack Hayford, ed., *New Spirit-Filled Bible: New King James Version* (Nashville, TN: Thomas Nelson Publishers, 1991), 1527.

10. Barbara L. Fredrickson, PhD, *Positivity* (New York: Crown Publishing, 2009), 6.

11. Peter Scazzero, *Emotionally Healthy Spirituality* (Nashville: Thomas Nelson, 2006), front cover.

12. Stephen Post, PhD, and Jill Neimark, *Why Good Things Happen to Good People* (New York: Broadway Books, 2007), 54–69.

13. Abbot Christopher Jamison, *Finding Happiness* (Collegeville, MN: Liturgical Press, 2008), 38.

14. C. S. Lewis, *Mere Christianity* (New York: HarperCollins, 1952), 92.

15. Keyes and Haidt, eds., *Flourishing*, 296.

16. Elizabeth J. Canham, "Pay Attention to How You Listen," *Weavings Journal* (November/December 2007): 17.

17. Ephesians 3:19 and Galatians 5:22–23.

18. Adapted from "Intercession" in the Catholic monthly reading of the *Magnificat* (Yonkers, NY: July 2010, Vol. 12, No. 5), 271.

CHAPTER 3

1. Alana B. Elias Kornfeld, "Mind Over Chocolate," *TIME*, April 6, 2009.

2. Dr. Earl Henslin, *This Is Your Brain On Joy* (Nashville, TN: Thomas Nelson, 2008), 19–20, 40.

3. William O. Paulshell, "Ways of Prayer: Designing a Personal Rule," *Weavings Journal* (September/October, 1987).

4. Jamison, *Finding Happiness*, 33.

5. Adele Ahlberg Calhoun, *Spiritual Disciplines Handbook: Practices That Transform Us* (Downers Grove, IL: InterVarsity Press, 2005), 21.

6. Martha Graham, "Dancer of the Century," *http://marthagraham .org/resources/about_martha_graham.php*.

7. Jeffrey Pfeffer, *What Were They Thinking? Unconventional Wisdom About Management* (Boston, MA: Harvard Business School Press, 2007), 39–45.

8. Ruth Haley Barton, *Sacred Rhythms: Arranging Our Lives for Spiritual Formation* (Downers Grove, IL: InterVarsity Press, 2006), 147.

9. Scazzero, *Emotionally Healthy Spirituality*, 198.

10. Marjorie J. Thompson, *Soul Feast: An Invitation to the Christian Spiritual Life* (Louisville, KY: Westminster John Knox Press, 2005), 145.

11. C. R. Snyder and Shane J. Lopez, *Positive Psychology: The Scientific and Practical Explorations of Human Strengths* (Thousand Oaks, CA: Sage Publications, 2007), 18.

12. A helpful modern manual adapted from *The Book of Common Prayer* is provided in a series by Phyllis Tickle, *The Divine Hours: A Manual for Prayer* (New York: Doubleday, 2000).

13. Some popular resource ideas include daily readings such as the classic *My Utmost for His Highest* by Oswald Chambers, *www .myutmost.org*; *www.pray-as-you-go.org*, which offers a daily online audio lectio divina devotional that you can listen to or download by clicking on the date you want on the main page; Our Daily Bread, *www.odb.org*; and Purpose Driven Daily Hope email devotional *http://profile.purposedriven.com/dailyhope*.

14. Leighton Ford, *The Attentive Life: Discerning God's Presence in All Things* (Downers Grove, IL: InterVarsity Press, 2008).

15. Julia Cameron, *The Artist's Way: A Spiritual Path to Higher Creativity* (New York, NY: Putman, 1992).

16. You can learn more about these in Richard Foster's books *Streams of Living Water* and *A Spiritual Formation Workbook*, which form most of the Renovare teachings. Richard Foster and James Bryan Smith, with Lynda Graybeal, *A Spiritual Formation Workbook* (New York: HarperCollins,1993), 30.

17. Henri J. M. Nouwen, *The Way of the Heart* (New York: Ballantine Books, 1981).

18. Frank C. Laubach, *Letters by a Modern Mystic* (Westwood, NJ: Revell, 1937), 7.

19. Gary Moon, *Falling for God: Saying Yes to the Extravagant Proposal* (Colorado Springs, CO: Waterbrook Press, 2004), 89.

20. Adapted from these resources on the Tabernacle as a model for prayer: Jon Courson, *Praying thru the Tabernacle* (Searchlight, 2007). Nancy Missler, *Be Ye Transformed* (Coeur d' Alene, ID: Koinonia House, 1996). *www.tabernacleexperience.com*.

CHAPTER 4

1. T. Berry Brazelton, Robert Coles, James P. Comer, Thomas Insel, Kathleen Kovner Kline, Alvin Poussaint, Allan N. Schore, Linda Spear, Stephen J. Suomi, and Judith Wallerstein, *Hardwired to Connect: The New Scientific Case for Authoritative Community* (New York: Institute for American Values, 2003), 14.

2. Kimberly Gaines Eckert and Cynthia Neal Kimball, "God As a Secure Base and Haven of Safety: Attachment Theory As a Framework for Understanding Relationship to God" in *Spiritual Formation, Counseling and Psychotherapy*, eds., Todd W. Hall and Mark R. McMinn (New York: Nova Science, 2003), 109.

3. Lee Kirpatrick, *Attachment, Evolution and the Psychology of Religion* (New York: Guilford Press, 2005), 63.

4. Sharon Hart Morris, *Safe Haven Marriage: Building a Relationship You Want to Come Home To* (Nashville, TN: W Publishing, 2003).

5. Sharon Morris May, *How to Argue So Your Spouse Will Listen* (Nashville, TN: Thomas Nelson, 2007).

6. Daniel J. Siegel, MD, and Mary Hartzell, M.Ed, *Parenting From the Inside Out: How a Deeper Self-Understanding Can Help You Raise Children Who Thrive* (New York: Penguin Group, 2003).

7. Eckert and Kimball, "God As a Secure Base and Haven of Safety," 111.

8. Adapted from Sharon Morris May, PhD, "Attachment Styles in Relationships" (Haven of Safety Relationship Center, 2010). Used by permission.

9. "Our Images of God Affect How We Relate to Prayer and Life," *www.jesuits.ca/orientations/image.htm*.

10. Dr. Beth Fletcher Brokaw and Todd W. Hall, "The Relationship of Spiritual Maturity to Level of Object Relations Development and God Image," *Pastoral Psychology* 43, no. 6.

11. Peter Scazzero, *Emotionally Healthy Spirituality*, 56.

12. Dr. Helen Roseveare, a missionary from England, dedicated her life to serving others even in the deep trials of life in Africa. This story of a little girl's prayer has been circulating on the Internet and was published in her now out of print book, *Living Faith*. Adapted from "A Little Girl's Prayer," *Heart 'n Souls, www.heartnsouls.com/stories/a/s99/shtml*.

13. Bob Sorge, *Secrets of the Secret Place* (Greenwood, MO: Oasis House, 2007), 172.

14. *www.palletmastersworkshop.com/kevin.html*

15. In his book *Sacred Pathways*, Gary Thomas helps us discover our spiritual temperaments through nine pathways to draw near to God. For more on the spiritual pathways and spiritual temperaments, you may also want to refer to *The Me I Want to Be* by John Ortberg and *What's Your God Language?* by Dr. Myra Perrine.

16. Dr. John Coe, "The Dark Night of the Soul in Psychology,"

(lecture, Christian Association for Psychological Studies [CAPS] West, Santa Clara, CA, 2000).

17. Edwina Gateley, "Let Your God Love You," *Psalms of a Laywoman* (Lanham, MD: Sheed & Ward, 1999). Sheed & Ward is an imprint of Rowman & Littlefield Publishers, Inc. Reprinted by permission.

18. A. W. Tozer, *The Pursuit of God* (Camp Hill, PA: Christian Publications, 1993).

19. Gary Moon, *Falling for God: Saying Yes to His Extravagant Proposal* (Colorado Springs, Colorado: WaterBrook Press, 2004), 3.

20. Hannah Whitall Smith, *The Christian's Secret of a Happy Life* (Uhrichsville, OH: Barbour Publishing, 2006).

21. M. Robert Mulholland Jr., *The Deeper Journey: The Spirituality of Discovering Your True Self* (Downers Grove, IL: InterVarsity Press, 2006), 93.

CHAPTER 5

1. Institute for Research on Unlimited Love, "About the Institute," *www.unlimitedloveinstitute.org/aboutus/index.html.*

2. Ibid., "Welcome," *www.unlimitedloveinstitute.org/welcome/index.html.*

3. George E. Vaillant, MD, *Spiritual Evolution: A Scientific Defense of Faith* (Broadway Books: New York, 2008), 101.

4. Dr. David Myers, "Psychology of Happiness," *Edinburgh Philosophy and Psychology,* May 2010.

5. Ed Diener, "Guidelines for National Indicators of Subjective Well-Being and Ill-Being," *Applied Research in Quality of Life* 1 (2005): 151–157.

6. Stephen J. Bavolek, PhD, ed., "Hardwired to Connect: The Scientific Case for Authoritative Communities" (report, Institute for American Values, New York, 2003), 17.

7. John Gottman, PhD, *Raising an Emotionally Intelligent Child* (New York: Fireside, 1997).

8. Adapted from "Attachment Theory and Safe Haven Model" by Dr. Sharon Morris May.

9. Sam Barkat (address given at InterVarsity Christian Fellowship Global Briefing, October 1999).

10. Stephen Kendrick and Alex Kendrick, *The Love Dare* (Nashville, TN: Broadman, 2008), 6.

11. Christopher Peterson and Martin E. P. Seligman, *Character Strengths and Virtues. A Handbook and Classification* (New York: Oxford Press, 2004).

12. To take the VIA Survey of Character Strengths, which measures 24 character strengths, go to *www.authentichappiness.com*. You may also refer to *Now, Discover Your Strengths* at *www.strengthsfinder.com*.

13. Post and Neimark, *Why Good Things Happen to Good People*.

14. Ibid., 1.

15. Anne Morrow Lindbergh, *Gift from the Sea* (New York, Vintage Books, 1975), 47.

16. The story of football player Michael Oher's path from poverty and homelessness to NFL stardom is told in the movie *The Blind Side*, and the Tuohys' book, *In a Heartbeat: Sharing the Power of Cheerful Giving* (New York: Henry Holt, 2010).

17. Good Morning America, "Real-Life 'Blind Side' Family on Giving Back," *http://abcnews.go.com/gma/real-life-blind-side-family-giving-back/story?id=11124741*.

18. Ibid.

19. Spiritual Media Blog, "Interview With Sean and Leigh Anne Tuohy on the Power of Cheerful Giving," *www.spiritualmediablog.com/2010/07/16/interview-with-sean-and-leigh-anne-tuohy*.

20. C. R. Snyder and Shane J. Lopez, *Positive Psychology: The Scientific and Practical Explorations of Human Strengths* (Thousand Oaks, CA: Sage Publications, 2007), 316.

21. Sharon Morris May, *How to Argue So Your Spouse Will Listen.*

22. Dr. John Gottman, *The Seven Principles for Making Marriage Work* (New York: Three Rivers Press, 1999), 40.

23. Everett L. Worthington Jr., *A Just Forgiveness: Responsible Healing Without Excusing Injustice* (Downers Grove, IL: InterVarsity Press, 2009), 74.

24. Lewis B. Smedes, *The Art of Forgiveness* (New York: Ballantine Books, 1996).

25. Dr. Martin Seligman and other psychologists have developed the Letting Go of Grudges Exercise as a way to decrease anger, which leads to depression, and promote increased positive emotion.

26. *http://thinkexist.com/quotation/feelings_of_worth_can_flourish_only_in_an/184239.html*

27. Hart and Hart Weber, *Is Your Teen Stressed or Depressed?*

28. George E. Vaillant, MD, *Spiritual Evolution: A Scientific Defense of Faith* (Broadway Books: New York, 2008).

CHAPTER 6

1. For further information about the relationship between joy and happiness, see Dr. Archibald Hart, *Fifteen Principles for Achieving Happiness* (Dallas, TX: Word Publishing, 1988). (Out of print, but reprints are available through *www.hartinstitute.com.*)

2. J. P. Moreland and Klause Issler, *Lost Virtues of Happiness: Discovering the Disciplines of the Good Life* (Colorado Springs, CO: Navpress, 2006), 28.

3. Linda M. Wagener and Richard Beaton, "Flourishing 101: Reflecting the Abundance of Creation," *Fuller Theology, News & Notes, Human Flourishing*, Spring 2010.

4. Henslin, *This Is Your Brain on Joy.*

5. Carlin Flora, "The Pursuit of Happiness," *Psychology Today,* January 1, 2009, *www.psychologytoday.com/articles/200812/the-pursuit-happiness.*

6. Dr. Seligman was elected President of the American Psychological Association and served in that capacity during the 1998 term. He has written several books about positive psychology. See his Web site: *www.authentichappiness.com.*

7. Daniel Gilbert, *Stumbling on Happiness* (New York: Random House, 2006).

8. Jonathan Haidt, *The Happiness Hypothesis* (New York: Basic Books, 2006), 91.

9. Earl Henslin, *This Is Your Brain on Joy,* 22–28.

10. Linda Petty, "Are we joyless working machines?" CNN, June 3, 2010, *www.cnn.com/2010/LIVING/worklife/06/03/pipher.joyless.working.machines/index.html.*

11. Dr. Archibald Hart, *Thrilled to Death: How the Pursuit of Pleasure Is Leaving Us Numb* (Nashville, TN: Thomas Nelson, 2007).

12. Gary Thomas, *Pure Pleasure: Why Do Christians Feel So Bad About Feeling Good?* (Grand Rapids, MI: Zondervan, 2009).

13. Adapted from the sections I contributed to writing for "Seven Steps to Recovering Your Pleasure," Dr. Archibald Hart, *Thrilled to Death: How the Pursuit of Pleasure Is Leaving Us Numb.*

14. Adapted from Henslin, *This Is Your Brain on Joy,* 39.

15. "Is God an Anti-Depressant? Studies Show That Religious People Are Happier," ABC News, January 23, 2005. *http://abcnews.go.com/print?id=435412.*

16. Henslin, *This Is Your Brain on Joy,* 22–28.

17. C. R. Snyder and Shane J. Lopez, *Positive Psychology.*

18. James H. Fowler and Nicholas A. Christakis, "The Contagion of Happiness. Dynamic Spread of Happiness in a Large Social

Network: Longitudinal Analysis Over 20 Years in the Framingham Heart Study," *BMJ* 337, no. 42 (December 2, 2008), *www.bmj.com/cgi/content/abstract/337/dec04_2/a2338*.

19. Dr. Archibald Hart, *Habits of the Mind: Ten Exercises to Renew Our Thinking* (Dallas, TX: Word Publishing, 1996), 116.

20. Barbara L. Fredrickson, PhD, *Positivity* (New York: Crown Publishers, 2009), 21.

21. Hennie Becker, *Music to Inspire Positive Thinking*. Soundtrack. Sonicaid. Avalon. 2008.

22. Advanced Brain Technologies, LLC. The Sound Health Series includes music to relax as well as enhance concentration, learning, and productivity. *www.advancedbrain.com/soundheath/sound-health.html*.

23. Val Willingham, "The Power of Music: It's a Real Heart Opener," CNN Health (May 11, 2009), *www.cnn.com/2009/HEALTH/05/11/music.heart/index.html*.

24. Travis J. Carter and Thomas Gilovich, "The relativity of material and experiential purchases," *Journal of Personality and Social Psychology* (2010), 98 (1): 146.

25. Lilach Sagiv, Sonia Roccas, and Osnat Hazan, "Value Pathways to Well-Being: Healthy Values, Valued Goal Attainment, and Environmental Congruence," in *Positive Psychology in Practice*, eds., P. Alex Linley and Stephen Joseph (Hoboken, NJ: John Wiley & Sons, 2004), 68.

26. *www.Cinematherapy.com*

27. Susan Hall, "Three Reasons to Love Flowers," *Health*, April 21, 2008, *http://living.health.com/2008/04/21/three-reasons-to-love-flowers/*.

28. JoAnne Brandi, "7 Tricks to Stay Positive in an Often Negative World," *Bottom Line/Personal* 30, no. 22, November 15, 2009.

29. P. J. Person and Mary Shipley, *Aromatherapy for Everyone* (Ridgefield, CT: Vital Health Publishing, 2004).

30. Luchina Fisher, "A Reading Rx for Emotional Relief," *Health*, May 5, 2008, *http://living.health.com/2008/05/05/reading-for -emotional-relief/*.

31. Adele Ahlberg Calhoun, *Spiritual Disciplines Handbook: Practices That Transform Us* (Downers Grove, IL: InterVarsity Press, 2005).

CHAPTER 7

1. Robert A. Emmons, *Thanks! How the New Science of Gratitude Can Make You Happier* (New York: Houghton Mifflin Books, 2007).

2. Nancy Leigh DeMoss, *Choosing Gratitude: Your Journey to Joy* (Chicago, IL: Moody Press, 2009), 71.

3. Sonja Lyubomirsky, *The How of Happiness* (New York: Penguin Group, 2007), 20.

4. Johnson Oatman Jr., "Count Your Blessings," 1897.

5. Robert A. Emmons, *Thanks!* 11.

6. Ibid., 12.

7. R. A. Emmons and M. E. McCullough, "Counting Blessings Versus Burdens: Experimental Studies of Gratitude and Subjective Well-Being in Daily Life," *Journal of Personality and Social Psychology* 84 (2003): 377–389.

8. Robert A. Emmons, *Thanks!* 40.

9. Dr. Sylvia Hart Frejd is a Flourish coach and leads worship for the Strength for the Journey retreats. She is also coauthor of the *Flourish* workbook and other resources.

10. Dr. Gary Oliver, "Surprised by Gratitude" (lecture, Fellowship Bible Church of Northwest Arkansas, July 18, 2009).

11. Jessica Ravitz, "The Power of Gratitude, a Year-Round Gift," CNN Living, November 25, 2009, *www.cnn.com/2009/ LIVING/11/25/giving.gratitude/index.html*.

12. Adapted from *Through All the Days of Life*, a collection of

prayers compiled by Fr. Nick Schiro, SJ.

13. St. Ignatius of Loyola describes our inner experience of grati-tude and flourishing as consolations and our struggles, dis-appointments, and languishing as desolations. Adapted from Dennis Linn, *Sleeping With Bread* (Mahwah, NJ: Paulist Press, 1995).

14. Adapted from Rollin McCraty, PhD, and Doc Childre, *The Appreciative Heart: The Psychophysiology of Positive Emotions and Optimal Functioning* (HeartMath Research Center, Insti-tute of HeartMath) *http://store.heartmath.org/store/e-books/ appreciative-heart* (accessed July 2010).

15. Ted Loder, *Guerrillas of Grace: Prayers for the Battle* (Min-neapolis: Augsburg, 1984, 2005), 81.

CHAPTER 8

1. Stephanie McClellan, MD, and Beth Hamilton, MD, with Diane Reverand, *So Stressed: The Ultimate Stress-Relief Plan for Women* (New York: Free Press, 2010), xx.

2. Abbot Christopher Jamison, *Finding Sanctuary: Monastic Steps for Everyday Life* (Phoenix, AZ: Orion Books, 2007), 22.

3. Dr. Archibald Hart. *Sleep: It Does a Family Good* (Carol Springs, IL: Tyndale, 2010).

4. American Psychological Association, "APA Poll Finds Women Bear Brunt of Nation's Stress, Financial Downturn," October 7, 2008, *www.apa.org/news/press/releases/2008/10/stress-women .aspx.*

5. Ed Stafford, a former British army captain, set out to become the first person to walk all along the 4,000 miles of the Amazon River. After three months he was joined by hiking buddy Gad-iel "Cho" Sanchez Rivera, a Peruvian forestry worker. "Hiker hopes to complete historic Amazon River trek on Monday," CNN.com, August 9, 2010, *www.cnn.com/2010/WORLD/ americas/08/08/brazil.amazon.hiker/index.html.*

6. Dr. Archibald Hart, *The Hidden Link Between Adrenaline and Stress* (Nashville, TN: Thomas Nelson, 1995), 24.

7. Archibald Hart and Catherine Hart Weber, *A Woman's Guide to Overcoming Depression* (Grand Rapids, MI: Revell, 2002).

8. McClellan, Hamilton, and Reverand, *So Stressed*, 57.

9. HeartMath provides products and tools to transform stress and better regulate emotional responses. *www.heartmath.com.*

10. Stephen Covey, A. Roger Merrill, and Rebecca R. Merrill, *First Things First* (London, UK: Simon & Schuster, 1999).

11. "Tend and Befriend," UCLA Social Neuroscience Lab, *http://taylorlab.psych.ucla.edu/research.htm#Tend_and_Befriend0* (accessed July 2010).

12. Miranda Hitti, "Holding Hands May Reduce Stress: Wives in Happy Marriages Feel Less Stress While Holding Hands With Husband," *WebMD Health News*, December 20, 2006, *www.webmd.com/balance/news/20061220/holding-hands-may -reduce-stress.*

13. Benedict Carey, "Holding Loved One's Hand Can Calm Jittery Neurons," *New York Times Health*, January 31, 2006, *www .nytimes.com/2006/01/31/health/psychology/31marr.html.*

14. Quoted in Jonathan Shaw, "The Deadliest Sin: From Survival of the Fittest to Staying Fit Just to Survive: Scientists Probe the Benefits of Exercise—and the Dangers of Sloth," *Harvard Magazine*. March–April 2004, *http://harvardmagazine .com/2004/03/the-power-of-exercise.*

15. Tal Ben-Shahar, *Even Happier: A Gratitude Journal for Daily Joy and Lasting Fulfillment* (New York: McGraw-Hill, 2009), 9.

16. Dennis Mann, "Sleep, Pray, Love—Survey Sheds Light on U.S. Bedtime Routine," CNN Health, March 8, 2010, *www.cnn .com/2010/HEALTH/03/08/sleep.pray.love.survey/index.html.*

17. Dr. Archibald D. Hart, *Sleep: It Does a Family Good.*

18. T. Byram Karasu, MD, "Breathe in the Holy Spirit," The Mystery

of Happiness blog, March 4, 2010, *www.psychologytoday.com/ blog/the-mystery-happiness/201003/breathe-in-the-holy-spirit.*

19. Mihaly Csikszentmihalyi and Isabella Selega Csikszentmihalyi, eds., *A Life Worth Living* (New York: Oxford Press, 2006), 128.

20. Richard Foster, *Celebration of Discipline: The Path to Spiritual Growth* (New York: HarperCollins, 1998), 98.

21. Blaise Pascal (French scientist, mathematician, physicist, philosopher, moralist, and writer), *Pensées* (1670, section 136).

22. Henri Nouwen, *Making All Things New: An Invitation to the Spiritual Life* (New York: HarperCollins, 1981), 79.

23. *Our Daily Bread*, May 5, 2010, *http://ourdailybreadonline .blogspot.com/2010/05/still-small-voice.html.*

24. Lynne M. Baab, *Sabbath Keeping: Finding Freedom in the Rhythms of Rest* (Downers Grove, IL: InterVarsity Press, 2005).

25. Jane Rubietta, *Resting Place: A Personal Guide to Spiritual Retreats* (Downers Grove, IL: InterVarsity Press, 2005).

CHAPTER 9

1. Daniel G. Amen, MD, "Kill the ANTs That Invade Your Brain," Amen Clinics, *www.amenclinics.com/cybcyb/brain-health-club/ seven-ways-to-optimize-your-brain-and-your-life/3-kill-the-ants -that-invade-your-brain/.*

2. Anxiety Disorders Association of America, "Facts and Statistics," 2010, *www.adaa.org/understanding-anxiety.*

3. Dr. Archibald D. Hart, *The Anxiety Cure* (Nashville, TN: Thomas Nelson, 1999).

4. James Allen, *As a Woman Thinketh*, trans., Dorothy J. Hulst (Camarillo, CA: De Vorss Publications), 11.

5. Dr. Martin Seligman, *Authentic Happiness* (New York: The Free Press, 2002), 40.

6. McClellan, Hamilton, and Reverand, *So Stressed*, 29.
7. Seligman, *Authentic Happiness*, 93.
8. Westwood Institute for Anxiety Disorders, "Dr. Jeffrey Schwartz' Four Steps," *http://hope4ocd.com/foursteps.php*.
9. To listen to a daily online Lectio Divina by Jesuits in London go to *www.pray-as-you-go.org*. Click on the date you want on the calendar on the main page.
10. Oswald Chambers, *My Utmost for His Highest*, "Think As Jesus Taught. May 26" (Westwood, NJ: Barbour and Company, 1935), 106.
11. Henslin, *This Is Your Brain on Joy*, 19.
12. Ibid.
13. Jeanie Lerche Davis, "Best Ways to Ease Anxiety Disorders," WebMD, February 3, 2006, *www.webmd.com/anxiety-panic/guide/20061101/best-ways-to-ease-anxiety-disorders*.
14. Elmer L. Towns, *Biblical Meditation for Spiritual Breakthrough: 10 Biblical Ways to Meditate and Draw Closer to the Lord* (Ventura, CA: Regal Books, 1998), 21.
15. "Christian Meditation," *http://en.wikipedia.org/wiki/Christian_meditation*.
16. Hart, *Anxiety Cure*, 241.
17. Towns, *Biblical Meditation for Spiritual Breakthrough*, 26.
18. Ibid., 29.
19. Gene Edwards, *100 Days in the Secret Place* (Shippensburg, PA: Destiny Image, 2001), 64–65.
20. *Our Daily Bread*, November 4, 2009, *http://odb.org/2009/11/04/seeds-and-faith*.
21. Lew Sterrett and Bob Smietana, *Life Lessons From a Horse Whisperer* (Grand Rapids, Michigan: Monarch Books, 2010), 16–19.
22. James Allen, *As a Woman Thinketh*, 61, 64.

CHAPTER 10

1. Jonathan Haidt, *The Happiness Hypothesis: Finding Modern Truth in Ancient Wisdom* (New York: Basic Books, 2006), 138.

2. Lewis B. Smedes, *Ministry and the Miraculous: A Case Study at Fuller Seminary* (Pasadena, CA: Fuller Theological Seminary, 1987), 42.

3. See *http://bethb.projectconnectonline.com/personal-essays/ playing-our-strings/*; *www.classicalnotes.net/classics/paganini .html*; *www.guitarramagazine.com/NicocoloPaganini.*

4. Haidt, *The Happiness Hypothesis*, 138–140.

5. Leadership journal.net. Cited in article by John Ortberg on Hope Management. Hope is the one responsibility no leader should delegate. Posted 2/11/2008. *http://www.christianity today.com/le/currenttrendscolumns/leadershipweekly/ cln80211.html.*

6. Collie W. Conoley and Jane Close Conoley, *Positive Psychology and Family Therapy* (Hoboken, NJ: John Wiley & Sons, Inc, 2009), 17.

7. This is one of the exercises used in research by Dr. Martin Seligman at *www.authentichappiness.com.*

8. "Trapped for Five Days," CNN News, January 24, 2010, *www .cnn.com/video/#/video/us/2010/01/23/lavandera.trapped.5.days .cnn?hpt=C2.*

9. "The Tap Code," *This Emotional Life*, PBS Series, *www.pbs .org/thisemotionallife/video/tap-code.*

10. Ibid.

11. James W. Pennebaker, PhD, *Opening Up: The Healing Power of Expressing Emotions* (New York: The Guilford Press, 1990).

12. Robert Biswas-Diener and Ben Dean, *Positive Psychology Coaching. Putting the Science of Happiness to Work for Your Clients* (Hoboken, NJ: John Wiley & Sons, Inc., 2007), 95.

CHAPTER 11

1. Walter Brueggemann, *Ichabod Toward Home: The Journey of God's Glory* (Cambridge, U.K: Eerdmans Publishing Co., 2002).

2. Tim Stafford, "The Third Coming of George Barna," *Christianity Today,* August 5, 2002, *www.christianitytoday.com/ct/2002/august5/1.32.html?start=3.*

3. Zedekiah's Cave, *http://en.wikipedia.org/wiki/Zedekiah%27s_Cave.*

4. Dr. Beth Fletcher Brokaw, "He Is Risen," Beth's Journey, April 4, 2010, *http://bethb.projectconnectonline.com/2010/04/04/he-is-risen/.*

5. Dr. Jack Hayford, Sermon: "When You Think You're at the End," Sunday, April 4, 2010, The Church On The Way, 1400 Sherman Way, Van Nuys, CA 91405.

Gratitude and Appreciation

I would like to begin by thanking the Lord God for the most amazing opportunity to share this book with you on your journey to flourish. Although the seeds have been germinating and sprouting for years, it all began to bear fruit when sharing the vision with Andy McGuire. I appreciate his partnership and support, which offered the most conducive environment for this book to truly flourish. I am also grateful to Ellen Chalifoux for her amazing editing expertise and patient persistence, as well as the rest of the Bethany House staff, who all contributed to preparing the book.

I would also like to thank my parents, Dr. Archibald and Kathleen Hart, who loved me before I was born, and continue to provide rich, nurturing love and support. They poured hours into reading every word, contributing significantly.

My dear "blood sisters" also labored alongside me in love. Dr. Sylvia Frejd walked daily with me across the miles, contributing her expertise as a coach, coauthoring the workbook and coaching programs. Dr. Sharon May sat with me, poring through pages, adding her expertise in attachment and faith-based emotion-focused therapy.

My husband, Rick, is God's great gift to me, continually

reflecting that it truly is God's loving-kindness that draws us to himself as He draws out our authentic beauty. He has been long-suffering and tremendously supportive.

My daughters, Nicole and Caitlin, are a living testimony to the value of flourishing in the presence of the love of God and one another. Being their mother as they have thrived has strengthened my faith and is a source of great joy to me.

The rest of my extended family—my niece, Ashley; my nephews, Vincent, Alan, Robbie, Daniel, Matt, and Mitch; and my brothers-in-law, Russ and Mike—deserve a tremendous thanks.

My dear friends and "sisters of the heart" prayed and toiled on this journey along with me. Dr. Beth Fletcher Brokaw spent hours into the night, by the light of the moon, pouring out her expertise on God attachment.

I thank all those who have fasted and prayed, seeded ideas, watered, cultivated, and weeded through the manuscript with me and across the miles. To the Strength for the Journey retreat companions, the Meaning Making Sister Gatherings, my Spiritual Direction Group, and other precious friends and colleagues. Deborah Montana, Cecelia Freeman, Linda Alleman, Debbie Linnamen, Dr. Theresa Tisdale, Anne Fletcher Grizzle, Kathy Scott Lewis, Dr. Judy Balswick, Dr. Laura Robinson Harbert, Jennifer Cisney, Georgia Shaffer, Sharon Jaynes, Dr. Chuck Shoemake and Tisha Shoemake-Lazare. My dear friend and "sacred soul brother," Dr. Gary Oliver, who contributed and inspired me immensely, from the depths of his painful life journey to the heights of authentic grace, wisdom, beauty, and sovereign joy that he radiates.

And to all those I walk alongside counseling, coaching, teaching, and leading in retreats: Thank you for enriching my life and allowing me to witness the harmonious graces of a redeeming, flourishing journey.

About the Author

Catherine Hart Weber, PhD, is a licensed marriage and family therapist and has been adjunct professor at Fuller Theological Seminary. Catherine has written, researched, and taught steadily over the years, providing helpful wellness resources in gender and marital enrichment, parenting teens, overcoming stress and depression, and personal and spiritual enrichment for women. She is the coauthor of *Secrets of Eve*, *A Woman's Guide to Overcoming Depression*, and *Is Your Teen Stressed or Depressed?* In addition to her PhD in Marriage and Family Therapy, Catherine also has an MA in Theology from Fuller Theological Seminary. She lives in Southern California with her husband, Rick, and their two daughters and three dogs.

For resources to help you flourish, including online downloads, assessments, a meditation exercise, and more, visit *www.howtoflourish.com*.

A portion of all proceeds related to *Flourish* products goes toward fair trade, supporting projects and microfinancing for women and orphans in Africa—to *flourish*.

Contact Information

Dr. Catherine Hart Weber
P.O. Box 905, Sierra Madre, CA 91025
www.howtoflourish.com